Grammar Acquisition and Processing Instruction

SECOND LANGUAGE ACQUISITION
Series Editor: Professor David Singleton, *Trinity College, Dublin, Ireland*

This series brings together titles dealing with a variety of aspects of language acquisition and processing in situations where a language or languages other than the native language is involved. Second language is thus interpreted in its broadest possible sense. The volumes included in the series all offer in their different ways, on the one hand, exposition and discussion of empirical findings and, on the other, some degree of theoretical reflection. In this latter connection, no particular theoretical stance is privileged in the series; nor is any relevant perspective – sociolinguistic, psycholinguistic, neurolinguistic, etc. – deemed out of place. The intended readership of the series includes final-year undergraduates working on second language acquisition projects, postgraduate students involved in second language acquisition research, and researchers and teachers in general whose interests include a second language acquisition component.

Full details of all the books in this series and of all our other publications can be found on http://www.multilingual-matters.com, or by writing to Multilingual Matters, St Nicholas House, 31–34 High Street, BS1 2AW, UK.

SECOND LANGUAGE ACQUISITION
Series Editor: David Singleton, *Trinity College, Dublin, Ireland*

Grammar Acquisition and Processing Instruction
Secondary and Cumulative Effects

Alessandro G. Benati and James F. Lee

Multilingual Matters
Bristol • Buffalo • Toronto

Library of Congress Cataloging in Publication Data
A catalog record for this book is available from the Library of Congress.
Benati, Alessandro G.
Grammar Acquisition and Processing Instruction: Secondary and Cumulative Effects
Alessandro G. Benati and James F. Lee.
Second Language Acquisition: 34
Includes bibliographical references and index.
1. Second language acquisition. 2. Grammar, Comparative and general.
I. Lee, James F. II Title.
P118.2.B453 2008
401'.93–dc22   2008026640

British Library Cataloguing in Publication Data
A catalogue entry for this book is available from the British Library.

ISBN-13: 978-1-84769-104-0 (hbk)
ISBN-13: 978-1-84769-103-3 (pbk)

Multilingual Matters

UK: St Nicholas House, 31–34 High Street, Bristol, BS1 2AW, UK.
USA: UTP, 2250 Military Road, Tonawanda, NY 14150, USA.
Canada: UTP, 5201 Dufferin Street, North York, Ontario M3H 5T8, Canada.

Copyright © 2008 Alessandro G. Benati and James F. Lee

All rights reserved. No part of this work may be reproduced in any form or by any means without permission in writing from the publisher.

The policy of Multilingual Matters/Channel View Publications is to use papers that are natural, renewable and recyclable products, made from wood grown in sustainable forests. In the manufacturing process of our books, and to further support our policy, preference is given to printers that have FSC and PEFC Chain of Custody certification. The FSC and/or PEFC logos will appear on those books where full certification has been granted to the printer concerned.

Typeset by Wordworks Ltd, Gairloch.
Printed and bound in Great Britain by Cromwell Press Ltd.

Contents

Acknowledgements vii

Introduction ix

1 A Theory of Input Processing: How Learners Work with Input . . . 1

2 Processing Instruction: Research and Practice in Assessing Primary Effects 24

3 From Processing Instruction on the Acquisition of Italian Noun–Adjective Agreement to Secondary Transfer-of-Training Effects on Italian Future Tense Verb Morphology 54

4 From Processing Instruction on the Acquisition of English Past Tense to Secondary Transfer-of-Training Effects on English Third Person Singular Present Tense (with Scott Dean Houghton) 88

5 From Processing Instruction on the Acquisition of French Imparfait to Secondary Transfer-of-Training Effects on French Subjunctive and to Cumulative Transfer-of-Training Effects with French Causative Constructions (with Cecile Laval) 121

Final Comments 158

Appendices 176

References 205

Index 210

Acknowledgements

From Alessandro G. Benati:

This is the third book of a very fruitful collaboration with James Lee. I must thank him for his support, priceless guidance and valuable feedback in the completion of this project. I admire the way James works so professionally with all his other commitments.

I would also like to thank and express my gratitude to Bill VanPatten for his guidance, support and friendship over the years.

I must thank Cecile and Scott for their hard work on two of the chapters of this book and also Jin Ho Chow for helping us to collect data for one of the classroom experiments. A special thanks to all students for taking part in the classroom experiments presented in this book and to the British Academy for its financial support.

I must also express my gratitude to several people who have supported me and helped me in this venture: among them Bernadette, my kids Grace and Francesco and all my colleagues at the University of Greenwich. A special thanks to everybody at Multilingual Matters who worked very hard to produce this book. We would also like to thank the anonymous reviewer for his priceless comments and for helping us to improve the content of this book.

Finally, I would like to dedicate this book to the memory of my mother, Anna Maria Ferrari.

From James F. Lee:

A fortuitous meeting at the 2005 Applied Linguistics Association of Australia in Melbourne brought me together with Alessandro Benati, who has, ever since, been motivating me to work and work and work. Over the course of the conference we exchanged ideas on language processing, second language learners, Processing Instruction and avenues for collaboration. This work is our third collaboration and arguably the most important in terms of the theoretical framework in which we conduct our research. Whereas our previous work moved the practice of Processing Instruction forward, the present work directly contributes to the theory of input processing. We must acknowledge and thank Bill VanPatten for his groundbreaking theorising and the line of research on Processing Instruction he spawned. His work drives ours.

Introduction

The research we present in this book establishes a unique line of research within the Processing Instruction model by assessing the transfer-of-training effects of this approach to grammar instruction on the way learners make form–meaning connections. In this work we will refer to direct or primary effects as well as to transfer-of-training effects. Each investigation of the effects of Processing Instruction has isolated and targeted for treatment a particular linguistic feature. Learners' knowledge of the target linguistic feature is assessed prior to treatment (pre-testing) and then again after treatment (post-testing). Their increased knowledge of the target linguistic item, resulting from the treatment, is what we refer to as a direct or primary effect. If the treatment also resulted in increased knowledge of some other linguistic item in addition to the target linguistic item, then we would have a transfer-of-training effect. We further categorise the transfer-of-training effects as being secondary effects or cumulative effects. We refer to an effect as secondary if the two linguistic items under focus present L2 learners with a similar processing problem. Word final morphology such as present tense *-s* and past tense *-ed* in English present L2 learners with similar processing difficulties. If Processing Instruction on past tense *-ed* also affected present tense *-s*, we would call it a secondary effect. Word final morphology such as French *imparfait* (past imperfective) and word order permutations such as French *faire* causative constructions present L2 learners with very different processing problems. Processing instruction on these two linguistic items attempts to instil very different processing strategies. Yet, if Processing Instruction on the French *imparfait* also affected French *faire* causative constructions, we would call it a cumulative effect.

As detailed in our review of literature in Chapter 2, research on Processing Instruction (PI) has so far focused on measuring only direct or primary effects on learning a specific/targeted linguistic feature. Typically, the research has compared Processing Instruction with traditional output-oriented instruction and/or meaning-based output instruction. The results of the empirical research have consistently shown that Processing Instruction is a better approach to grammar instruction than are output-based approaches, because those receiving PI develop knowledge of the target as measured by both interpretation and production tasks, whereas those receiving output-based instruction typically develop only knowledge of target as measured by production tasks not by interpretation tasks.

Processing Instruction is a very effective approach to grammar instruction in that it teaches L2 learners to alter inappropriate processing strategies as well as helping them instil appropriate ones. We have accumulated a large body of positive results that have measured the primary effects of Processing Instruction. Even so, no research has yet been conducted to determine, what, if any, are the transfer-of training effects of this approach. In his critical review of the then extant research on Processing Instruction, Lee (2004) generated 11 hypotheses and stated that they showed a robust future for Processing Instruction research. Indeed, we pursue two of the hypotheses in our current work:

- *Hypothesis 9:* learners who receive training on one type of processing strategy for one specific form will appropriately transfer the use of that strategy to other forms without further instruction in PI.
- *Hypothesis 11:* the cumulative effects of PI will be greater than its isolated effects. (Lee, 2004: 322)

The main aims of this book are to provide empirical evidence that will show that second language (L2) learners receiving Processing Instruction can transfer their training on one linguistic feature to other forms or linguistic features without further instruction on the other forms and to determine what the cumulative effects of PI might be. The data were gathered in order to address the following two questions.

- *Question 1:* Will learners who receive training on one type of processing strategy for one specific form appropriately transfer the use of that strategy to other forms without further instruction in PI?

In Chapter 3, we present research on the acquisition of Italian as a second language. L2 learners of Italian will receive PI focused on noun–adjective agreement (*-o* and *-a* at end of words). They will be taught to develop a word final processing strategy appropriate to Italian. Can they then transfer that training to another word final morphological form? Can these L2 learners also process future tense forms located at the ends of words?

In Chapter 4 we present research on the acquisition of English as a second language. L2 learners of English will receive PI focused on past tense *-ed* that occurs in word final position. This form is made redundant when accompanied by a lexical temporal indicator. L2 learners will be taught to rely on the morpheme to assign tense, an appropriate processing strategy for this linguistic feature of English. Can they then transfer that training to another word final temporal morpheme? Can these L2 learners also process present tense forms located at the ends of words?

- *Question 2:* What are the cumulative effects of receiving PI instruction on the different types of processing strategies needed for different types of linguistic features?

In Chapter 5 we present research on the acquisition of French as a second language. L2 learners of French will receive PI focused on French past imperfective aspect, the *imparfait*, which occurs as a word final morpheme and can be made redundant with a lexical temporal/aspectual indicator. L2 learners will be taught to rely on and process the morpheme as a tense and aspect indicator. Can they then transfer that training to another word final verb morpheme? The other linguistic feature we assess is the French subjunctive, a form that is triggered by the meaning expressed in the main clause of the sentence. We also explore if learners can transfer their training on processing verb morphology to the appropriate processing of a word-order phenomenon, the French causative construction with *faire*.

Research on Processing Instruction has so far investigated its effects in isolation. That is to say, one study has investigated the relative effects of Processing Instruction on one specific form. Another study has investigated another set of learners and taught them via Processing Instruction to process a different linguistic form. PI research has, to date, taken the appropriately conservative approach of assessing the direct effects of instruction, seeking only to determine if Processing Instruction would indeed alter inappropriate processing strategies and/or instil appropriate ones. As seen in Chapter 2, the empirical evidence has shown that Processing Instruction has been highly effective across many types of forms and in many languages.

In this volume we will present the results of new and unpublished empirical work that investigates transfer-of-training effects, both secondary and cumulative, of Processing Instruction. This is achieved by:

(1) presenting and explaining the processing principles as part of the input processing model so that readers can appreciate the foundation on which our work is based;
(2) reviewing the empirical research conducted, to date, on the primary effects of Processing Instruction;
(3) presenting the results of three studies that have investigated transfer of training effects (secondary and cumulative effects) for Processing Instruction; and, finally,
(4) drawing appropriate conclusions about transfer-of-training effects and indicating possible future directions for research in the PI model.

Contents

In Chapter 1 we provide a synopsis of VanPatten's theory of input processing, (VanPatten, 1996, 2003, 2004b). This theory captures as a set of Principles what second language learners do with meaning-bearing, comprehensible input. We first present the theory as VanPatten does, as a set of principles. The two major principles of this theoretical model (the

Primacy of Meaning Principle and the First Noun Principle) are reviewed along with their corollaries. After presenting these principles, we undertake to demonstrate their empirical underpinnings. In doing so, we further explicate the scope of each principle. This chapter provides the theoretical background for the empirical work presented in Chapters 3, 4 and 5, in which the transfer-of-training effects of Processing Instruction are measured.

Chapter 2 is divided into two parts. In Part 1 we review all the research to date on the effects of Processing Instruction that has addressed a specific processing problem. Research on the effects of PI has been conducted using both syntactic and perceptual strategies. Within this research framework (which intended to measure the primary effects of Processing Instruction), we can identify various lines or strands of research. In this chapter we revise four main lines of reserach.

(1) First of all, we provide a summary of the findings of the existing body of research that has compared the effects of Processing Instruction to other types of instruction, the former having focused on language processing and the latter having emphasised language production. That is, traditional instruction consists of form-focused output practice, whereas meaning-based output instruction consists of communicatively-focused output practices. The fundamental question Processing Instruction had to address at the outset was whether or not it was effective instruction.

(2) We revise the empirical work conducted on measuring the effects of the individual components of Processing Instruction. Processing Instruction comprises of two elements: explicit information about the grammatical item, including information about processing strategies, and structured input activities. The question as to which element was the causal variable in the positive findings of PI emerged early in the trajectory of PI research.

(3) We summarise very recent research on the effects of Processing Instruction delivered via different modes (i.e. online vs. pencil and paper) or in different contexts (i.e. virtual or classroom). The question this strand of investigation addressed was whether a self-guided learner doing work online would be more, less, or equally influenced by Processing Instruction.

(4) Finally, we evaluate classroom-based studies that have manipulated Processing Instruction materials with the idea of potentially increasing the number of form–meaning connections learners would make. To that end, the research compared the effects of using Processing Instruction materials that had undergone input enhancement techniques with the same materials that lacked those enhancements.

In Part 2 of the chapter, we present Processing Instruction as a viable approach to grammar instruction. We review a set of guidelines for developing structured input activities and look very closely at the activities that learners are engaged in and how they are derived from the input processing principles presented in Chapter 1.

In Chapter 3 we present the results of our first investigation of transfer-of-training effects of Processing Instruction on the acquisition of Italian. In this work we focused on what we have termed the secondary effects. We investigated whether learners who are exposed to Processing Instruction on one linguistic item will transfer that training and use it to process another linguistic item that presents a similar processing problem to the first. The two linguistic items we selected for this investigation were Italian noun–adjective agreement and the morphological future tense. These two forms are respectively affected by two processing problems/principles: *The Preference for Nonredundancy Principle* and *The Lexical Preference Principle*. In the case of the first processing problem, adjective ending in Italian is an agreement feature affected by this principle. We isolate gender agreement. Here is an example. In the sentence *la ragazza bella* the adjective (*bella*) must agree in number and gender with the noun it modifies (*ragazza*). This feature of grammar (*a* = singular feminine) is highly redundant, as there are a number of -*a* markers of feminine gender (*la ragazza bella*). It is also very low in semantic value, as it does not contribute very much to the meaning of the utterance. There is no difference in meaning between *ragazza bella* and *ragazza bello*; the difference is grammaticality.

Future tense morphology is also word final, but it is affected by the Lexical Preference Principle. If learners can establish the temporal framework or assign tense with a lexeme (a content word), then they do not need the verb form to also do that. For example in the sentence *Domani Paolo giocherà a Pallone* both the lexical item *domani* and the -*à* verb ending communicate future tense. According to the Lexical Preference Principle learners will naturally rely on the lexical item over the verb inflection in order to gather semantic information. Unlike adjective agreement, future tense morphology has semantic value and, in the absence of a lexical temporal indicator, would be the only way to assign tense. The two linguistic items are formally similar (word final) but represent different processing problems. Processing Instruction on adjective agreement in Italian directs learners to process the ends of words. Would learners receiving PI transfer that training to another linguistic item and thereby be able to process Italian future tense forms? The main question in the first study is, does processing instruction on adjective agreement aid learners in processing future tense?

Because this is the first study on transfer-of training effects for PI, we compared PI with another type of instruction. Processing Instruction (which is input-based) was compared with traditional output-based instruction. Three groups were used. One group received Processing Instruction and a second group received traditional output-based instruction. The third was a control group that did not receive instruction on the target items over the duration of the experimental treatments. Pre-tests and post-tests were developed for this study and consisted of an aural interpretation task and a written form-completion text. All groups received pre-tests on both linguistic features. After the pre-tests learners were randomly assigned to one of three groups. The two treatment groups received instruction only on the first linguistic feature (adjective agreement). After the end of the instructional period all three groups were administered post-tests on both the target linguistic feature (adjective agreement) and the additional linguistic feature (future tense). Learners' performance on the future tense post-tests will allow us to measure any possible secondary effects on processing and production.

In Chapter 4 we present the results of a classroom study that also investigated secondary transfer-of-training effects of Processing Instruction, but this time we investigated native speakers of Korean learning English as a second language. It is important for generalising the results of Processing Instruction that we investigate different second languages as well as learners with different native language backgrounds. We selected two linguistic items from English for this investigation: the past tense marker -*ed* and the third person singular present tense marker -*s*. As temporal markers both linguistic items are affected by the Lexical Preference Principle, which is that, if there are lexical temporal indicators present, learners would prefer to use these to establish the time frame. In essence, a lexeme would make the verb morphology redundant. The following sentence, for example, doubly conveys past time: 'Yesterday the dog chased the cat up the tree'. Once learners establish the temporal framework with a lexeme (content word, 'yesterday'), then they do not also need the verb form to do that. In the absence of a lexical temporal indicator, the verb morphemes become very important for establishing time. The present tense marker -*s* presents another processing problem in that it carries not only temporal information but (unlike the past tense marker) also indicates person and number. The processing problem for learners is that in English the subject of the verb must be stated explicitly, which always makes the person/number feature of the morpheme redundant. Given that Processing Instruction on past tense helps learners process the ends of words, because it directs their attention there to find the form and connect it to its meaning, would learners receiving Processing Instruction on past tense transfer the strategy and use it to process present tense? The main question in the study is: does processing instruction on past tense aid L2 learners' processing of future tense?

As in Chapter 3, we compared Processing Instruction with another type of instruction. Processing Instruction (input-based) was compared with traditional output-based instruction and, again, three groups were used. One received Processing Instruction and a second group received traditional output-based instruction. The third was a control group that did not receive instruction on either of the target items (past tense and present tense) over the duration of the experimental treatments. Pre-tests and post-tests were developed for this investigation and consisted of an aural interpretation task and a written form-completion text. All three groups received pre-tests on both linguistic features. After the pre-tests learners were randomly assigned to one of three groups. The two treatment groups received instruction only on the first linguistic feature (past tense *-d*). After the end of the instructional period all three groups were administered the post-tests on both the target linguistic feature (past tense *-d*) and the additional linguistic feature (present tense, third person singular *-s*). Learners' performance on the present tense, third person singular *-s* post-tests will allow us to determine whether there are any secondary effects of Processing Instruction, and if those effects are found in the area of processing or production or both.

In Chapter 5 we present the results of a classroom study that explored both secondary and cumulative transfer-of-training effects. The learners were native speakers of English learning French. The form targeted for instruction was the French past imperfective tense, the *imparfait*, which is a verb final morphological marker. As with the other tense markers discussed above in relation to Chapters 3 and 4, this past imperfective tense marker is subject to the Lexical Preference Principle. Its meaning can be conveyed via lexical temporal aspectual indicators, for example, 'every summer of my childhood' conveys past imperfective time. The French subjunctive mood marker is also affected by the Lexical Preference Principle, albeit in a different way. Unlike tense morphemes, this mood marker is completely redundant. It can be realised only in the presence of a lexical marker. Additionally, the subjunctive occurs in a subordinate clause while the lexical marker is the verb in the independent clause. The subjunctive, therefore, is also subject to the Sentence Location Principle. It does not occur in a favoured processing location. The first question we aim to address is: would learners receiving Processing Instruction on the *imparfait* transfer that training to another linguistic item and thereby be able to process French subjunctive mood forms? The first question in this study is: does processing instruction on verb tense and aspect aid learners in processing mood markers in subordinate clauses?

This study makes another very important contribution to our knowledge base by investigating what we have termed cumulative effects. The French *imparfait* is a tense and aspect verb morpheme. The French faire causative constructions present a very different processing problem, a word order processing problem. In the sentence '*Jean fait laver la voiture à Marc*', learners use an inappropriate word order processing strategy that assigns the first noun in the sentence the role of agent. That is, L2 learners interpret the sentence as 'Jean washes the car'. The true meaning of the sentence is, however, that 'Marc washes the car'. The sentence reads 'Jean makes Marc wash the car'. The question we aim to address is, will learners receiving Processing Instruction on the *imparfait* transfer that training to another linguistic item that requires the use of a different processing strategy, and thereby be able to process French *faire* causative constructions? The second question in this study is, does processing instruction on verb morphology aid learners in processing syntactic constructions?

Three groups were used in this study. One received Processing Instruction and a second group received traditional output-based instruction. The third was a control group that did not receive instruction on the target items over the duration of the experimental treatments. Pre-tests and post-tests were developed for this study and consisted of an aural interpretation task and a written form-completion test examining sentence level production. All groups received pre-tests on the three linguistics features. After the pre-tests, learners were randomly assigned to one of three groups. The two treatment groups received instruction only on the first linguistic feature (imperfective past tense). After the end of the instructional period all three groups were administered post-tests on the target linguistic feature (imperfective past tense) and the two additional linguistic features (subjunctive mood morphology and *faire* causatives). Learners' performance on the subjunctive mood morphology post-tests will allow us to measure any possible secondary effects on processing and production. Their performance on the faire *causative* constructions will allow us to measure any possible cumulative effects across different processing principles. Additionally, we will also determine if those effects are found in the area of processing or production, or both.

In Chapter 6 we summarise our findings and discuss their importance in two contexts. First, we consider our work in the broader context of other research conducted on Processing Instruction. Secondly, and more importantly, we explore the contributions that our research makes to the theoretical underpinnings of Processing Instruction as we examine issues such as the role of the learners' first language in second language acquisition as well as the limited role that output plays in second language development. Finally, we consider how instructed language acquisition might have a role in incidental acquisition and what mechanism that role takes.

Chapter 1
A Theory of Input Processing: How Learners Work with Input

There are many theories and theoretical orientations that guide contemporary research on second language acquisition (SLA). Mitchell and Myles (2004: 2) comment that '... although the field of second language learning research has been extremely active and productive in recent decades, we have not yet arrived at a unified or comprehensive view as to how second languages are learnt'. VanPatten and Williams (2007a) ask why just one comprehensive theory to account for all of second language acquisition does not exist. Their response to the question is amusing but insightful nonetheless.[1]

> To understand [why there isn't just one theory to account for SLA], one might consider the parable about the four blind men and the elephant. These sightless men chance upon a pachyderm for the first time and one, holding its tail, says, 'Ah! The elephant is very much like a rope'. The second one has wrapped his arms around a giant leg and says, 'Ah! The elephant is like a tree'. The third has been feeling along side the elephant's massive body and says, 'Ah! The elephant is very much like a wall'. The fourth, having seized the trunk cries out, 'Ah! The elephant is very much like a snake'. For us, SLA is a big elephant that researchers can easily look at from different perspectives ... Thus, researchers have grabbed onto different parts of the elephant as a means of coming to grips with the complex phenomenon. (VanPatten & Williams, 2007a: vii–viii)

While we do not make any assertions as to which part of the elephant we are grabbing, we can assert that, as far as second language acquisition is concerned, we are working with input and examining the ways in which learners work with input. What is input? 'The raw linguistic data (oral or written) to which learners are exposed' (Farley, 2005: 109). 'Samples of language that learners are exposed to in a communicative context or setting' (Wong, 2005: 119). 'Samples of second language that learners hear or see to which they attend for its propositional content (message)' (VanPatten, 1996: 10).

We can also assert that we are working with input processing, the process by which learners make the initial connection between a grammatical form and its meaning.

Indeed, it is common ground among all theorists of language learning, of whatever description, that it is necessary to interpret and to process incoming language data in some form, for normal language development to take place. There is thus a consensus that language input of some kind is essential for normal language learning. (Mitchell & Myles, 2004: 20)

We are working, in particular, with VanPatten's theory of input processing (VanPatten, 1996, 2000, 2002, 2004a, 2007).

VanPatten's theory of input processing in adult second language acquisition frames the research questions, methods and procedures we used in the work we present in this book. It is critical, then, that we begin with an account of this theory. We draw from several sources to present our account. We draw extensively from the work of its principal theoriser (VanPatten, 1996, 2000, 2004b, 2007) as well as from our own work with and within this theoretical framework (Lee & Benati, 2007a, 2007b). As a theoretical framework, input processing is concerned with three fundamental questions that involve the assumption that an integral part of language acquisition is making form–meaning connections:

- Under what conditions do learners make initial form–meaning connections?
- Why, at a given moment in time, do they make some and not other form–meaning connections?
- What internal strategies do learners use in comprehending sentences and how might this affect acquisition? (VanPatten, 2007: 116)

We can add to this list of three umbrella question more specific ones that the research on input processing has attempted to delineate.

- What linguistic data do learners attend to during comprehension? Why?
- What linguistic data do learners not attend to? Why?
- How does a formal feature's position in the utterance influence whether it gets processed?
- What grammatical roles do learners assign to nouns based on their position in an utterance?

In its current form, VanPatten's theory consists of two overarching organising principles, each of which is further explicated with subprinciples. We quote here from VanPatten (2004b: 14–18) noting and footnoting, of course, the differences in the development of some principles from 1996 to 2004b to 2007. The two overarching principles address two different aspects of processing. The first, the Primacy of Meaning Principle asserts that when learners are engaged in communicative, meaningful interchanges, they are primarily concerned with meaning. The second, The First Noun Principle, asserts that the order in which learners encounter sentence elements is a powerful factor in assigning grammatical relations amongst sentence elements. These two principles are as follows.

- Principle 1 (P1): *Primacy of Meaning Principle*: learners process input for meaning before they process it for form.
- Principle 2 (P2): *First Noun Principle:* learners tend to process the first noun or pronoun they encounter in a sentence as the subject or agent.[2]

The Primacy of Meaning Principle is further subdivided into six subprinciples (a–f). Some of these subprinciples had previously been referred to as the corollaries of the principle (VanPatten, 1996) and some are new developments to the framework, adding as such to its explanatory adequacy. These subprinciples are meant to capture the interplay of various linguistic and cognitive features during comprehension. The subprinciples to the Primacy of Meaning Principle are as follows.

- (P1a) *Primacy of Content Words Principle*: learners process content words in the input before anything else.
- (P1b) *Lexical Preference Principle*: learners will tend to rely on lexical items as opposed to grammatical form to get meaning when both encode the same semantic information.[3]
- (P1c) *Preference for Nonredundancy Principle*: learners are more likely to process nonredundant meaningful grammatical form before they process redundant meaningful forms.
- (P1d) *Meaning-Before-Nonmeaning Principle*: learners are more likely to process meaningful grammatical forms before non-meaningful forms, irrespective of redundancy.[4]
- (P1e) *Availability of Resources Principle*: for learners to process either redundant meaningful grammatical forms or non-meaningful forms, the processing of overall sentential meaning must not drain available processing resources.
- (P1f) *Sentence Location Principle:* learners tend to process items in sentence initial position before those in final position and those in medial position.

When we listen to an utterance or read a sentence, we are presented with the linguistic elements of the sentence in a rigidly linear fashion. One sentence element precedes the next such that we must comprehend the sentence 'as it comes' to us. While regression is possible in some reading contexts, it is rarely possible in listening contexts. Research in both first and second language acquisition has found that the order of the words plays a role in comprehension and hence in language acquisition (e.g. Slobin, 1973;

Lee, 2003). VanPatten's First Noun Principle captures one powerful processing strategy, that is, assigning the grammatical role of subject to the first noun encountered in an utterance. Between 1996 and 2004, we gathered more data on learners' misassignment of the first noun so that VanPatten has developed a set of subprinciples that describe factors that might attenuate learners' misuse of the first noun. The subprinciples are as follows.

- (P2a) *Lexical Semantics Principle*: learners may rely on lexical semantics, where possible, instead of word order to interpret sentences.[5]
- (P2b) *Event Probabilities Principle*: learners may rely on event probabilities, where possible, instead of word order to interpret sentences.
- (P2c) *Contextual Constraint Principle*: learners may rely less on the First Noun Principle if preceding context constrains the possible interpretation of a clause or sentence. (VanPatten, 2004b: 14–18)

These principles model 'what guides learners' processing of linguistic data in the input as they are engaged in comprehension' (VanPatten, 2007: 116). We will examine each of these principles in turn and provide some of the evidence that supports them. It is important to keep in mind that learners are doing two things with the language to which they are exposed and with which they are engaged. They are making meaning and they are making form–meaning connections (Lee & VanPatten, 1995, 2003). Making meaning is comprehending, arriving at an idea of what the propositional content of the message is. Making form–meaning connections is input processing, attending to the grammatical forms/features in the input so as to connect the forms with their meanings. While related and often intertwined, these are not the same processes. As we further explore VanPatten's theory of input processing, we will see both types of processes at work.

The Push to Make Meaning

To assert the primacy of meaning in input processing is to take as the point of departure that learners are primarily motivated to understand messages be they delivered orally during an interaction or visually while reading print. If someone is talking to us, we assume they have something to say that we are meant to understand. Our task as listeners is to put forward at least an effort, if not our best effort, to understand the speaker. When we see a billboard, for example, and read what it says, we assume that someone has something to communicate to us about a product or service. There is a message that we are meant to grasp and we put forth the effort to do so. Second language learners assume the same thing; there are messages in what they hear and read and they are meant to put forward an effort to understand them. 'Simply put, P1 states that learners are *driven* [emphasis added] to look for the message in the input ("What is this person saying to me?") before looking for how that message is encoded' (VanPatten, 1996: 17).

Meaning first

Research has repeatedly uncovered the varying conditions under which learners successfully make meaning from the input. Lee (1987), for example, showed that L2 learners of Spanish can extract the lexical meaning of verbs that are morphologically marked as subjunctive even though they had never been exposed to subjunctive forms in the classroom setting. They extracted meaning as successfully as a group of learners who had already been taught subjunctive forms. Lee and Rodríguez (1997) compared the effects of morphosyntactic modifications on passage comprehension. Keeping content constant, they manipulated subordination and whether that subordination required subjunctive mood or not. They found that L2 learners of Spanish comprehended the three versions of the passage equally well. Additionally, they substituted the target verbs (those that were subordinated and made into subjunctive mood forms) with nonsense words that conformed to the orthographic structure of Spanish. This substitution had no effect on passage comprehension. Manipulating both verbal and lexical forms did not affect passage comprehension because the readers' task was to get the meaning of the text and they did.[6]

More evidence for how learners process input for meaning before they process it for form comes from the recall data reported in Lee (2002, 2003). The learners read a passage about the future of telecommunications technologies in which the last few sentences in the passage warn of the dangers of society's growing dependence on technology. The last sentence they encountered was as follows:

> *El hombre,* Homo sapiens, *se convertirá en* Homo electrónicus.
> (Man, *Homo sapiens*, will become *Homo electrónicus*.)

Most learners understood the meaning of the sentence and understood its meaning in the context of the passage. Few, however, wrote the exact form of what they had seen in the text. That is, few learners wrote *Homo electrónicus*. Some learners produced graphemically-based renderings such as *Homo electricity* and *Homo erectus* (the anthropological facts were not quite accurate in this recall). Others made a semantic substitution such as *Homo technology* and *Homo technologicalus*. Clearly, the semantic substitutions show us that learners processed the input for meaning before they processed it for form.

Lee and Rossomondo (2004) analysed other elements of the input passage reported on in Lee (2002, 2003) and Rossomondo (2007). The passage they used in their research targeted learners' processing of future tense verb forms in Spanish, which are morphologically marked word finally for person/number and tense. The first verb in the passage was *dependerá* (will depend). Lee and Rossomondo's analyses revealed that learners recalled this verb in a variety of forms. The forms varied, but the meaning always centred on the idea of dependence. They noted both verbal and nominal rendering of the target verb. Among the verbal forms they found: *will depend on, depend or depends on, rely upon, relies* and *will use*. Among the nominal forms they found *dependency, dependence upon, are dependent* and *will become dependent*. These forms show us that learners were primarily working to get the meaning not the form.

Content words

VanPatten's theory differentiates between the value of content words and function words for their contribution to meaning from the learners' perspective and from the perspective of the push to get or make meaning. Which words are the most helpful for getting the meaning out of the input? The answer is content words, those words that represent major lexical categories as opposed to functional or minor lexical categories.[7] In layman's terms we might refer to content words as the 'big' words and functional words as the 'little' words. Learners must bring some metalinguistic knowledge with them to the task of second language acquisition such that they can differentiate content and function words in the L2. That discussion is, however, beyond the scope of this chapter. We do, however, present several empirical works that have demonstrated the greater value of content words to second language learners.

Bernhardt (1992) discussed the different text-processing strategies employed by native and inexperienced non-native readers of German. In tracking their eye movements across the lines of a text, she showed that native readers of German fixated (i.e. placed their central focal point) far more frequently than inexperienced non-native readers did. Because non-native readers fixated less frequently, they did not take in as much of the text as native readers did. In other words, native readers read more densely and intensely than the non-natives did. Moreover, Bernhardt found that the native readers fixated quite frequently on the ends of words, that is, on word final morphology. The non-native readers tended to fixate on the centres of words, leaving word final morphology in peripheral vision. And, with their less numerous fixations, non-native readers tended to process content words over function words. This eye movement data is very interesting because it contrasts the approaches native and non-native readers take to processing. Non-native readers, the language learners, valued content words highly and valued word final morphology much less. The eye movement evidence very directly supports the value of content words to learners. In VanPatten (1990) we see what happens when we focus learners on word final morphology.

VanPatten (1990) conducted an experiment in which he demonstrated the interplay of content words, function words and verb morphology with comprehension. He asked learners of Spanish to listen to a short passage on inflation in Latin America. He assigned learners to one of four conditions. One group simply listened to the passage and had no secondary processing task to perform; VanPatten termed this the 'content-only' group. Another group listened to the passage and indicated each time they heard the word *inflación*, which was also the title of the passage. VanPatten termed this the 'content + lexical item' group. A third group listened to the passage and indicated each time they heard the word *la*, the feminine singular form of the definite article. It occurred prior to each occurrence of the word *inflación*. VanPatten termed this the 'content + functor' group. Finally, a fourth group listened to the passage and indicated each time they heard an *n* at the end of a word. This verbal inflection is the morpheme that marks third person plural in Spanish. He termed this group the 'content + inflection' group. As they listened to the passage, the three groups with simultaneous listening tasks placed a checkmark on a page for each occurrence of the target item. After listening to the passage, the learners recalled as much as they could of what they had heard. VanPatten found that listening for content alone and listening for content + lexical item were complimentary activities insofar as learners in both conditions comprehended equal amounts of the passage. Listening for the functor and for the verbal inflection were equally detrimental activities in that comprehension fell off significantly in these conditions. From Bernhardt (1992) we know that learners tend not to process word final morphology and from VanPatten (1990) we know that if they are directed to it, they lose some of the meaning. These data support the thesis that content words are the building blocks of comprehension. Drawing learners' attention to non-content elements of a passage, be they verb morphemes or definite articles, makes learners lose some of the content.[8]

More evidence of how learners process content words over other sentence elements comes from examining the products of comprehension. VanPatten and Wong (2004) demonstrated that learners misinterpret French causative constructions using an inappropriate word order processing strategy. They give the following example:

Jean fait promener le chien à Marie.
John-makes-to-walk-the-dog-to-Mary.
John makes Mary walk the dog. (VanPatten & Wong, 2004: 98–99)

The target sentence contains two verbs each with its own subject/agent. Learners, however, tend to take the first subject, Jean, and make it the agent of the second verb, *promener*. The second subject, Marie, tends to be interpreted as the dog's owner. In the end the learners misinterpret the sentence (by misassigning grammatical and semantic roles) to mean the following:

John walks the dog for Mary.

Whereas VanPatten and Wong address this processing problem from the perspective of word order and the First Noun Principle (P2), we can also see the effects of processing content words over other sentence elements. We underline the content words to demonstrate that they are the words learners focused in on.

Jean fait promener le chien à Marie.

Two important grammatical elements are not processed, *fait* and *à*. They are important because they signal the underlying semantic relationships between Jean and Marie.

A similar example of collecting content words to make meaning comes from Lee (1990). After early stage learners read a short passage about feudalism, they were asked to recall in writing as much as they could remember. Here are the first two sentences of the passage:

> *Entre los años 900–1000, Europa Occidental estaba en gran desorden. El imperio de Carlomagno, que había logrado unir esa parte del mundo, se estaba dividiendo en pequeños estados.*
> (Between the years 900 and 1000, Western Europe was in great disorder. The empire of Charlemagne, that had managed to unite that part of the world, was being divided into small states.)

One subject recalled these two sentences as follows (misspellings in the original are preserved here).

> In the years around 900-1000, there was an emporer Carlomagna (sp?) that ruled an area in the world. (Lee, 1990: 147)

If we go back to the original text and underline the words that appear in the recall, we see the way the learner has collected words from the input and put them together. We also see the way the learner left out some words, most likely due to the effort required to accomplish the task:

> *Entre los años 900–1000, Europa Occidental estaba en gran desorden. El imperio de Carlomagno, que había logrado unir esa parte del mundo, se estaba dividiendo en pequeños estados.* (VanPatten, 2007; Lee, 1999).

This learner did not process an important function word, the preposition *de* in the noun phrase *imperio de Carlomagno* (empire of Charlemagne). The preposition is important because it establishes the relationship between the two content words. The learner put the two content words together and misassigned the meaning of one of them, making it emperor not empire. What do emperors do? They rule, which is something the learner inserted into the recall. Another learner recalled these two lines as follows.

Charlemagne was the ruler. He divided the country into small states ... (Lee, 1990: 146).

The content words that this learner collected to make meaning attribute agency to Charlemagne (whose death in 814 was not an historical fact known to this group of readers). Attributing agency to Charlemagne occurred quite frequently in the recalls. The learners who did so did not process the entire verb phrase, *se estaba dividiendo*, but rather used only the content word, *dividiendo*, to make meaning. The verb phrase in the original text is marked for past (*estaba*) as well as for imperfective aspect (*-aba*) and progressive aspect (*-ndo*). The learner uses a perfective past form in his recall. We can, therefore, infer that he did not process these formal elements in the input. He collected content words but not their formal features in order to make meaning.

We find additional evidence of the value of content words to language learners from their own accounts of what they do to understand. Lee (1999) analysed think aloud protocols for the interplay between input-processing strategies and comprehension strategies. He asked beginning-level learners to perform a retrospective think aloud of a passage in which eight past tense verb forms were the targeted linguistic items. The following excerpt of one learner's think-aloud protocol was not included in Lee (1999), but comes from the data set that he analysed. The task of the second language learner was to read the passage sentence by sentence and then think aloud his comprehension process. With regard to two of the target sentences, he stated the following about his use of key words. We can understand the learner's use of the term 'key words' as content words.

> Um, you can see from like different words like, um, *contacto* and *consecuencia*, like the, um, different like structure of the sentence, like if you can get the key words like that then you can kinda see what should follow it ... Um, a word like *disco* is kind of a humorous tip-off 'cause you can tell that's something related to music.

This learner collects content words to build up his comprehension. In all he refers to his use of words to comprehend sentence meaning seventeen times. At a later point in the think-aloud he offers another example of using key/content words and other words, too:

> Um, *'filme'*, um, *'ofer-'*, *'oferta'*, *'aceptó'*, 'Hollywood' all give you like, you know, key words, like 'offer', 'accept', 'Hollywood', uh, would tell you what the sentence is going to be about. And those are all cognates, and then other words that you already know or can figure out would tell you pretty much the meaning of that sentence.

Finally, the learner also makes a distinction between key words and another type, the small words. He stated the following:

> Um, *múltiples* is a good cognate. And then there's a lot of pretty small easy words like 'with' and 'to see', 'is'.

Another type of evidence supporting the primary role of content words in comprehension comes from Carroll (2004), who points to their role in the negotiation of meaning. She specifies content words as those in major lexical categories and refers to them as prosodic words. In a footnote to her commentary on VanPatten's model of input processing, she notes that content words have the linguistic properties that make them repeatable 'as single utterances in situations where a speaker has failed to make herself understood and believes that the learner has limited language abilities' (Carroll, 2004: 298). She provided the following example to underscore the point.

NS: The exercises are all on my homepage.
NNS: (...) [looks confused]
NS: EXERCISES ... HOMEPAGE
NNS: oh ... yes ... EXERCISES. (Carroll, 2004: 298)

The native speaker has isolated and repeated the two content words from her initial utterance. Content words are important not only to learners but also to native speakers who, apparently, assign them value for insuring comprehension.

Lexical preference

Languages have ways of encoding and thus signalling the same information in multiple ways; we refer to this as the natural redundancy of languages. Given the availability of limited resources to second language learners VanPatten's theory tries to account for where learners direct their processing resources. The background research VanPatten uses to support the Lexical Preference Principle has all been focused on tense assignment. Likewise, the research on the effects of Processing Instruction framed by the Lexical Preference Principle has focused on tense assignment. The background research on tense assignment has manipulated the input to include or exclude lexical and grammatical cues to tense. Preferring lexical cues to tense is connected to learners' use of content words to make meaning.

Lee *et al.* (1997) gave two groups of learners of Spanish different versions of the same passage to listen to. One version contained lexical temporal adverbs referring to the past, while the other version contained no such lexical temporal markers. In this second version, only the verb final morpheme indicated tense, for example, *admitió* (he admitted). After listening, the learners performed a tense identification task. The results showed that the learners who listened to the passage with adverbials identified correctly more of the temporal references than did the learners who listened to passages with only verb morphology to mark tense.

Lee (1999) examined the comprehension and input-processing strategies of a small number of learners of Spanish as they performed a retrospective think aloud. Half the learners read a passage that contained lexical temporal adverbs whereas the other half read a version of the passage that did not contain the adverbs. As Lee (1999: 53) put it, 'when subjects have adverbs they use them [to comprehend temporal reference]. Those in the +adverb condition only sporadically refer to verb forms'.

Rossomondo (2007) demonstrated a very dramatic difference in tense assignment due to the presence or absence of lexical temporal markers. She conducted introspective think aloud protocols on two groups of learners. One group was reading and introspecting on a passage that contained Spanish future tense verb forms along with lexical temporal markers. The other group read and introspected on a version of the passage that contained only verb forms but no lexical temporal markers. Rossomondo found that, in the presence of a lexical temporal marker, learners comprehended (i.e. rendered it in the introspection) the future meaning of the verb form on average 52%; the scores per individual verb ranged from 0% comprehension of the future meaning to 92%. In the absence of the temporal marker, learners comprehended the future meaning of the target verbs only 0.8%. The learners did not comprehend the future meaning of 12 of the 13 target verbs. They managed a future meaning for one verb only 11% of the time.

Lee (1990) examined the recall protocols of first year learners of Spanish in order to reveal the processes through which they constructed the meaning of the passage. The passage referred to the social-political system known as feudalism. The first line of the passage referred to the years 900–1000. The passage also contained the number 400, which was the number of years the feudal system helped maintain order, and a reference to the year 1200, the year feudalism was at its zenith. All learners read the same version of the passage, i.e. there was no version of the passage in which temporal markers had been removed. Relevant to the current discussion of the Lexical Preference Principle is that 11 of the 13 learners Lee (1990) examined used the years 900–1000 to construct the temporal framework for their recalls. One learner, who had a particularly difficult time comprehending used the years to structure the second part of his recall.

> In the beginning there was nothing. (STOP!)
> There was a society change in the era of Charlemagne
> a change from honour to a society of justice.
> I remember many years 900 – start of Charlemagne
> 1100 – ?
> 1200 – justice and equality. (Lee, 1990: 148)

Musumeci (1989) conducted a cross-linguistic study (Italian, French and Spanish) in which she examined how successfully learners assigned tense at sentence level under different exposure conditions. She manipulated both linguistic and nonlinguistic cues to temporality. In one condition, the baseline condition, she presented learners with sentences in which the only cue to temporal reference was the verbal inflection. In each of the subsequent conditions, the learners received the verbal inflections as well as some other cue or cues. In the next condition Musumeci added a lexical temporal adverbial as an additional cue to temporal reference. In the third condition, she gave learners the additional cue of a typical teacher gesture performed as the learners heard the sentences. For example, to indicate past, the speaker pointed her thumb over her shoulder, pointing backwards. To indicate future, the speaker gestured with her hand moving it away from her body and outward toward the side. In the fourth condition Musumeci supplied learners with all the cues: verbal inflections, adverbials and gestures.

Overall, the results confirmed that the main factor influencing correct tense assignment was the presence or absence of temporal adverbials in the input sentences (Musumeci, 1989: 127). Specifically, Musumeci found that learners assigned tense more correctly in the two conditions that included a lexical temporal adverbial than in the other two conditions, i.e. verbal inflections only and verbal inflections plus gestures. Lexical items are more useful to the learners for assigning tense than are the verb forms or a teacher's gesturing.

Redundancy and meaningfulness

VanPatten (1985) introduced the idea that formal features of a second language, from a learner's perspective, would be either of high or low communicative value. 'Communicative value refers to the relative contribution a form makes to the referential meaning of an utterance and is based on the presence or absence of two features: inherent semantic value and redundancy within the sentence-utterance' (VanPatten, 1996: 24). VanPatten extrapolated his original principle regarding processing meaningful versus non-meaningful morphology (1996: 24) from the morpheme acquisition studies. Why, for example, is the progressive aspect marker *-ing* acquired before third person singular *-s* in English? VanPatten's answer is that because *–ing* contributes unique information to the sentential meaning (an event in progress), learners direct attention to it during processing. They do not direct attention to the third person *-s* because it does not offer them unique information. He provides two examples:

> The cat is sleeping.
> The cat sleeps ten hours everyday. (VanPatten, 2007: 119)

'Thus, if learners are confronted with something like *-ing* on verb forms, they will be forced to make this form–meaning connection sooner than, say, third person *-s* because the latter is redundant and the former is not' (VanPatten, 2007: 119). As we saw with the Lexical Preference Principle, a grammatical marker might well have semantic value, but other sentence elements might make it redundant. Removing the lexical item, as is done in Processing Instruction, makes the grammatical marker nonredundant. And so, the Preference for Nonredundancy Principle is highly related to the Lexical Preference Principle.

Some grammatical markers do not carry any meaning; they express no real world semantic information. We can offer several examples (Lee & Benati, 2007b). Grammatical gender marking in Romance languages is an example of non-meaningful morphology. The surface-level agreement features are such that adjectives agree in number and in grammatical gender with the nouns they modify. In other words, the characteristics of the noun determine the form of adjective. That an adjective is marked as masculine or feminine does not change its meaning. In Italian, both *bassa* and *basso* mean *short*. Which form to use is determined by the noun they are describing. Additionally, gender markings on adjectives are often a redundant marking. Consider the noun phrase *mio fratello basso* (my short brother) and the gender markings on the three words. The gender marking on *basso* is the third masculine marker in the string. Being non-meaningful as well as redundant contribute to the processing problems that face second language learners.

Subjunctive mood verbal morphology is another grammatical form that is non-meaningful and redundant in sentences that express doubt and opinion in Italian and other Romance languages. We use the subjunctive mood markings on the verb in a subordinate dependent clause when the verb of the main clause expresses doubt or opinion. The following two sentences demonstrate the processing problems learners encounter with subjunctive mood morphology.

Dubito che George sia intelligente.
(I doubt that George is intelligent.)

So che George e intelligente.
(I know that George is intelligent.)

The meanings of the verbs *dubito* and *so* trigger the forms *sia* and *e*, respectively. *Sia* and *e* mean exactly the same thing, *is*.

Resources

It is not impossible for learners to direct their attention to meaningful but redundant grammatical forms or to non-meaningful grammatical forms.

As VanPatten (1990) and Bransdorfer (1991) showed with their simultaneous processing tasks, learners can be directed to attend to non-meaningful forms but at a loss to comprehension.

> Comprehension for learners is initially quite effortful in terms of cognitive processing and working memory. This has consequences for what the input processing mechanisms will pay attention to. At the same time, learners are limited capacity processors and cannot process and store the same amount of information as native speakers can during moment-by-moment processing. (VanPatten, 2007: 116)

To capture this loss to comprehension when focused on non-meaningful form, VanPatten proposed the Availability of Resources Principle. The principle states that comprehending overall sentential meaning can not be overly effortful if learners are also to process redundant meaningful grammatical forms or non-meaningful forms.

Lee (1999) analysed the comprehension and input processing strategies of second language learners. He states:

> the comprehension strategies of low comprehenders may circumvent processing text for form. It is an interesting paradox to consider that learners' attempts to manage their comprehension has the less than desirable effect of dislocating from their attention key aspects of the input. (Lee, 1999: 57)

Comprehension difficulties can impede processing forms in the input. In the following example, the target form is the verb *decidió* (decided) or more specifically, the *-ó* morpheme indicating past tense. Beginning-level learners performed a retrospective think aloud of a passage that contained eight target items. In the think aloud (below), comprehension of the initial adverbial phrase was so effortful that the learner then miscomprehended the temporal and lexical meanings of the target form. The learner ultimately abandoned the attempt to make meaning and in abandoning the attempt to make meaning, the learners could not have made a form–meaning connection.

> *Hace siete años decidió volver a la universidad para hacer un Master en leyes.*
>
> *Translation:* Seven years ago, [he, Rubén Blades] decided to return to university to do a Masters in Law.
>
> *Think aloud:* Um, for seven years he, seven years old he's coming to the university... but I'm not sure and seven sounds awfully young. I would probably just disregard that sentence. (Lee, 1999: 50)

Another example from this research also demonstrates the interplay between comprehension and input processing. In this example, the learner initially miscomprehends the verb *actuó* (he acted) as the adverb 'actually'. What follows in the think-aloud protocol is the learner's various efforts to make sense of the meaning of the sentence.

> *En la década pasada , actuó en varias películas, como por ejemplo, Crossover Dream y The Milagro Beanfield War.*
>
> *Translation:* In the past decade, [he, Rubén Blades] acted in various films, for example, Crossover Dream and The Milagro Beanfield War.
>
> *Think aloud:* So, in the decade past, actually in various films. I don't think that's actually but it looks like actually so that's why I guessed that. Um, maybe it's act. Act in various films, like the example Crossover Dream and The Milagro Beanfield War. So that just speaks of like if you know the context of the paragraph you can follow along and probably guess that, that, uh, it's talking about how he worked on the different [films].

Interestingly, the learner's second rendering of *actuó* was 'act', not 'acts' nor 'acted' although in the end he placed the sentence in a past time frame (he worked). Moreover, the learner assigned no subject even though this is the sixth of eight statements about Rubén Blades. In this think aloud we can see both the push to get and make meaning and the effortful nature of comprehension. In his own words the learner told us he used context to follow along the meaning and guesswork. His last statement about the meaning of a sentence demonstrates that he is aware of the past temporal framework of the passage he read; he states that Blades worked on films.

As part of the think-aloud procedure, the researcher made inquiries about the target forms, in this sentence *actuó*. This learner does make a form–meaning connection with the target, but only after he is certain about the meaning, with which he works intensively. The rest of the think-aloud protocol now follows.

Researcher: Why did you decide that this word *actuó* does or doesn't mean 'actually'?
Learner: Um, well, actually wouldn't be like the word to fit in there. Well as least to me it wouldn't because it wouldn't make sense to say actually in various films.
Researcher: So what makes more sense to you then?
Learner: Um, he, he acted in various films. And also, we just learned the past tense last night. And it looks like the past tense, *actuó*. I don't know. Good guess at least.

Location

Again referring to the availability of processing resources, VanPatten (2004b) proposed the Sentence Location Principle. He states

> ... elements that appear in certain positions of an utterance are more salient to learners than others, namely, sentence initial position is more salient than sentence final position that in turn is more salient than sentence internal or medial position. (VanPatten, 2004b: 13)

That sentence initial position is the most favourable processing position is logical. Those elements are the first encountered and are the first on which processing resources get aligned. Through the medial portion of a sentence, the processing resources may likely still be processing the initial elements but then get redirected when the end of the sentence comes into focus.

The evidence for the Sentence Location Principle strongly affirms that initial position is the most favoured processing position. Barcroft and VanPatten (1997) and Rosa and O'Neill (1998) varied the location of target elements in sentences; the locations were initial, medial and final position in the sentence. They also used both acoustically stressed and unstressed forms. They asked learners to repeat the sentences they heard and then determined how successfully the learners repeated the target items in each position. Barcroft and VanPatten (1997) found that learners repeated items most successfully in initial position, more so than in medial position and more so than in final position. They did not find a difference between medial and final position. They also found that learners more successfully repeated the stressed targets over the unstressed ones. Rosa and O'Neill (1998) found interactions between location and acoustic stress. Both factors affect processing. By and large Rosa and O'Neill's results confirm that initial position is the most favourable processing position and that final position is more favourable than medial position.[9]

Summary of Principle 1

To summarise, so far we have discussed one of the two major principles of VanPatten's theory and the six subprinciples that fall out from the discussion of the primacy of meaning when learners are engaged in processing. These principles, when taken together, help us understand under what conditions learners make form–meaning connections as well as why they might make only some connections and not others.[10] By way of summary, we offer Table 1.1 in which we have paired each principle with an explanatory statement from VanPatten's work. This table captures the Primacy of Meaning Principle for the reader 'at-a-glance'.

Processing Grammatical and Semantic Relationships

As noted in our introduction, VanPatten's theory of input processing encompasses two main principles. In this section we address the second of these, the First Noun Principle, which asserts that learners tend to

Table 1.1 At-a-glance summary of Principle 1 and its subprinciples

Principles	In other words ...
P1: Primacy of Meaning Learners process input for meaning before they process it for form.	'Learners are driven to look for the message or communicative intent in the input.' (VanPatten, 2004b: 7)
P1a: Primacy of Content Words Learners process content words in the input before anything else.	'... second language learners in particular know there are "big words" that can help them get the meaning of what is being said to them and their internal processors attempt to isolate these aspects of the speech stream during comprehension.' (VanPatten, 2004b: 8)
P1b: Lexical Preference Learners will tend to rely on lexical items as opposed to grammatical form to get meaning when both encode the same semantic information.	'Learners will thus seek out lexical forms of semantic notions in the input before they seek grammatical forms that encode the same semantic notions.' (VanPatten, 2007: 118)
P1c: Preference for Nonredundancy Learners are more likely to process nonredundant meaningful grammatical form before they process redundant meaningful forms.	'Learners will be forced to make a form–meaning connection sooner for a nonredundant meaningful form but only later for a redundant meaningful form.' (VanPatten, 2007: 119)
P1d: Meaning before Nonmeaning Learners are more likely to process meaningful grammatical forms before non-meaningful forms irrespective of redundancy.	'... such [non-meaningful] formal features of language will be processed in the input later than those for which true form–meaning connections can be made.' (VanPatten, 2007: 120)
P1e: Availability of Resources For learners to process either redundant meaningful grammatical forms or non-meaningful forms, the processing of overall sentential meaning must not drain available processing resources.	'... increased comprehensibility results in increased likelihood of a form being processed in the input.' (VanPatten, 2004b: 11)
P1f: Sentence Location Principle Learners tend to process items in sentence initial position before those in final position and those in medial position.	'... grammatical form or linguistic elements in sentence initial position are more likely to be processed than elements in other positions (all other processing issues being equal).' (VanPatten, 2004b: 13)

misassign the grammatical role of subject or semantic role of agent to the first noun or pronoun they encounter in a sentence.[11] This processing strategy has been documented in child first language acquisition (Bever, 1970; Slobin, 1966), child second language acquisition (Ervin-Tripp, 1974; Nam, 1975) and adult second language acquisition (Lee, 1987; LoCoco, 1987; VanPatten, 1985). In a sense, initial position works against a grammatical object being correctly interpreted. The problem with learners' use of this processing strategy goes beyond miscomprehension to the heart of acquisition. VanPatten states:

> ... this particular principle may have a variety of consequences in a variety of languages. It is not just that learners may get word order wrong, it is also that they may not process case markings for some time, will have difficulties with the pronoun system in some languages, and so on. (VanPatten, 2004b: 16)

Word order

Even though languages have a typologically canonical word order, such as SVO (subject, verb, object) for English and SOV for Japanese, other word orders are permissible. González (1997) documented the acquisition of different word orders for learners of Spanish with SVO being the first acquired and OSV and OVS being the last acquired. Children acquiring Spanish as a first language also acquire these word orders last (Echevarría, 1978 cited in González, 1997). LoCoco (1987) presented learners of Spanish and German with three different sentence types, in each of which the first noun was an object (direct object, indirect object or the object of a preposition). She found that learners assigned the first noun the grammatical role of subject from 7% to 72% of the time. LoCoco's research documents the use of the first noun strategy and also teases out factors that attenuate learners' use of it. VanPatten (1985) and Lee (1987) presented learners of Spanish with OVS and OV sentences, respectively, in which the objects were pronominalised. VanPatten documented that learners assigned the grammatical role of subject to the object pronoun from 35% to 70% of the time. Lee (1987) documented learners' use of the first noun strategy between 27% and 73% of the time. Under certain circumstances, learners are heavily reliant on word order to assign grammatical roles.[12]

VanPatten and Wong (2004) and Allen (2000) demonstrated that learners of French use the first noun strategy to assign the semantic role of agent to the first noun in *faire-causatif* sentences. As mentioned above in the section on the Primacy of Content Words Principle, learners incorrectly interpret that the agent performing the action of the second verb is the first noun. Instead of indicating that Henri reads the newspaper in the sentence *Jean-Paul fait lire le journal à Henri* (Jean-Paul makes to read the newspaper to

Henri/Jean-Paul makes Henri read the newspaper) they indicate that Jean-Paul reads it (VanPatten & Wong, 2004: 104).

Lexical semantics

Learners do not simply and categorically use the first noun strategy to assign grammatical and semantic roles. They are sensitive to several factors, one of them being lexical semantics, that attenuate their use of the first noun strategy. The lexical semantics of the verb 'kick', for example, requires an animate agent. A sentence such as 'The ball was kicked by the child' is unlikely to be misinterpreted because a ball cannot perform the action. Among her target sentences LoCoco (1987: 124) included the following.

> *La cerveza le trae el muchacho a la muchacha./Das bier bringt der Junge dem Mädchen.*
> The beer to her brings the boy to the girl.
> The boy brings the beer to the girl.
>
> *Las flores le da el muchacho a la niña./Die blumen gibt der Junge dem Mädchem.*
> The flowers to her gives the boy to the girl.
> The boys gives the flowers to the girl.

The learners of Spanish and German never identified the first noun in these sentences as the grammatical subject/agent. The lexical semantics of the verbs 'bring' and 'give' do not allow inanimate subjects.

Event probabilities

We also use what we know about the world to interpret sentences. In the following sentences, both nouns are capable of performing the action but one interpretation is more likely than another. The event probabilities are low for the first noun being the agent and are higher for the second noun being the agent.

> The farmer was kicked by the horse.
> The child was bitten by the dog.

Likewise, learners of French are unlikely to interpret that the professor is doing the studying in the following sentence:

> *Le professeur fait étudier le verbe 'être' à l'élève.*
> The professor makes the student study the verb '*être*'. (VanPatten & Wong, 2004: 101)

Learners use event probabilities to attenuate their use of the first noun strategy.

We might also consider learners' background knowledge of a set of characters as a type of real world knowledge. Houston (1997) showed that learners use their knowledge of a set of characters to overcome their use of the first noun strategy. He had learners interpret two sets of sentences, in both of which he used OVS word order. One set of sentences used the names of characters from a video series the learners were seeing in class. The other used random names. As can be seen in the following example, the sentences are structurally and semantically identical.

Characters: Random names:
A Raquel la contrata don Pedro.   *A Silvia la contrata Ricardo.*

Learners used the first noun strategy only 28% of the time to misassign the grammatical role of subject to the character-based sentences. In the random-name sentences, they misassigned the grammatical role of the first noun 48% of the time.

Contextual constraints

Whereas background knowledge is an extra-linguistic type of context, VanPatten (2004b, 2007) has added sentence-internal linguistic context as a possible constraint on learners' use of the first noun strategy. VanPatten and Houston (1998) demonstrated the effects of context on sentence interpretation. They created ten target sentences containing OVS word order in which a clause preceding the object pronoun provided contextual information. The target sentences were paired with ten sentences that contained a preceding clause that did not provide a contextual cue. The target sentences were constructed with the verbs attacked, insulted, rejected, greeted, and kissed. Note the following examples from VanPatten and Houston (1998). The OVS constructions are underlined.

Context:

Ricardo está enojado porque <u>lo insultó Susana</u> en la reunión.
Ricardo is angry because him insulted Susana in the meeting.
Ricardo is angry because Susana insulted him in the meeting.

Roberto está en el hospital porque <u>lo atacó María</u> con un cuchillo.
Robert is in the hospital because him attacked María with a knife.
Robert is in the hospital because María attacked him with a knife.

No context:

Ricardo me dice que <u>lo insultó Susana</u> en la reunión.
Ricardo me tells that him insulted Susana in the meeting.
Ricardo tells me that Susana insulted him in the meeting.

Gloria contó a sus amigas que <u>la atacó Ramón</u> en su casa.
Gloria told to her friends that her attacked Ramón at home.
Gloria told her friends that Ramón attacked her at home.

A Theory of Input Processing

VanPatten and Houston found that sentence-internal context attenuated learners' use of the first noun strategy for assigning grammatical roles. In the context condition, learners assigned the grammatical role of subject to the object pronoun 59% of the time; in the no-context condition they did this 84% of the time. Learners use of the first noun strategy to assign grammatical roles is quite strong in both the context and no-context sentence types, but context does give learners an additional clue for processing the formal elements of the sentence.

Summary of Principle 2

In the preceding section, we discussed the second of the two major principles of VanPatten's theory and the three subprinciples that fall out from the discussion of the effects of word order in input processing. This set of principles, when taken together, helps us understand some of the internal strategies learners use in comprehending sentences, specifically, in comprehending semantic relationships underlying surface-level word order. By way of summary, we offer Table 1.2 in which we have paired each principle with an explanatory statement from VanPatten's work. This table captures the First Noun Principle and does so for the reader 'at-a-glance'.

Table 1.2 An at-a-glance summary of Principle 2 and its subprinciples

Principles	In other words...
P2: First Noun Principle Learners tend to process the first noun or pronoun they encounter in a sentence as the subject or agent.	'... the human mind may be predisposed to placing agents and subjects in a first noun position.' (VanPatten, 2004b: 15)
P2a: Lexical Semantics Learners may rely on lexical semantics, where possible, instead of word order to interpret sentences.	'... only one noun is capable of the action... ' (VanPatten, 2007: 124)
P2b: Event Probabilities Learners may rely on event probabilities, where possible, instead of word order to interpret sentences.	'... it is possible (though not necessary) that real-life scenarios might override the First Noun Principle... ' (VanPatten, 2007: 123)
P2c: Contextual Constraint Learners may rely less on the First Noun Principle if preceding context constrains the possible interpretation of a clause or sentence.	'... contextual information... would push [learners] away from interpreting the targeted clause the wrong way.' (VanPatten, 2004b: 17)

Conclusion

Input processing is one part, albeit a rather important one, of what we could refer to as the entirety of second language acquisition. Input is essential to second language acquisition. In this chapter we have presented VanPatten's theory of input processing. The theory offers a set of principles and subprinciples designed and formulated to explain how learners work with input, that is, how they make a connection between a form in the input and its meaning. In this chapter we not only presented and explained each principle and subprinciple, we also supplied empirical evidence to support them. These are the foundations on which Processing Instruction (PI) has been built (Lee & VanPatten, 1995, 2003; VanPatten, 1993, 1996, and elsewhere). When we know what learners do with input and how they work with it, we can then derive instructional techniques and write instructional materials that intervene at the time learners are working with input to make form–meaning connections and not at the time when they are practicing making output. Our thesis in the present work is that working with learners while they work with input has cumulative effects on the developing system. The results of Processing Instruction have consistently demonstrated a direct positive effect on the target item investigated (see reviews in Lee & Benati, 2007a, 2007b). We now ask whether Processing Instruction has indirect or secondary effects. Does learning to process one grammatical form help learners become better processors of other grammatical forms?

Notes

1. VanPatten likens SLA to building construction. It is less amusing than the elephant parable, but also insightful: 'In a sense, understanding SLA is like understanding how a building works. There is the electrical system, the plumbing, the foundation, the frame, the heat and air system, and so on. All are necessary; one alone is insufficient. But like those who work in house construction and are electrical contractors or plumbing contractors, in SLA some of us are interested in matters dealing with input. Others are interested in output' (VanPatten, 2004b: 27).
2. VanPatten (2007: 122) opens up the First Noun Principle to the possibly attenuating effects of L1 transfer. These effects have yet to be empirically tested. VanPatten parenthetically includes an L1 parsing procedure in the Lexical Semantics Principle and L1 transfer in the Contextual Constraint Principle.
3. VanPatten (2007: 118) casts the Lexical Preference Principle as follows, 'learners will process lexical items for meaning before grammatical forms when both encode the same semantic information'. He then goes on to revise this principle as follows. 'If grammatical forms express a meaning that can also be encoded lexically (i.e. that grammatical marker is redundant), then learners will not initially process those grammatical forms until they have lexical forms to which they can match them.' This revision does not materially affect our research because in the research we structure input so that it does not contain a lexical form for learners to process. We structure the input in a way that forces learners to process the grammatical form.

4. VanPatten (2007: 120) uses the word *markers* instead of *forms* when stating this principle and does not include the reference to redundancy that he had developed in 2004b: 'Learner are more likely to process meaningful grammatical markers before non-meaningful grammatical markers'.
5. VanPatten (2007) replaces the phrase *word order* with the *First Noun Principle* in his wording of the Lexical Semantics and Event Probabilities Principles.
6. VanPatten (1996: 17) supported Principle 1 (The Primacy of Meaning Principle) with work in first and second language acquisition. For first language acquisition, he cited Peters' (1985) operating principle that guides children during input processing. This principle states that children pay attention to utterances that have a readily identifiable meaning. For second language acquisition, he cited the work of Sharwood Smith (1986), who posited the difference between processing for communication (i.e. meaning) and processing for acquisition (i.e. form).
7. Carroll hypothesised that: 'a number of distinct phonetic cues might lead learners to segment and phonologically encode words from the major lexical classes of English precisely when they are realised as prosodic words, and that would lead them not to segment and encode clitics (determiners, auxiliaries, complementisers, tense morphemes, number morphemes, etc.). This is true despite the fact that many of the functional categories express important semantic distinctions' (Carroll, 2004: 9). Her hypothesis is useful for considering why content words are attended to over function words.
8. VanPatten (1996: 19–20) supports the subprinciple of content words with research by Klein (1986) and Mangubhai (1991). Klein (1986) showed that, when asked to repeat utterances, early stage learners tended to repeat only the content words. Only advanced level learners could repeat the utterances correctly with content words plus functors. Mangubhai (1991) showed that learners who were being taught via Total Physical Response methodology routinely extracted the content words from the stimuli commands in order to physically respond.
9. We use the phrase 'by and large' here to indicate that in three out of four processing contexts the results demonstrated that learners more successfully repeat the targets that occur in sentence initial position than in medial position. Likewise, in three out of four processing contexts, learners more successfully repeated target items that occur in sentence final position than in sentence medial position.
10. We are not asserting here that form does not affect meaning extraction. Lee (1998) expanded on his 1987 research by substituting the subjunctive forms with infinitives in one version of the text and an invented form in another version. He showed that L2 learners of Spanish found passage comprehension easier when the form was not the subjunctive but was an infinitive or invented form. He attributed this to the consistency of the forms in the infinitive and made-up versions versus the inconsistent morphological endings on the subjunctive forms. In this case, the form affected meaning extraction.
11. The wording of the first noun principle has changed significantly from 1996 to 2004. It once read as follows. 'Learners possess a default strategy that assigns the role of agent to the first noun (phrase) they encounter in a sentence. We call this the "first noun strategy" ' (VanPatten, 1996: 32). It now reads as the First Noun Principle: 'Learners tend to process the first noun or pronoun they encounter in a sentence as the subject or agent' (VanPatten, 2004b: 15). The modification from default strategy to tendency better reflects the empirical research on this phenomenon.
12. Lee (2003) provides a critical review of the research on the second language acquisition of Spanish object pronouns. He includes a more thorough review of learners' use of the first noun strategy.

Chapter 2
Processing Instruction: Research and Practice in Assessing Primary Effects

PART 1: THE PRACTICE OF PROCESSING INSTRUCTION

There have been considerable changes in terms of second language instruction. Much of this has been undoubtedly the shift from the explicit focus on language itself (i.e. grammar, phonology and vocabulary) to an emphasis (implicit focus) on the expression and comprehension of meaning through language. Behind this shift is the belief that L2 learners can develop greater second language communicative abilities through the kind of instruction that is more similar to the naturalistic environment (Krashen, 1982). Traditional methods such as the grammar–translation method, and the Audio-Lingual Methodology were very ruled-based. In traditional methodologies, grammar teaching in the L2 classrooms included the paradigmatic presentation of grammatical rules, which was followed by mechanical practice of the rules (e.g. drills), and then by a series of meaningful and communicative drills (see Paulston, 1972).

With the advent of the communicative language teaching approach, comprehensible and simplified input was considered the main ingredient for acquisition. According to a communicative approach to language teaching, we should provide focus on form (see Long, 1991, for a definition of 'focus on form' and 'focus on forms') and this practice should be meaning-based and tied to input or communication. When learners produce language it should be for the purpose of expressing some kind of meaning. Learners make use of the targeted forms through activities that involve communication and negotiation of meaning.

However, as suggested by VanPatten (1993), communication and comprehension do not necessarily trigger the processing of input. Focus on input should take into consideration how learners process input. Learners have limited capacity for processing, and they find it arduous to attend to linguistic forms at the same time as they are trying to comprehend someone else's speech or become involved in more interactive activities. Output practice as argued by Lee and VanPatten (1995, 2003) may help learners in becoming more fluent but does not necessarily bring changes in learners' developing system. Lee and VanPatten (1995: 95) have argued that grammar instruction that is intended to cause a change in the developing system, 'is akin to putting the cart before the horse when it comes to acquisition; the learner is asked to produce when the developing system has not yet had a chance to build up a representation of the language based on input data'.

VanPatten (2003: 27) has strongly argued that output practice is not responsible for the making of an implicit system. Grammar instruction follows Paulston's (1972) hierarchy in which mechanical practice precedes meaningful and communicative practice. In contrast to this approach, VanPatten (1996) has proposed a new pedagogical approach called Processing Instruction (PI), which offers more instructional benefits than output practice. What are these benefits and characteristics?

First of all PI is theoretically grounded in the input processing model. One of the main implications for instruction drawn from this theoretical framework is that it should take into account the psycholinguistic processes utilised in input processing (strategies and mechanisms used by L2 learners to process input). The main role of instruction is therefore to manipulate, enhance and alter input processing in order to make intake grammatically richer. PI should structure and manipulate the input in such a way so as to push learners to process a greater proportion of the input and make correct one-for-one-meaning binding.

Secondly, assuming that acquisition occurs when learners perceive and process comprehensible and meaning-bearing input and then are able to make form–meaning connections (binding the meaning with its form), PI will guide and focus learners' attention when they process input. PI is consistent with the input-processing perspective in SLA. It is for this reason that PI (as shown in Figure 2.1), in its attempt to alter the way L2 learners process input, should have a greater impact on learners' developing system than an output-based approach to grammar instruction (see Figure 2.2) whose aim is to alter how L2 learners produce the target language. There is a clear mismatch between classroom teaching and what really happens

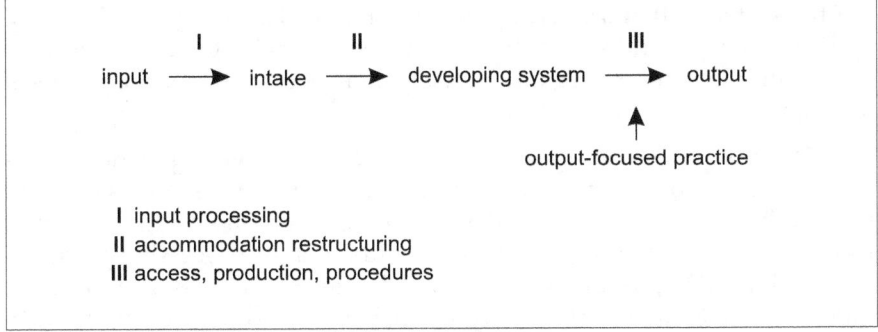

Figure 2.1 Input processing model (traditional practice)

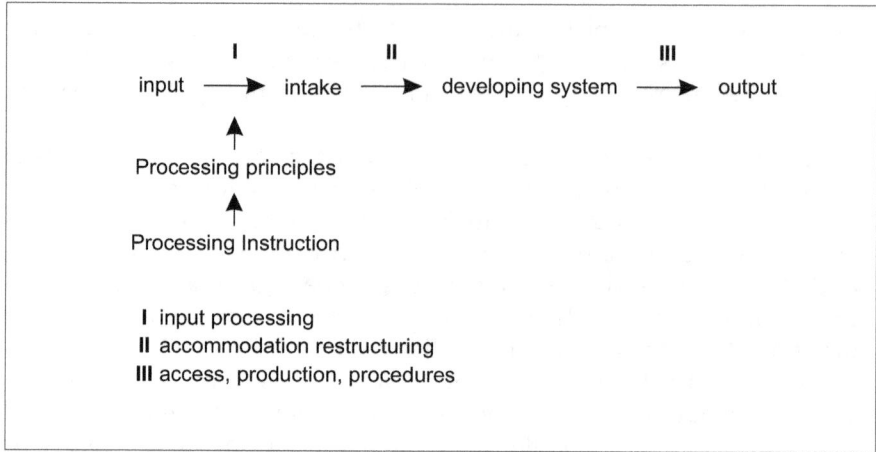

Figure 2.2 Input processing model (processing grammar instruction)

when learners process the input they receive. This is because L2 learners have internal mechanisms responsible for how input is processed. In order to provide better input, teachers must take these mechanisms into consideration.

Unlike output-focused practice, where the emphasis is on the mastery of the grammatical rule and production practice, the purpose of Processing Instruction is to alter how learners process input and to encourage better form–meaning mapping, which results in a grammatically richer intake.

PI is a new type of grammar instruction that is concerned with learners' awareness of how grammatical forms and structures are acquired. PI is a focus on form which draws on the principles of the input processing model (VanPatten, 1996, 2004a). In the model of SLA proposed by VanPatten:

> input provides the data, input processing makes (certain) data available for acquisition, other internal mechanisms accommodate data into the system (often triggering some kind of restructuring or a change of internally generated hypotheses), and output helps learners to become communicators and, again, may help them become better processors of input. (VanPatten, 2002: 760)

PI is a more effective method for enhancing language acquisition as it is used to ensure that learners' focal attention during processing is directed toward the relevant grammatical items, and not elsewhere in the sentence. Its main objective is to help learners to circumvent the processing problems (processing principles are described in Chapter 1) that they use to derive intake data by making them rely exclusively on form and structure to derive meaning from input. Processing Instruction consists of three basic components:

(1) learners are given explicit information about how a linguistic structure or form works, and are presented with one form at a time;

(2) learners are informed about a particular processing problem that may negatively affect the way they process a form or structure during comprehension;

(3) learners are given structured input activities in the hope of pushing them away from non-optimal processing principles described in Chapter 1. In structured input activities the input is manipulated in particular ways to push learners to become dependent on form and structure to get meaning.

The ultimate scope of VanPatten's pedagogical approach to grammar instruction is to make learners appreciate the communicative function of a particular form, and consequently enrich learners' intake.

Structured Input Activities

Wong (2004a: 35) has described PI as a pedagogical approach to grammar instruction that 'pushes learners to abandon their inefficient processing strategies for more optimal ones so that better form–meaning connections are made'. Structured input activities are the main component in the PI approach (see the review of studies comparing PI and its component in Part 2 of this chapter). In order to develop good structured input activities we need to follow a step-by-step procedure. First, it is important to identify the processing problem that affects a particular form. What is/are the processing principle/s causing the processing problem for learners? Sometimes a form can be affected by a processing problem or a combination of processing problems. The second subprinciple of the Primacy of Meaning Principle (VanPatten, 2004b: 14) suggests that learners prefer processing lexical items to grammatical items for semantic information (the Lexical Preference Principle, P1b; see Table 1.1 in the previous chapter). In the sentence, *Ieri mia madre mi ha chiamato per invitarmi a cena* (Yesterday, my mother called me to invite me for dinner), learners will process the lexical item *Ieri* before the grammatical form *chiamato* to encode pastness in the sentence. The grammatical form (past tense in Italian) expresses meaning that can also be encoded lexically by the adverb of time (*Ieri*). Another example is the German past tense for regular verbs. This tense is marked by lexical items like *gestern* (yesterday) and by morphological markers (verb ending) as indicated in the following sentence: *Gestern arbeitete er lange* (Yesterday he worked long). Learners will process the adverb of time *gestern* before the grammatical form *arbeitete*, as both features encode the same semantic information.

Learners prefer to process lexical items before grammatical items in the input they receive when they are asked to comprehend the meaning of the sentence. We therefore need to think of a form of intervention, a new kind of grammar instruction that will guide and focus learners' attention when they process input. In the previous section, we said that learners should be given information about the target linguistic structure or form. Learners should also be informed about a particular processing strategy that may negatively affect their picking up of the form or structure during comprehension. However, the most important component in PI is the structured input practice. Learners must be pushed to process the targeted form or structure during activities with structured input. Input must be structured and manipulated in a way that will push learners to become dependent on form and structure to get meaning. Structured input activities are structured so that L2 learners have to attend to meaning (see Guidelines later in this chapter).

In the referential Activity 2.1, learners have to listen to statements made by a journalist about the life of Pele and decide whether each statement is referring to his past life as a football player or to his present life as a Sports Minister. In order to accomplish the task they must pay attention to the grammatical marker to establish whether the sentence is referring to the past career of the player or to his current career as a Minister of Sport.

Activity 2.1

- Listen to the following statements made by a journalist about the life of Pele and decide whether each statement is referring to his past life as a football player or his present life as a sport minister.

	football player	sport minister	[Sentences heard]
(1)	☐	☐	*Ha giocato per il Brasile.*
(2)	☐	☐	*Fa una nuova legge per l'educazione sportiva.*
(3)	☐	☐	*Ha vinto due coppe del mondo.*
(4)	☐	☐	*Ha rappresentato il suo paese all'estero.*
(5)	☐	☐	*Ha segnato molti goal.*
(6)	☐	☐	*Incontra spesso il primo ministro.*
(7)	☐	☐	*Aiuta i giovani.*
(8)	☐	☐	*Ha giocato per il Santos.*
(9)	☐	☐	*Lavora per il governo brasiliano.*
(10)	☐	☐	*Va spesso nelle scuole in Brasile.*

Another processing problem is redundancy. The Preference for Nonredundancy Principle (P1c: VanPatten: 2004b) indicates that learners are more likely to process nonredundant meaningful grammatical form before they process redundant meaningful forms. In the case of Italian grammatical gender agreement between nouns and adjectives, the adjective is marked to agree with the gender of the noun. To indicate that a *ragazzo* (male person) is attractive, the adjective would be *bello* whereas *bella* indicates that a *ragazza* (female person) is attractive. Italian word order typically places descriptive adjectives after the nouns they modify. This particular form is affected by a combination of processing problems:

(1) *(Non)Meaningfulness:* Adjective agreement is a purely grammatical marker devoid of any semantic meaning. Nonmeaningful morphology is unlikely to be processed at all (Learners prefer processing more meaningful morphology before less or non meaningful morphology: the Meaning-Before-NonMeaning Principle, P1d).

(2) *Redundancy:* The noun establishes the grammatical gender and so the adjective marking is redundant (Preference for Nonredundancy Principle, P1c). Learners tend not to process redundant forms. The form of the adjective would be made all the more redundant if there were an indefinite or definite article preceding the noun; it, too, would agree in gender with the noun, *un ragazzo bello* versus *una ragazza bella*.

(3) *Location:* Because we read Italian from left to right, learners would first encounter an article, then the noun and finally the descriptive adjective. Being in final position would make the adjective marking less likely to be processed than if it were in initial position. Learners tend to process items in sentence initial position before those in final position and those in medial position (Sentence Location Principle, P1f).

(4) Acoustic saliency. The agreement marker on the adjective occurs in an unstressed syllable and so lacks acoustic saliency. It is difficult to perceive when embedded in a sentence.

Structured input activities will help learners to process one form and one meaning and circumvent the processing problems. In the case of adjective agreement in Italian, in affective Activity 2.2, learners are asked to read some statements about a famous actress and then indicate whether according to them the statements are true or false. After this, they have to compare their views with those of a classmate and establish whether they have a positive or negative view of the famous actress.

In the referential structured input activities (see Activity 2.3) learners must establish whether the adjectives refer to Brad Pitt or Claudia Schiffer. The input is structured in such a way that learners are given the opportunity to attend to the grammatical marker (o = masculine and a = feminine) to

Activity 2.2

- Read the following statements about Uma Thurman and for each one indicate whether it is true or false.

		Vero	*Falso*
(1)	È brutta.	☐	☐
(2)	È acuta.	☐	☐
(3)	È una brava attrice.	☐	☐
(4)	È chiusa.	☐	☐
(5)	È limitata.	☐	☐
(6)	È dotata.	☐	☐
(7)	È aperta.	☐	☐
(8)	È stupida.	☐	☐
(9)	È fredda.	☐	☐
(10)	È una persona calda.	☐	☐

- Compare your answers with a classmate: *Sei d'accordo?* Or *No sei d'accordo?* And establish the following:

  ☐ I have a positive view of Uma. ☐ I have a negative view of Uma.

Activity 2.3

- Listen to each sentence in which a person is described and determine which person is described.

	Claudia Schiffer	Brad Pitt	[Sentences heard]
(1)	☐	☐	È bella.
(2)	☐	☐	È bello.
(3)	☐	☐	È Americano.
(4)	☐	☐	È Tedesca.
(5)	☐	☐	È bruno.
(6)	☐	☐	È bionda.
(7)	☐	☐	È viva.
(8)	☐	☐	È antipatico.
(9)	☐	☐	È alto.
(9)	☐	☐	È magra.
(10)	☐	☐	È alto.

Activity 2.4

- Read each phrase about Ricky Martin and decide if the speaker is expressing certainty about the statement or uncertainty.

(1)... è celebre in tutto il mondo
Non penso che ...
So che ...

(2)... sappia cantare molto bene
Sono sicuro che ...
Non credo che ...

(3)... possa ballare
Dubito che ...
Sono certo che ...

(4)... ha molti soldi
Non credo ...
So che ...

(5)... ha una bella voce
E certo che ...
Dubito che ...

(6)... è bello e affascinante
Penso che ...
Si sa che ...

(7)... sia popolarissimo tra le donne giovani
So che ...
Dubito che ...

(8)... abbia una bella fidanzata
Si sa che ...
Non credo che ...

(9)... non è molto intelligente
Sono certo che ...
Non penso che ...

(10)... non piaccia a molte persone
Temo che ...
So che ...

- Which statements best describe your feelings about Ricky Martin?

establish the form–meaning connection. All the other elements (article and nouns) have been removed from the sentence so that learners must process the grammatical marker in order to get meaning.

In the affective structured input activities (see Activity 2.2) learners are asked to process input for meaning and establish whether the sentences are true or false. The second step in this structured input activity is for the learners to compare their answers and establish whether they have a positive or negative view about Uma Thurman. When they are processing the input, they need to focus their attention on the adjective to understand the meaning and accomplish the task.

Another example is the Italian subjunctive of doubt and opinion. In Italian when we intend to express doubt, disbelief, uncertainty or opinion, the verb in the dependent clause must be in the subjunctive mood. If we intend to express certainty, then the verb in the dependent clause must be in the indicative mood. This form is affected by two main processing problems. First of all, the subjunctive form occurs near or at the end of the sentence and therefore it is not in the most favoured position for processing (the Sentence Location Principle); secondly the subjunctive forms are redundant (the Preference for Nonredundancy Principle). Because of these processing problems with structured input activities, we must encourage learners to process the subjunctive morphology as the trigger for doubt/

opinion. In Activity 2.4, the activity is structured in such a way that learners must pay attention to the verb in medial position to establish whether the sentence expresses certainty or doubt. L2 learners would not process this grammatical form as they would process the item in first position (Sentence Location Principle). Structured input activities will ensure that L2 learners will process the form in medial position in order to understand the meaning of the sentence.

Following the guidelines of VanPatten and Sanz (1995) for structured input activities (see Figure 2.3), we shall now develop structured input activities to circumvent the processing problems that affect Italian gender agreement previously described. The guidelines are as follows:

(1) Paradigms and rules should be broken down into smaller parts and taught one at a time during the course of the lesson. Students are presented with the linguistic feature before being exposed to structured input activities.
(2) Learners should be encouraged to make form–meaning connections through structured input activities. Meaning must be kept in focus. Learners must pay attention to meaning to complete the activity.
(3) Learners must move from sentence level to discourse level activities.
(4) Activities that combine oral and written input should be used, as some learners respond better to one than the other. This is in order to account for individual differences.
(5) Learners must do something with the input. Learners must be engaged in processing the input sentences, and must respond to the input sentence in some way through referential and affective types of structured input activities.

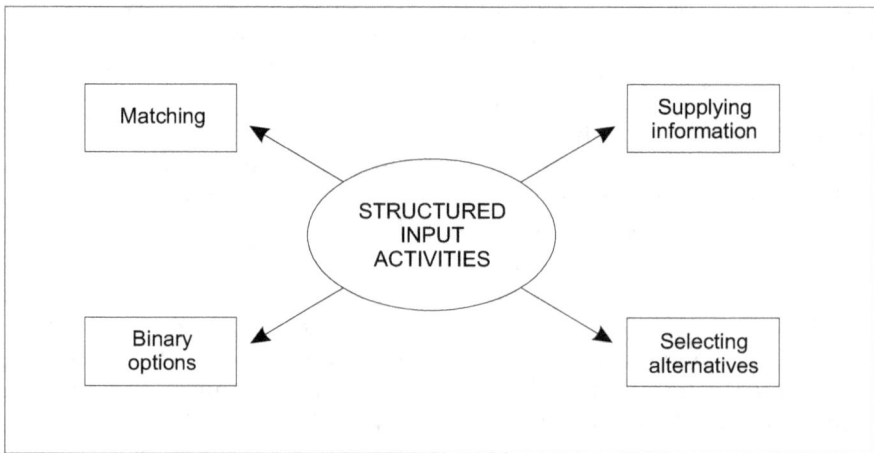

Figure 2.3 Types of structured input activities

(6) Processing principles should be kept in mind. Learners' attention should be guided not to rely on natural processing strategies. Structured input activities (referential and affective) in which the input is structured to alter learners' reliance on one particular processing principle should be created. Referential activities are those for which there is a right or wrong answer and for which the learner must rely on the targeted grammatical form to get meaning. Affective structured input activities are those in which learners express an opinion, belief or some other affective response and are engaged in processing information about the real world.

Lee and VanPatten (1995, 2003) have proposed various type of structured input activities (see Figure 2.3, adapted from Lee & VanPatten, 1995). In these activities the input is structured so that learners can process the grammatical markers that otherwise will not be processed (see processing principles, VanPatten, 2004b) and at the same time make correct form–meaning connections. These different types of structured input activities involve learners in accomplishing different tasks: providing information, selecting alternatives, choosing between two options or matching. Learners must notice the grammatical form/structure in the input and at the same time they are asked to process the input in order to accomplish a communicative task.

In the case of Activity 2.5, learners must choose between two options. In this case, learners are required to listen to each sentence and indicate if each activity is physically sedentary or active.

Activity 2.5

- Each sentence describes Chris's events last week. Listen to each sentence and indicate if each activity is physically sedentary or active.

	Sedentary	Active	[Instructor's script]
(1)	☐	☐	*Tenisu o shimashita.* (I played tennis.)
(2)	☐	☐	*Hon o yomimashita.* (I read a book.)
(3)	☐	☐	*Terebi o mimashita.* (I watched TV.)
(4)	☐	☐	*Paatii o shimashita.* (I had a party.)
(5)	☐	☐	*Depaato ni ikimshita.* (I went to a department store.)
(6)	☐	☐	*Rajio o kikimashita.* (I listened to a radio.)
(7)	☐	☐	*Chokoreeto o tabemashita.* (I ate a chocolate.)
(8)	☐	☐	*Koohii o nomimashita.* (I drank coffee.)
(9)	☐	☐	*Kaban o kaimashita.* (I bought a bag.)
(10)	☐	☐	*Dansu o shimashita.* (I danced.)

Activity 2.6

- Look at the statements below. Tick the boxes that indicate the statements that are more logical to describe your teacher's life.

(A) *Durante il giorno:*
Insegna ☐
Studia ☐

(B) *Il pomeriggio:*
Pranza alla mensa ☐
Mangia a casa ☐

(C) *La sera:*
Incontra i figli ☐
Lavora in un bar ☐

Activity 2.7

- Match logically the event in column A to the person/country in column B.

A	B
(1) *Ha scoperto l'America.*	(a) Van Morrison
(2) *Ha attaccato l'Iraq.*	(b) Germania
(3) *Ha conquistato la Luna.*	(c) Armani
(4) *Ha fatto successo nel cinema.*	(d) Papa
(5) *Ha recitato in Mission Impossible III.*	(e) Cristoforo Colombo
(6) *Ha creato un nuova moda.*	(f) George Bush
(7) *Ha visitato L'Irlanda.*	(g) Tom Cruise
(8) *Ha organizzati i mondiali di Calcio.*	(h) Bill Gates
(9) *Ha suonato a Londra.*	(i) Steven Spielberg
(10) *Ha rivoluzionato il mondo dei computer.*	(l) America

In the case of Activity 2.6 (adapted from Lee & VanPatten, 1995) learners are given a stimulus and must select from two alternatives. Learners must indicate whether each statement is appropriate to be referred to their teacher.

In the case of Activity 2.7, learners must indicate how two sentences are logically connected. Learners are asked to match an event (column A) and connect logically this event to a person or country in column B.

PART 2: RESEARCH IN PROCESSING INSTRUCTION, AN OVERVIEW

Introduction

To date, research on the effects of Processing Instruction has addressed specific processing problems. We must keep in mind that PI always addresses a processing problem. Its goal is to help learners to derive richer intake from the input they are exposed to. Structured input activities have the role of pushing learners away from a non-optimal processing strategy/principle and creating correct form–meaning bindings.

Research on the effects of PI has been conducted in both syntactic and perceptual strategies as described by Lee (2004). Within this research framework, which intended to measure the primary effects of PI, we can identify various lines of research.

The first line of research has investigated the relative effects of PI compared with different types of output-based instruction, which emphasised language production, not language processing. PI has mainly been compared with traditional instruction (TI) (see Table 2.1) and meaning-based output instruction (MOI) which is a more communicatively-focused output practice. In a second line of research the internal components of PI have been tested. PI comprises two elements: explicit information about the grammatical item (including information about processing strategies) and structured input activities. This line of research has sought to establish the causative factor responsible for the positive effects of PI. The third line of research has focused on measuring the effects of delivering PI via different modes (e.g. computer vs. pencil and paper). Another line of research has investigated long-term effects for PI (see VanPatten & Fernández, 2004).

A recent and new line of research has attempted to compare PI to other input enhancement (a term coined by Sharwood-Smith, 1993) techniques.

Measuring Primary Effects of PI

The first study that measured the effects of PI was carried out by VanPatten and Cadierno (1993), who investigated whether PI would alter a processing problem known as the First Noun Principle (P2). This principle might cause learners of Spanish a number of problems. VanPatten and Cadierno (1993) investigated the impact of PI on the acquisition of direct object pronouns, as learners seem to misinterpret sentences containing direct object pronouns in Spanish. When processing object pronouns in Spanish, learners assign the first noun of an input sentence to the role of subject. VanPatten and Cadierno (1993) set out to compare three groups of students of Spanish at intermediate level (80 subjects participated in this study) who received different instructional treatments over two consecu-

Table 2.1 Primary effects of PI vs. TI

Study	Linguistic feature/ language	Processing principle	Subjects/L1	N	Design	Tests	Results
VanPatten & Cadierno (1993)	Spanish object pronouns	First noun	Intermediate English native	80	Pre-test Post-tests: immediate & delayed	Interpretation (aural) Production (written)	Int = PI > (TI = C) Prod = (PI = TI) > C
Cadierno (1995)	Spanish preterite tense	Lexical preference	Intermediate English native	60	Pre-test Post-tests: immediate & delayed	Interpretation (aural) Production (written)	Int = PI > (TI = C) Pro= (PI = TI) > C
Benati (2001)	Italian future tense	Lexical preference	Beginners English native	39	Pre-test Post-tests: immediate & delayed	Interpretation (aural) Production (written)	Int = PI > TI > C Pro= (PI = TI) > C
Cheng (2004)	Spanish copula	Preference for nonredundancy	Intermediate English native	197	Pre-test Post-tests: immediate & delayed	Interpretation (aural) Production (written)	Int = PI > (TI = C) Prod = (PI = TI) > C
VanPatten & Wong (2004)	French causative	First noun	Intermediate English native	76	Pre-test Post-tests: immediate & delayed	Interpretation (aural) Production (written)	Int = PI > TI > C Prod = (PI = TI) > C

PI = Processing Instruction, TI = Traditional Instruction, C = Control group, Int = Interpretation test, Prod = Production test

tive days of instruction. One group received TI, which is an instructional approach based on grammar explanation of a form or structure followed by oral or written production practice; the second group received PI as described in the previous paragraph; and a third group was used as a control and received no instruction. A pre-test and post-test design was used to measure the possible effects of instruction. Two different assessment tasks were developed by the researchers. The first was an interpretation task in which learners heard 10 sentences and 5 distracters. Five of these sentences were of the order object pronoun-verb subject and the other five were of the order object marker + noun-object pronoun-verb subject. The five distracters were simply subject-verb-object sentences. The group of learners, after hearing a sentence, had just a few seconds to select one of the drawings projected on an overhead screen in front of the class. The other assessment task was a sentence-level written production task in which the three groups were given five items to complete. Each item consisted of a two-part sentence that corresponded to a two-part drawing. The second part of the sentence was incomplete, and the student's task was to complete it based on the visual cues. The results showed that PI is superior to TI and very beneficial for learners. PI improved learners' ability at correctly interpreting object pronouns in Spanish and the study furthermore demonstrated that PI was also effective in improving learners' production, as its positive effects were not limited to input processing but were also observable in learners' accuracy in producing the target feature. PI was overall superior to TI and the control group.

Cadierno (1995) set out to investigate the effects of PI on a different processing problem (Lexical Preference Principle, P1b). This study was a replication of the previous study in terms of the design used (pre-post tests) and the overall aims. The linguistic items of Spanish which was researched was the Spanish 'preterite tense' (equivalent to the simple past tense in English). Considering how the processing problem affected the targeted form, the aim of PI in this study was to push learners to attend to the grammatical element in the input that might be otherwise get missed. The participants in this study were 60 English native speakers studying intermediate Spanish at undergraduate level. PI was compared with TI on the acquisition of this grammatical feature. As in the previous study, two assessment tests were used (interpretation and a production written task).

The results showed that the group who received PI was superior to the TI group and the control group in the interpretation task and, again as in the first study (VanPatten & Cadierno, 1993), the PI group (although never engaged in production-type activities during instruction) was able to perform as well as the TI group in the production test.

These findings support the hypothesis that PI might have an effect on learners' developing system, and eventually on their output.

Benati (2001) conducted an investigation into the effects of two types of PI and TI on the acquisition of a feature of the Italian verbal morphology system, the future tense. He investigated the impact of the two instructional treatments (PI vs. TI, and a control group) on the Lexical Processing Principle (P1b), which has an effect on the linguistic item under investigation. TI was operationalised in the same way as in the previous study. For PI the input was 'structured' so that the grammatical form carried a meaning and the learner had to attend to the form in order to complete the task. In the PI treatment, temporal adverbs were removed from the structured input activities so that the learner's attention was directed toward the verb endings as an indicator of tense. Since the lexical indicators of tense were absent, learners should use verbal morphology as an indicator of tense. This approach was used to circumvent the processing problem caused by reliance on the lexical item when processing a sentence that contains the lexical item and the grammatical feature encoding the same meaning.

Beginner undergraduate students (the final pool consisted of 39 students) of Italian participated in this study; all were English native speakers. One interpretation test and two production tests were used for this study and consisted of an aural interpretation task, a written completion text and an oral limited-response production task. The results obtained in this research provide clear evidence that PI has positive effects on the acquisition of Italian verbal morphology and greater effects on the developing system of beginner L2 learners than instruction of the output-based type.

Cheng (2004) measured the effects of PI on the acquisition of copular verbs in Spanish (*ser* and *estar*). The Preference for Nonredundancy Principle (P1c) was particularly relevant for this study, as copular verbs in Spanish are of low communicative value for L2 learners and are redundant features of Spanish. The study involved 197 subjects studying Spanish in their third year of a University college level course. Cheng used a very similar research design to that of VanPatten and Cadierno (1993), comparing three groups in a pre-test and post-test format including three type of tests (interpretation, sentence completion, guided composition).

The results showed that, in the interpretation task, students receiving PI outperformed those receiving no instruction (control group) and those receiving TI. Once more the effects of PI were observable on output tasks, whereas the effects of the traditional type of instruction are not observable on interpretation tasks.

With the intention of generalising the findings from previous studies to a different language and linguistic feature, VanPatten and Wong (2004) carried out a study comparing the effects of PI and TI on the French *faire* causative. The relevant principle in this study was the First Noun Principle (P2). Some 76 undergraduate students learning French participated in the classroom experiment. As in previous studies investigating primary effects for PI, students were assigned to three groups (PI, TI and a control group). As in previous PI studies two separate instructional packagess were used. The main difference was that the structured input activities in the PI group required learners to process input for meaning and form in order to complete the task. The activities were designed to alter the First Noun Principle and learners were never involved in any type of production practice. In the traditional treatment learners instead received the paradigmatic explanation of the target structure and a series of mechanical activities to produce the target forms. The assessment tasks consisted of an interpretation test and a production test.

The results confirmed the previous findings that compared PI with TI and showed that the PI group was superior to both the TI group and the control group on the interpretation test, and there was no statistical difference between the two instructional groups in the production test.

Other studies have measured the primary effects for PI compared with a different and more meaning-based output instruction (MOI), see a summary of these studies in Table 2.2). Farley (2001b, 2004a) compared the effects of PI versus MOI on the acquisition of the Spanish subjunctive. Unlike TI, the MOI contained no mechanical drills and the activities developed for the treatment were based on the tenets of structured-output activities proposed in Lee and VanPatten (1995, 2003). The subjunctive was selected because of the Sentence Location Principle (P1d). This processing strategy has been investigated in relation to Spanish subjunctive in previous studies (Farley, 2001a, see Table 2.2). In Spanish the subjunctive is located in medial position where it is least likely to be processed. In the sentence *Non pienso que entienda el problema* (I do not think he/she understands the problem) the subjunctive inflection (the *-a* of *entienda*) is in the middle of the sentence and the Sentence Location Principle predicts that learners will overlook the subjunctive inflection because it is not located in a more salient position.

The 129 undergraduate students who participated were assigned to two instructional groups (PI and MOI). Both the PI and the MOI groups of students were assessed following a pre-test/post-test design that included interpretation and production tasks. Farley's results differed from previous studies comparing PI with TI. Both the PI and MOI groups made equal and significant improvements on both the interpretation and the production tests. Farley attributed the equal performance of the two treatments to one main factor. The MOI treatment is different from TI as it does not contain mechanical drills practice and its communicative and interactive nature might have resulted in incidental input.

Benati (2005) conducted a similar and parallel classroom experiment investigating the effects of PI, TI and MOI on the acquisition of English past simple tense. The relevant processing principle in this case was the Lexical

Table 2.2 Primary effects of PI vs. MOI

Study	Linguistic feature/language	Processing principle	Subjects/L1	N	Design	Tests	Results
Farley (2001a)	Spanish subjunctive	Lexical preference Sentence location	Intermediate English native	29	Pre-test Post-tests: immediate & delayed	Interpretation (aural) Production (written)	Int = PI > MOI Prod = PI = MOI
Farley (2001b, 2004a)	Spanish subjunctive	Lexical preference	Intermediate English native	129	Pre-test Post-tests: immediate	Interpretation (aural) Production (written)	Int = PI = MOI Prod = PI = MOI
Benati (2005)	English simple past	Lexical preference	Beginners Greek and Chinese native	30	Pre-test Post-tests: immediate & delayed	Interpretation (aural) Production (written)	Int = PI > TI = MOI Prod = PI = TI = MOI
Morgan-Short & Bowden (2006)	Spanish object pronouns	Preference for nonredundancy	Intermediate English native	47	Pre-test Post-tests: immediate & delayed	Interpretation (aural) Production (written) T1: pre-test, T2: immediate post-test, T3: one week	PI = MOI T1: PI = MOI = C T2: (PI = MOI) > C T3: (PI > MOI) > C

PI = Processing Instruction, TI = Traditional Instruction, MOI: Meaning-based output instruction, C= Control group, Int = Interpretation test, Prod = Production test

Preference Principle (P1b). The subjects involved in the present studies were Chinese (47 subjects) and Greek (30 subjects) school-age learners of English residing in their respective countries. The participants in both schools were divided into three groups: the first group received PI; the second was exposed to TI and the third received MOI. One interpretation and one production measure were used in a pre- and post-test design.

The results showed that PI had positive effects on the processing and acquisition of the target feature. In both studies the PI group performed better than the TI and MOI groups in the interpretation task, and the three groups made equal gains in the production task. The PI treatment was superior to the TI and MOI treatment in terms of helping learners to interpret utterances containing the English past tense. The findings on the sentence-level task involving the interpretation of the English past simple tense support previous findings on PI research which indicated that PI is successful in altering learners' processing default strategy (P1b). The results of the statistical analysis indicated that PI, TI and MOI made an equal improvement (from pre-test to post-test) on the production task (sentence-level task). Even in this case, the findings from the present experiment support the main results of previous research on PI which showed that the PI group made significant similar gains from the pre-test to the post-test compared with the TI and MOI groups in production tasks. The evidence obtained in this study on the production task suggests that the effects of PI not only have an impact on the way learners interpret sentences, but also on the way they produce sentences. PI has clearly altered the way learners processed input and this had an effect on their developing system and subsequently on what they could access for production.

Morgan-Short and Bowden (2006) have also investigated the effects of PI and MOI. They assigned 45 first semester Spanish students to PI, MOI and control groups. The structure targeted in this study was the Spanish direct object pronouns and the processing problem was the First Noun Principle (P2). The findings revealed that both PI and MOI group were equal in the interpretation task adopted in this study and the MOI group was better than the PI group on the first production post-test only.

Summary

The primary effects of PI have been investigated in a number of studies (see Table 2.1 and Table 2.2) that have compared PI with two different types of output-based instruction, TI and MOI. The TI approach was chosen as it is still the dominant approach to grammar teaching in foreign language classrooms. It typically involves the explanation of the target feature (all forms presented at once) and mechanical output practice. Form oriented activities are followed by more meaningful practices. Lee and VanPatten

(1995, 2003) have defined mechanical activities as those activities that L2 learners can complete without attending to meaning and for which there is only one possible answer as in the following example:

- Change sentences using the past tense according to the model below:
  John plays tennis → John played tennis

The results in all the studies comparing PI vs. TI and reported in this chapter (Table 2.1) showed the following:

(1) PI is a more effective approach to grammar instruction than TI, as it seems to have a direct effect on learners' ability to process input (various processing problems, various linguistic forms, different languages and populations).
(2) PI also seems to provide learners with the ability to produce the target linguistic features during output practice. The PI groups performed as well as the TI groups on the production task, and this is a remarkable finding given that subjects in the PI group were never asked to produce the target features through output practice.

PI has also been compared to MOI, which consists of structured output activities that are meaningful activities in nature. They all carry a meaningful context and the target forms are produced not with the sole intention of practicing the target item, but rather to communicate opinions, beliefs, or other information related to designated topic.

The results in all the studies comparing PI vs. MOI and reported in this chapter (Table 2.2) showed that overall PI was superior to MOI.

Measuring the Effects of PI Components

The second line of research reviewed in this chapter is the line of research that has investigated and teased out the components of PI that are considered to be responsible for the positive outcomes of previous research. The main purpose of this classroom-based research was to establish which factor is the main causative variable for learners' improved performance in PI studies (see Table 2.3). Is it the explicit information or the structured input practice? Or perhaps a combination of the two?

VanPatten and Oikkenon (1996) carried out the first study to investigate whether the results obtained in VanPatten and Cadierno (1993) were due to the explicit information component of PI or to the positive effects of the other component of PI: namely the structured input activities.

The 50 students who participated in this classroom experiment were from a secondary school and all were studying Spanish in their second year. The item investigated was the same as in VanPatten and Cadierno's study (1993): object pronouns in Spanish. The materials, design and assessment tasks were also the same, as the main purpose of the research was to establish which of the following variables, explanation, structured input activities or a combination of the two, is the most significant in accounting for the post-tests results. Three groups were tested, following the same design as VanPatten and Cadierno (1993): one group received only explicit instruction, the other received structured input activities and the third received full PI. The outcome of this study was that structured input activities were found to be responsible for learners' gains. The gains made (on both the interpretation and production tasks) by both the PI group and the structured input activities group were greater than those of the group receiving only explicit instruction on the targeted form. A very significant finding of this study is that the structured input activities group performed as well as the PI group.

As indicated by VanPatten (1996: 126), these findings strongly suggest that it is the structured input activities and the form–meaning connections being made during input processing that are responsible for the relative effects observed in the present and previous studies.

Benati (2004a) reports an experimental investigation of the relative effects on the acquisition of the future tense of PI, structured input activities and explicit information. This study addressed the Lexical Preference Principle (P1b). The material and assessment measures were the same as the one used for the study carried out comparing PI vs. TI (Benati, 2001). The 38 subjects studying Italian at undergraduate level who participated in this classroom experiment were divided into three groups receiving respectively PI, structured input (SI) only and explicit information (EI) only. The results confirmed the findings obtained in VanPatten and Oikkenon's study (1996). Another replication study was conducted by Benati (2004b) on the acquisition of Italian gender agreement. This study addressed the Preference for Non Redundancy Principle (P1c). The structured input activities were developed with the intention of helping learners to process the target form efficiently and correctly. The 31 students studying Italian at undergraduate level who formed the population in this study were divided into three groups: the first received PI, the second group received SI only and the third group received EI only. One interpretation and two production measures were used in a pre- and post-test design. Once more the results were similar to those of VanPatten and Oikkenon (1996). The PI group and the SI group made significant gains on a sentence-level interpretation test and a sentence-level production test, while the EI group made no gains. The SI group also made identical gains to the PI group in the oral production task, compared with the EI group.

Farley (2004b) conducted a study measuring the effects of PI and structured input activities only on the acquisition of the Spanish subjunctive of doubt; the relevant processing principle was the Sentence Location Principle (P1f). The 54 students who participated were divided into two groups:

one received full PI and the other received SI practice. The results were slightly different from the previous ones. Despite the fact that both groups made significant improvements from pre- to post-tests, the PI group outperformed the SI practice group in both the interpretation and the production task.

Wong (2004b) found positive results for SI practice alone in a study where she compared the effects of PI, SI practice and EI only, and a control group in the acquisition of French negative + indefinite article. In a negative or non-affirmative statement (*ne ... pas*), *de* is used before nouns beginning with a consonant and *d'* is used before nouns beginning with a vowel. However, owing to the Lexical Preference principle (P1b) learners will process *ne ... pas* before *de* or *d'* to get the meaning of the French negation.

Some 94 undergraduate, intermediate students of French participated in this study. The materials were designed to alter the processing problem, and an interpretation and a production task were developed. The results in both the interpretation and the production task showed that the PI group and the SI group were not different from each other. These two groups were better than the EI group and the control group. The SI component seemed to be the causative factor for the beneficial effects of PI.

Lee and Benati (2007a) compared the relative effects of two types of instructional intervention (SIA vs. TI) on the acquisition of Japanese past tense form. Their study extended previous research which suggested that learners' strategy for processing input could be altered through structured input activities (SIA) which eventually enhance the acquisition of the target grammar feature. This feature of Japanese was selected because of the processing principles investigated in this study: The Lexical Preference Principle (P1b). In a sentence such as *Kinô kaisha ni ikimashita* (Yesterday, I went to the office) both the lexical item *Kinô* and the verb ending *ikimashita* communicate past tense. Again the main purpose of SIA in this study is to push learners to process the past tense marker that otherwise may not be processed because learners do not need to process it to assign pastness to the meaning of the sentence. The 27 beginner students of Japanese who participated in this study were all Italian native speakers and were studying Japanese in a school. They were assigned to two groups and two sets of materials were developed. One for the TI group consisted in grammar teaching and output practice, while the one for the SIA group involved teaching the subjects to process input sentences. The output-based activities required the subjects to accurately produce past tense forms. The SIA required learners to interpret sentences containing past tense forms and make form–meaning connections.

Two tests were produced: one for the interpretation task and one for the production task. The results of the interpretation and the production data confirmed the key role for structured input activities practice. The evidence

Table 2.3 Primary effects of PI vs. SIA and EI

Study	Linguistic feature/language	Processing principle	Subjects/L1	N	Design	Tests	Results
Van Patten & Oikennon (1996)	Spanish object pronouns	First noun	Intermediate English native	59	Pre-test Post-tests: immediate & delayed	Int (aural) Prod (written)	Int = (PI = SI) > EI Prod = (PI = SI) > EI
Benati, (2004a)	Italian future tense	Lexical preference	Beginners English native	38	Pre-test Post-tests: immediate	Int (aural) Prod (written)	Int = (PI = SI) > EI Prod = (PI = SI) > EI
Farley (2004b)	Spanish subjunctive	Lexical preference	Bntermediate English native	54	Pre-test Post-tests: immediate & delayed	Int (aural) Prod (written)	Int = PI > SI Prod = PI > SI
Wong (2004)	French negative + indef. article	First noun	Intermediate English native	94	Pre-test Post-tests: immediate	Int (aural) Prod (written)	Int = (PI = SI) > (EI = C) Prod = (PI = SI) > C PI > EI, EI=S, EI = C
Benati (2004b)	Adjective agreemen	Preference for nonredundancy	Beginners English native	31	Pre-test Post-tests: immediate	Int (aural) Prod (written)	Int = (PI = SI) > EI Prod = (PI = SI) > EI
Lee & Benati (2007a)	Japanese past tense	Lexical preference	Beginners Italian native	27	Pre-test Post-tests: immediate	Int. (aural) Prod (written)	Int = SI > TI Prod= SI = TI

PI = Processing Instruction comprising EI and SI, SI = Structured input activities only, EI = Explicit Information only, C = Control group, Int = Interpretation test, Prod = Production test

collected in this study has shown that SIA is a better instructional treatment than TI practice, as the SIA group outperformed the TI group in the interpretation task and the two instructional groups improved equally in the production task.

Summary

The main finding of the second line of research in PI confirmed that it is the structured input component practice that is responsible for the changes in learners' developing system and eventually in their output. As a result of the empirical evidence collected in the research that has compared PI with its components, we are able to conclude that the causative factor in the positive effects for PI is the structured input activities. These have been proved and observed in different processing principles, languages, linguistic items and assessment tasks. Structured input activities within PI, represent the most significant variable. As indicated by VanPatten (1996: 126), structured input activities and the form–meaning connections being made during input processing are responsible for the relative effects observed.

Measuring the Effects of PI Delivered via Different Modes

In this third line of research in PI, researchers have attempted to measure whether PI delivered in different ways would bring about the same results (see Table 2.4).

Lee *et al.* (2007) have compared the effects of three modes of delivering PI on preterite/imperfect distinction and negative informal commands in Spanish. In this study they manipulated three variables: mode of delivery (textbook/classroom, computer/ terminals, individualised downloads of computer materials), linguistic item (preterite/imperfect distinction, negative informal commands), and time (pre-test, immediate post-test, delayed post-test). The linguistic items selected for this investigation was the preterite/imperfect aspectual distinction in Spanish. The processing problem addressed was one of redundancy (the Preference for Nonredundancy, P1c), and 25 undergraduate students constituted the final subject-pool in this study.

The materials were developed out of the existing textbook materials (VanPatten *et al.*, 2006), which were transposed into the virtual environment so that the computer materials were as exact a replica of the textbook materials as possible.

The computer materials were downloaded and individualised, paper and pencil packets of materials for learners were created. For both interpretation and production tests, pre-tests and post-tests were used for assessing the effects of modes of delivering PI on different linguistic items in Spanish.

Table 2.4 Primary effects of PI delivered via different modes

Study	Linguistic feature/ language	Processing principle	Subjects/L1	N	Design	Tests	Results
Lee, Benati, Aguilar-Sánchez & McNulty (2007a)	Preterite/ imperfect distinction Negative informal commands in Spanish	Preference for nonredundancy	Intermediate English native	25	Pre-test Post-tests: immediate & delayed	Interpretation (aural) Production (written)	PI delivered via computer = individualised = textbook in the following tests: multiple choice test, negative informal command test
Lee & Benati (2007a)	French and Italian subjunctive	Lexical preference Sentence location	Intermediate English native	27	Pre-test Post-tests: immediate & delayed	Interpretation (aural) Production (written)	Int = PI = PIcomp > (MOI = MOIcomp) Prod = PI = PIcomp = MOI comp

PI = Processing Instruction, MOI = Meaning-based output instruction, Int = Interpretation test, Prod = Production test

The results showed no significant interactions involving modes of delivering PI. The study proved rather conclusively that delivering PI in three different modes is equally effective in addressing learners' processing problems. The instruction itself is what is important to learning, not the mode of delivery.

In a second study Lee and Benati (2007a) set out to compare modes of delivering PI and MOI in the acquisition of Italian and French Subjunctive. Materials were developed for use in a classroom (instructor + students + interaction) and in a computer environment (terminal + individual student). The subjunctive was chosen as it presents learners with several processing problems. The subjunctive form occurs in a subordinate clause that typically follows the main clause of the sentence. The target form is, therefore, located medially in the sentence. VanPatten's Sentence Location Principle (P1f) indicates that this position is not favoured during processing: learners have difficulty detecting formal features in medial position. Additionally, it is the main clause of the sentence, in which speakers choose verb phrases that lexically encode doubt/opinion, that learners prefer to process. The subjunctive forms are redundant. The same design as in previous studies was used to assess the effects of treatment. The 27 participants were assigned to four groups (PI classroom, PI computer, MOI classroom, MOI computer). Additionally, we gave all groups the same explicit information, that is, the same explanation. The results coincided with the one obtained by Lee *et al.* (2007). PI can be delivered with equal effectiveness in both classroom and computer environments. This result also supported previous findings comparing PI vs. MOI (see Table 2.2) and strongly support VanPatten's model of language processing. That is, language production practice does not affect the way learners process input.

Summary

To summarise we can confidently argue that PI is a very effective instructional intervention for addressing a variety of L2 processing problems, in Romance and non-Romance languages, and with native speakers of a variety of L1s. The studies reviewed in this paragraph have clearly demonstrated that PI is an effective intervention no matter the mode (computer or classroom) in which it is delivered to L2 learners.

Comparing the Effects of PI with Other Types of Input Enhancement Techniques

In the final line of research in PI, researchers have brought together two areas of investigation: input processing and input enhancement (see Table 2.5). VanPatten's (1996, 2004a) theory of Input Processing captures in a set of principles what learners do with the input to which they are exposed. To

Table 2.5 Primary effects of PI vs. input enhancement techniques

Study	Linguistic feature/language	Processing principle	Subjects/L1	N	Design	Tests	Results
Lee & Benati (2007b)	Italian adjective agreement and subjunctive	Preference for nonredundancy / Sentence location	Beginners English native / Intermediate English native	20 / 24	Pre-test Post-tests: immediate	Interpretation (aural) Production (written)	SIA = SIAE SIA = SIAE PI = PIE = PIEcomp
Lee & Benati (2007b)	Italian future tense	Lexical preference	Beginners English native	20	Pre-test Post-tests: immediate	Interpretation (aural) Production (written)	SIA = SIAE
Lee & Benati (2007b)	Japanese past tense	Lexical preference	Beginners Italian native	26	Pre-test Post-tests: immediate	Interpretation (aural) Production (written)	Int. = (SIA = SIAE) > C Prod = PI = TI = MOI Prod = (SIA = SIAE) > C

PI = Processing Instruction, PIE = PI enhanced, PIE comp = PIE delivered via computer terminals, SIA = structured input activities, SIAE = SIA enhanced, C = control group, Int = Interpretation test, Prod = Production test

address processing problems, VanPatten devised Processing Instruction (PI) with structured input activities (SIA). The latter is considered as a type of input enhancement since these activities direct learners to process form for its meaning. Input enhancement (e.g. Sharwood-Smith, 1991; Wong, 2005) proposes that grammatical forms in the input can be made more salient to learners through a variety of techniques. This line of research has measured the effects of structured input activities and enhanced structured input activities on a variety of grammatical items that present processing problems to second language learners. Learners improve by practicing structured input activities. The question that we have to address is: 'Do learners improve even more if they are exposed to enhanced structured input activities?' The languages that have been examined are Italian, Spanish and Japanese. The linguistic features targeted are adjective agreement, future tense, past tense and subjunctive.

Lee and Benati (2007b) investigated the effects of structured input unenhanced and structured input enhanced tasks on the acquisition of Italian gender agreement and subjunctive of doubt. The main aim of this study was to measure the effects of two different techniques of delivering SIA in order for learners to process non-meaningful and redundant morphology (the Preference for Nonredundancy principle, P1c). Some 20 English native speakers students of Italian were randomly assigned to two instructional groups, SIA enhanced vs. SIA unenhanced. In both treatments learners were asked to pay attention to the adjective endings in the input through structured input practice, the only difference in the two instructional treatment is that in the enhanced treatment both aural and written stimuli were enhanced. In aural activities the enhancement was obtained by pronouncing the targeted gender agreement ending by raising our voices (louder) and by tightening the muscles of the phonal apparatus (tenser). In the written activities, grammatical forms (endings -*o* and -*a*), but not the rest of the verb, were made bold and underlined, so that attention was drawn to the verbal element that we expected learners to process.

The results of the interpretation and production tasks developed for this classroom experiment showed that enhanced structured input practice and unenhanced structured input practice were equally successful in altering the processing principles under investigation while helping learners to interpret and produce accurate sentences containing the correct adjective agreement forms. Structured input practice, with or without enhancement, helped learners to process the input more efficiently and helped them to make better form–meaning connections. Structured input practice, with or without enhancement, helped learners to produce the target features accurately.

In a similar study Lee and Benati (2007b) investigated the effectiveness of PI enhanced vs. PI unenhanced delivered through different modes at directing learners' attention to sentence final position (the Sentence Location Principle, P1f). Some 24 students were randomly assigned to three groups (PI vs. PI enhanced vs. PI enhanced delivered via computer terminals). The first group received the PI treatment via classroom instruction; the second group received the same PI treatment but with the target grammatical form enhanced; the third group received the PI treatment enhanced but via a computer terminal delivery. The results of the interpretation and production tasks confirmed that PI is an approach that is equally effective no matter how the SIA practice is delivered. Enhanced and unenhanced SIA have the same success in altering the processing problem investigated in this study.

In a third study, Lee and Benati (2007b) investigated whether learners improve even more if they are exposed to enhanced structured input practice. The processing principle under investigation in this case was the Lexical Preference Principle (P1b) and the grammatical feature was the Italian future tense. First semester English native speaker undergraduate students of Italian participated in this study. In order to compare the effects of enhanced and unenhanced structured input activities on the acquisition of the Italian future tense, two groups were set. The final pool consisted of 20 students who went through a process of randomisation to sort them into groups. The material for the SIA was the same as the one used by Benati (2001, 2004a). The SIA were the same for both treatments. The only difference between the two treatments was the fact that the forms were unenhanced for the first group and enhanced for the second group. The results of the interpretation and production tests confirmed previous results and showed that the two instructional treatments helped learners to improve their performance in an equal way.

In a final study Lee and Benati (2007) compared the effects of PI to other types of input enhancement techniques. They compared the effects of SIA vs. SIA enhanced type of delivery on the acquisition of Japanese past tense forms. Once again the grammatical item was selected because of the processing principle called The Lexical Preference Principle (P1b) which indicates that learners will naturally rely on the lexical item over the verb inflection in order to gather semantic information.

Data from 26 participants were analysed. All subjects were adult Italian native speakers who were studying Japanese at beginner level in a private school. The subjects were assigned to three groups receiving SIA, SIA enhanced and a control group. The results of the interpretation and production tasks again confirmed previous results. The findings showed that the participants who received both structured input activities and enhanced structured input activities obtained equal statistical results in both the interpretation and the production tests. The two instructional groups were significantly better than the control group.

Summary

Overall, the results of the studies reviewed in this section (see Table 2.5) have shown that SIA practice is a successful approach for addressing various processing problems (position, redundancy and lexemes versus verbal morphology) that were targeted in these studies. Structured input practice, with or without enhancement, helped learners to process the input better and make better form–meaning connections. Structured input practice, with or without enhancement, helped learners to produce the target features accurately. The main outcome from the studies reviewed is that it reaffirms the positive effects of structured input activities as a successful type of input enhancement in altering learners' processing strategy. Consequently it has positive effects on learners' developing system. We may conclude that it is the nature of the SIA practice that can cause changes in learner performance. Structured input activities are designed with processing principle in mind and, as stated by Wong (2005: 76), 'stand the most chance at altering learners' inefficient strategies so that optimal input processing can take place'.

Enhancing the input through input enhancement techniques is a very useful tool for directing learners' attention to grammatical properties of a targeted L2. However, it is only through structured input activities that we help learners make form–meaning connections and cause a change in learners' developing systems.

Other Issues

Previous research on the effects of PI has sought to illuminate one other issue, long-term effects of PI. VanPatten and Fernández (2004) controlled a curriculum so that learners received no further instruction in the targeted linguistic item (Spanish object pronouns). They tracked learners eight months after receiving their one and only PI treatment. They compared the results of the pre-tests (interpretation and production) with the 8-month delayed post-tests and found that learners' scores were significantly higher on the delayed post-tests than on the pre-tests. These delayed post-test scores were, however, significantly lower than those on the immediate post-test. There are, then, long-term yet diminished effects for PI.

Conclusion

Research on PI has so far focused on measuring its direct and primary effects by comparing this type of instruction with traditional and meaning-output based instruction. The results of the empirical research have shown that PI is a better approach than output-based approaches. PI is a very effective approach towards altering inappropriate processing strategies and instilling appropriate ones in L2 learners. Despite the positive results obtained on measuring the primary effects of PI, no research has yet been conducted to look into the secondary effects of this approach. In the next chapters we will present the results of classroom studies that have addressed this new question. These studies have attempted to determine whether learners receiving processing instruction can transfer that training to the acquisition of other forms without further instruction. The data were gathered in order to address the following two questions (Lee, 2004):

(1) Will learners who receive training on one type of processing strategy for one specific form appropriately transfer the use of that strategy to other forms without further instruction in PI?
(2) What are the cumulative effects of receiving PI instruction on the different types of strategies? Do learners who have been exposed to a processing strategy pick up a second strategy more quickly and efficiently than they pick up the first one?

In the next chapters of this book we will present, review and discuss results from studies that have investigated the secondary effects of this very successful input technique called Processing Instruction.

Chapter 3

From Processing Instruction on the Acquisition of Italian Noun–Adjective Agreement to Secondary Transfer-of-Training Effects on Italian Future Tense Verb Morphology

Introduction

In this chapter we present the results of a classroom study on the secondary effects of Processing Instruction. The main purpose of this study is to address a lacuna in the Processing Instruction database by investigating whether learners who are exposed to Processing Instruction will develop better intuitions about the L2 than learners who receive other, different type of instruction. Processing Instruction focuses on input, whereas the other types of instruction focus on output. Also, the term 'intuitions' probably conjures images of grammaticality judgement tasks, as the two terms are quite interwoven in the literature. We take, however, a broader view of the term 'intuitions' and include under the term any change in how learners approach processing the second language as evidence of developing intuitions. Evidence of better intuitions (see Chapter 6 for a full discussion) would come, not only from grammaticality judgements or preferences, but from processing data. Specifically, when presented with a new or novel linguistic item, do learners revert to previous, perhaps L1-based, inappropriate processing strategies or do they attempt to use newer, L2-based, processing strategies? Attempting the latter would demonstrate that the L2 learners are developing intuitions about how to approach the L2.

For the current study, we selected two linguistic items from Italian: noun–adjective agreement and future tense verb morphology. The processing problems associated with these two forms are captured by two processing principles (see Figure 1.1), specifically, the Preference for Non-redundancy Principle (P1c) and the Lexical Preference Principle (P1b) (VanPatten, 2004b). The aim of Processing Instruction on noun–adjective agreement in Italian is to direct learners' attention toward processing the ends of words. Given that, would learners receiving Processing Instruction develop better intuitions (processing strategies) grounded in the L2 such that they would be able to process Italian future tense verb-final forms? Again, the processing problems associated with both the target form and the transfer-of-training form are captured by the same processing principles.

We will present the findings of this experiment which investigates the possible training effects of two types of form-focused instruction on the acquisition of noun–adjective agreement and future tense verb morphology in Italian. Processing Instruction (input-based) will be compared with traditional output-based instruction TI). Three groups will be used. One receiving PI, one receiving TI and the third, serving as a control group, that did not receive instruction on the two linguistic items over the duration of the investigation.

Target and Secondary Linguistic Items

In order to examine any transfer-of-training effects we must select a target or primary linguistic item and a transfer-of-training, and in this case a secondary, linguistic item. These two linguistic items are, respectively, noun–adjective gender agreement and future tense verb morphology in Italian.

Primary target item

Italian has grammatical gender agreement between nouns and adjectives. In a sentence adjectives must agree in gender with the noun they are modifying. To indicate that a *casa* (house) is beautiful, the adjective *bello* (beautiful) will have to be appropriately inflected as *bella* so as to agree in gender with the noun to which it is referring. Italian word order typically places descriptive adjectives after the nouns they modify. Two of the characteristics that we emphasised about gender-agreement morphology are: (1) any gender agreement of an adjective with a noun is a purely grammatical marker devoid of any semantic meaning; and (2) the noun establishes the grammatical gender and so, consequently, marking the adjective is redundant. This linguistic feature, i.e. noun–adjective gender agreement, is a grammatical feature with low communicative value. Communicative value is a function of both semantic value and redundancy. Adjectives in Italian must agree in number and gender with the noun they modify. In the phrase *la casa bella* the word final *-a* marks feminine gender. This feature of grammar (*a* = singular feminine) is highly redundant (*la casa bella*) and low in semantic value, as it does not contribute anything to the meaning of the utterance. There is no difference in meaning between *bella* and *bello* so, if a learner said *la casa bello*, the error would be grammatical but not semantic.

VanPatten (1996, 2002) asserts that a form's relative communicative value is important in processing because, the greater communicative value a form has, the more likely it is to be processed and, consequently, to be made available for acquisition. Bardovi-Harlig (2007) uses the term 'functional load' to refer to a similar phenomenon from a language production perspective. L2 learners tend to make form–meaning connections sooner in the case of forms that are semantic and nonredundant as opposed to redundant nonmeaningful forms such as gender morphology. This observation of a form's redundancy leads to an input processing principle, the Preference for Nonredundancy Principle (P1c), which states that ' learners are more likely to process nonredundant meaningful grammatical forms before they process redundant meaningful forms' (VanPatten, 2004b: 14).

Noun–adjective gender agreement poses a number of processing challenges for L2 learners. First of all, learners, when faced with processing forms that are redundant, tend not to process these forms, either at all or only in some minimal way, because learners are focused on getting content words first (The Primacy of Content Words Principle). Secondly, in a sentence containing gender agreement (*la casa bella*) there is no semantic reason why either *bello* or *bella* should be used because they are identical in meaning. As argued by VanPatten (2004a: 120), features such as these agreement markers would be processed later than the ones for which true form–meaning connections can be made. VanPatten (2004b: 14) captured this observation as *The Meaning-Before-Non Meaning Principle* (P1d), which states that 'Learners prefer processing more meaningful morphology before less or non meaningful morphology'. In the typical syntactic arrangement of a noun and a descriptive adjective in Italian, we would first encounter an article (definite or indefinite) followed by the noun, and then that would be followed by the descriptive adjective.

In addition to the processing challenge that redundancy presents is the position of the adjective in the noun phrase. It is in final position and serially, in the direction in which words and their forms are encountered, it is the third gender-marked word of the three gender-marked words in the phrase. This position would make the adjective marking even less likely to be processed than if it were, for example, in initial position. Finally, the agreement marker on the adjective occurs in an unstressed syllable and so, without accentuation, it lacks acoustic or perceptual saliency, a factor that has been shown to be important in morpheme acquisition (Ellis, 2007). It is difficult and extremely challenging for L2 learners to perceive a noun adjective agreement marker when it is embedded in a sentence delivered in conversation.

Secondary target item

The future tense in the Italian language was chosen as a secondary target item for two main reasons: the fact that it is meaning-bearing and for its morphological and phonological characteristics. The Italian future is equivalent semantically to the English 'will + verb' (compound tense).

Whereas 'will' lexically marks future in English, Italian depends on verb morphology to mark tense, person and number. The Italian future is formed by first dropping the final -*e* of the infinitive and then adding different person-number endings to the base. The *'are'* verbs, however, change the *'a'* (thematic vowel) of the infinitive ending to an *'e'*. Here are some examples of third person singular future tense forms in Italian.

*arrivare > arriver*à   *prendere > prender*à   *partire > partir*à

The future is used (as in this study) to express future action, make plans, express probability or possibility, and make resolutions.

One of the characteristics of the Italian language is that the verb stem encodes the action/event; it is the lexical base. Verb morphology encodes tense, aspect and the grammatical subject. The verb form, to a much greater extent than in English, carries a high semantic load by virtue of its morphology. Italian is considered a null-subject language morphologically. Verb forms are marked distinctly both morphologically and phonologically for grammatical subject. The appearance of a subject pronoun is not essential. In the future, the appearance of accent marks for first and third person singular in their written form reflects their acoustic properties. The written accent indicates strong stress on the final vowel. Here are examples of the first person singular future tense in Italian:

arrivare > arriverò   *prendere > prenderò*   *partire > partirò*

Musumeci's (1989) study examined L2 learners' ability to assign tenses at sentence level under different conditions. Despite the morphological and phonological properties of the future tense, the presence or absence of a temporal adverbial to accompany the morphology was the main factor enabling L2 learners to assign tenses correctly. Musumeci's findings revealed that early stage learners use lexical items in order to assign tense and, in particular, this was the case for the future where the effects of the adverbial were strongest for early-stage learners. Musumeci concluded that the future, despite the clues (*ò* and *à*), is the least accessible for early-stage learners. Also, Musumeci points out that learners appear to assign tenses using a binary option strategy: for them the sentence is either present or future. Italian future tense morphology is an inflection for person, number and tense that appears in verb final position. This tense marker can be high in communicative value to L2 learners, but only when it is the only indicator of tense. The marker's communicative value to L2 learners drops significantly when it co-occurs with a lexical temporal indicator. The lexical temporal indicator makes the verb morphology redundant.

This linguistic feature presents several processing challenges to L2 learners. The first challenge is captured in VanPatten's Lexical Preference Principle (VanPatten, 2004b: 14). Learners tend to process lexical items over morphological markers when both encode the same semantic information. If learners can establish the temporal framework with a lexeme or content word, then they do not also need the verb form to do that. For example in the sentence *Domani James visiterà il suo amico Alessandro* both the lexical item *domani* and the *-à* verb ending communicate future tense. According to the Lexical Preference Principle, learners will naturally rely on the lexical item over the verb inflection in order to gather semantic information.

In other words, if a grammatical marker is redundant as it is in this case, it might not get processed at all as L2 learners are focused on getting content words first and derive tense from these content words (e.g. temporal adverbs).

Review of Previous PI Research on the Target Linguistic Items

The purpose of the classroom experiment discussed in this chapter was to investigate the possible transfer-of-training effects of PI. Based on previous research reviewed in Chapter 2 of this book which investigated primary effects for PI, it was hypothesised that PI would not only be an effective approach to grammar instruction in terms of its primary effects, but it might also have secondary effects on L2 learners.

Previous research on the acquisition of gender agreement in Italian has shown that through PI and structured input activities, learners can improve both their interpretation and production of adjective forms (Benati, 2004a; Lee & Benati, 2007b). We offer a summary of results of these studies in Table 3.1.

The main and rather consistent findings from research on the effectiveness of PI and its components are that when learners receive PI or structured input activities (SIA) practice alone, they make significant improvement in their performance on both interpretation and production tasks. Benati's previous research (Benati, 2001, 2004b; Lee & Benati, 2007b) on the acquisition of Italian future tense morphology has demonstrated that learners who receive PI or structured input activities significantly improve on interpretation and production tasks and their improvement is statistically significant

Table 3.1 Summary of previous findings on the effects of Processing Instruction on Italian adjective gender agreement

Studies	Interpretation task	Production task
Benati (2004b)	PI = SIA > EI	PI = SIA > EI
Lee & Benati (2007b)	SIA = SIAE	SIA = SIAE

PI = Processing Instruction, SIA = Structured input activities, SIAE = SIA enhanced, EI = Explicit information

Table 3.2 Summary of previous findings on the effects of Processing Instruction on Italian future tense

Studies	Interpretation task	Production task
Benati (2001)	PI > TI and C TI > C	PI = TI > C
Benati (2004b)	PI = SIA > EI	PI = SIA > EI
Lee & Benati (2007b)	SIA = SIAE	SIA = SIAE

PI = Processing Instruction, SIA = Structured input activities, SIAE = SIA enhanced, EI = Explicit information, TI = Traditional Instruction, C = Control group

when compared with L2 learners receiving traditional instruction (TI). We offer a summary of the results of these studies in Table 3.2.

Research questions

The present study was designed to examine the primary and possible transfer-of-training effects of PI. To do this, we compared PI with traditional instructional treatments (TI) of the target linguistic feature and included a control group who did not receive instruction. The research questions that guide this study are framed in terms of this comparison. The questions are as follows.

(Q1) What are the primary effects of PI and TI on the acquisition of Italian noun–adjective agreement as measured by an interpretation task?

(Q2) What are the primary effects of PI and TI on the acquisition of Italian noun–adjective agreement as measured by a production task?

(Q3) Are there any secondary transfer-of-training effects of PI and TI from receiving instruction on noun–adjective agreement to the acquisition of Italian future tense morphology as measured by an interpretation task?

(Q4) Are there any secondary transfer-of-training effects of PI and TI from receiving instruction on noun–adjective agreement to the acquisition of Italian future tense morphology as measured by a production task?

Based on previous empirical findings presented in Chapter 2 and in this section on the primary effects of PI and TI in second language acquisition, the following hypotheses related to research questions 1 and 2 on can be formulated as follows:

(H1) PI will be a more effective type of instruction than TI and the control group in helping learners to interpret correctly and efficiently sentences containing noun–adjective gender agreement in Italian.

(H2) PI will be an equally effective type of instruction to TI in helping learners to produce correctly and efficiently sentences containing noun adjective gender agreement in Italian.

The main objective of the present study was, however, to discover whether the positive and primary effects of PI can be transferred/applied by L2 learners to other features affected by the same or a similar processing problem. Previous research has clearly and consistently demonstrated that PI has direct and primary effects on learners as it helps them to alter inappropriate processing strategies. Based on this, we will hypothesise that we will uncover transfer-of-training effects. We are, in essence hypothesising that after PI instruction on noun–adjective agreement, learners will use the more appropriate L2-based processing strategy in a novel situation. That is, we hypothesise that they will develop an L2-driven intuition about processing. PI instruction will, to paraphrase Ellis (2007), help the learners not be so committed and tuned to their first language.

(H3) Learners receiving PI on noun–adjective agreement in Italian will transfer that training and process future tense morphology better than those receiving TI as measured by an interpretation task.

(H4) Learners receiving PI on noun–adjective agreement in Italian will transfer that training and process future tense morphology better than those receiving TI as measured by a production task.

Methods and Procedures

Participants

Three groups of subjects, numbering 25 in the final data pool, participated in this study. They were all native speakers of English who were learning Italian as part of their undergraduate degree at the University of Greenwich. The initial subject pool, numbering 37, was reduced to 25 subjects as only subjects who scored less than 50% of the maximum score in the pre-tests, both the interpretation and production tests, were included in the final pool. In addition to the cut score on the pre-tests, we used the following set of criteria to select the population of this study:

(1) all participants had to be English native speakers of English;
(2) they all had to be beginning-level learners of Italian;
(3) they should not have been taught or should not have been previously exposed to the primary and secondary target linguistic items (noun–adjective agreement and future tense verb morphology).

As the pre-test means show (Tables 3.5 to 3.8 below), the mean scores of subjects in the final data pool was less than 1% across the different pre-tests and the different treatment groups. Their knowledge of the primary and

Secondary Effects of Processing Instruction (Italian)

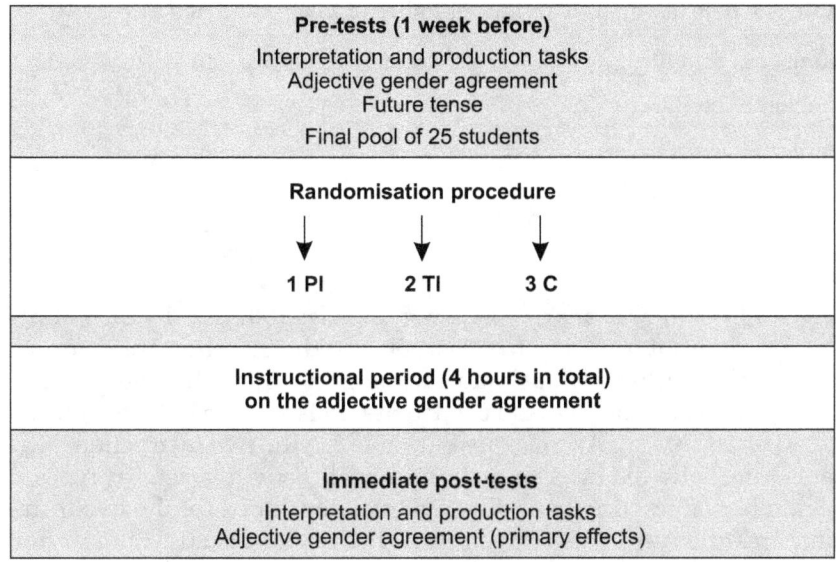

Figure 3.1 Overview of the experiment

secondary linguistic targets was minimal and the random correct answer on the pre-tests was most likely due to pure chance.

The final pool consisted of 11 males and 14 females, ranging in age from 18 to 20 years old. A randomisation procedure was adopted to assign learners to one of the three groups. The two instructional groups consisted of the PI group ($n = 9$) and the TI group ($n = 10$). These students participated in the two-day instructional treatment period that was then followed immediately by the post-test after the end of instruction. A control group ($n = 6$) was also used in this experimental study. They did not receive instruction on the primary or secondary linguistic targets during the two-day treatment period. We provide an overview of the experiment in Figure 3.1.

Materials

Two packs of instructional materials were developed for the noun–adjective gender agreement linguistic item: one for the group receiving the PI instructional treatment and another for the group receiving the TI instructional treatment. The pack used for the PI group consisted of explicit information about the forms and functions of the target as well as information on processing strategies. This was followed by structured input activities as the means of practising the target. During the PI treatment, learners were taught how to process input sentences using the gender morpheme on the adjective. The TI group received a type of instruction that consisted of a

Table 3.3 Instructional materials: Number of tokens and activities

Number of activities	10
Number of utterances	100
Pair activities	5
Whole class activities	5
Visuals	5

more traditional grammar explanation of rules followed by output practice. This output practice has learners producing the target form by performing both mechanical and meaningful drills. The two packets of materials had been piloted and used in previous experiments (Benati, 2004; Lee & Benati, 2007a). As presented in Table 3.3, the two instructional treatments were balanced in terms of the number of activities, activity types and the number of practice items. The material developed for the two instructional treatment was also balanced in the use of visuals, the classroom dynamic of paired and whole class activity formats (see Table 3.3). And, finally, the vocabulary used in the instructional materials across the two treatments was roughly the same and consisted in highly frequent and familiar vocabulary for beginning level L2 learners of Italian.

The amount of instruction about the linguistic form subjects received was exactly the same for the two treatments. The two groups received the same amount of information about how noun–adjective gender agreement works in Italian. The materials differed, however, in the way the information was presented. As can be seen in Figures 3.2 and 3.3, Processing Instruction on a particular linguistic item is non-paradigmatic. One of the guidelines for creating structured input activities is 'one thing at a time' (Lee & VanPatten, 1995, 2003). Traditional instruction, on the other hand is normally operationalised with the use of paradigms presenting all forms for all persons and for both singular and plural.

The two treatments differed as to whether they were receptive or productive. The PI treatment could be defined 'receptive' as practice focused on comprehension/interpretation activities. As is the hallmark of Processing Instruction as formulated for research purposes, those learners receiving PI never produce the target form during the instructional treatment. Better than the term 'receptive' would be the term 'input-oriented' because there is nothing receptive or passive about teaching learners how best to work with input. The TI treatment is considered to be 'productive', as all practice focused on production activities. Perhaps a better term is 'output-oriented'. Although the grammar explanations were different in the two instructional treatments (paradigmatic vs. non-paradigmatic) the

Gender agreement

ATTENZIONE

- As you have probably noticed, descriptive adjectives have different gender: in Italian, adjectives must agree in number and gender with the noun they modify.

    Masculine = -o   Feminine = -a
    bello   bella
    un ragazzo   una ragazza
    Clinton è bello.   Claudia Schiffer è bella.

- You must pay attention to the adjective ending in order to understand who and what we are referring to. In addition to that, you need to understand the meaning of the sentence containing the adjective.

Figure 3.2 Explicit information for Processing Instruction

Gender agreement

- An adjective describes a noun or pronoun. The adjective has to match in gender with the noun or pronoun it describes. The position of adjectives is not the same as in English.

- Regular adjective with a masculine singular ending in -o change the ending to -a in the feminine form.

Masculine singular	Feminine singular
-o	-a

Examples:
Il figlio bello (The beautiful son)
La figlia bella (The beautiful daughter)
Il ragazzo bravo (The good boy)
La ragazza brava (The good girl)

- Regular adjective with a masculine plural ending in -i change the ending to -e in the feminine plural form.

Masculine plural	Feminine plural
-i	-e

Examples:
Il figli belli (The beautiful sons)
Le figlie belle (The beautiful daughters)
I ragazzi bravi (The good boys)
Le ragazze brave (The good girls)

Figure 3.3 Explicit information for TI

Table 3.4 Main characteristics of the two instructional treatments

Processing Instruction (PI)	Traditional Instruction (TI)
• Explanation of rules in a non paradigmatic way. • Practice in processing input. • Focus on form to extract the meaning.	• Explanation of rules in a paradigmatic way. • Practice in output. • Mechanical practice devoid of any focus on meaning.

time allocated to grammatical explanation was exactly the same in the two treatments. The activities presented to the PI group could all be considered meaningful and communicative, whereas the activities presented to the TI groups contained some mechanical and some meaningful form-oriented practices. The main characteristic of the PI treatment is that structured input activities were designed to help learners in this group to process input better. The main differences between PI and the output-based type of instruction used in this study are summarised in Table 3.4.

Processing Instruction (PI)

The pack of materials for PI had been constructed and used by the researchers in previous studies (Benati, 2004b; Lee & Benati, 2007a, 2007b). In addition to the sample activities that follow, more activities can be found in the Appendix. This material reflects one approach to the teaching of grammar that encourages L2 learners to focus their attention on noun–adjective gender agreement in Italian in the input. In contrast with the TI treatment where the presentation of the adjective gender agreement rules was followed by subsequent practice in how to make sentences making the right agreement (masculine -o vs. feminine -a), PI aimed at teaching learners how to interpret and comprehend these rules. The PI treatments had the following components: explanation and practice. However, learners in this group were not engaging in production practice.

The explanation of noun–adjective agreement was limited to only the singular endings, -o and -a, of regular adjectives (see Figure 3.2). In the presentation of the target forms the relation between form and meaning was always in focus. As can be seen in Activities 3.1 and 3.2, there were two types of structured input activities, referential and affective. For either type of structured input activity, the L2 learners had to respond to the content sentences. Never during instruction were the students assigned to the PI group asked to produce a sentence making the correct noun–adjective gender agreement, but rather, they were engaged in processing input sentences so that they could make better form–meaning connections. PI

Secondary Effects of Processing Instruction (Italian)

aims at making learners interpret and comprehend the linguistic feature in oral and written form, and not producing it.

The use of both referential and affective structured input activities has been discussed by several authors (Farley, 2005; Lee & VanPatten, 1995, 2003; Wong, 2005). Activity 3.1 is an example of a referential activity. In the referential activities learners were asked to identify at sentence level who was the subject of the sentence based on the form of the adjective they heard or read. Referential activities are, then, those that have right or wrong answers. For example, learners had to determine which of two people, either a male or a female, was being described. The input sentences that learners processed were stripped of any cue to the referent other than the form of the adjective such that extraneous nouns and any other reference to gender were removed. Contrast the two sentences *È bello* and *È un ragazzo bello*. In the former, only the adjective encoded gender whereas in the latter, the noun and article also encode gender. Only *È bello* is suitable for use in PI because it means that learners are obliged or forced to attend to the grammatical markers in order to establish to whom the sentence refers.

In the affective activities, learners had to perform different types of tasks based on the informational content of the input. The affective activities

---

Activity 3.1 Referential activity

- Listen to each sentence in which a person is described and determine which person is described.

	Claudia Schiffer	Brad Pitt	[Sentences heard]
(1)	☐	☐	*È bella.*
(2)	☐	☐	*È bello.*
(3)	☐	☐	*È Americano.*
(4)	☐	☐	*È Tedesca.*
(5)	☐	☐	*È bruno.*
(6)	☐	☐	*È bionda.*
(7)	☐	☐	*È viva.*
(8)	☐	☐	*È antipatico.*
(9)	☐	☐	*È alto.*
(9)	☐	☐	*È magra*
(10)	☐	☐	*È alto.*

required learners to respond with an opinion or information about themselves or people around them. For example, in Activity 3.2, learners were asked to tick boxes to show whether they agreed or disagreed with each of a series of statements about George Bush. As we will see, this activity adheres to a guideline for creating structured input activities: 'have learners do something with the input' (Lee & VanPatten, 1995, 2003). Each statement consisted of a copular verb plus descriptive adjective inflected for masculine singular. Based on the number of ticks indicating agreement versus the number indicating disagreement, learners had to conclude whether they had a positive or negative view about this person. In this activity learners' attention is directed to the adjective form through a task in which the adjective endings must be attended to. At the same time learners must process each sentence for its meaning in order to complete the task of agreeing or disagreeing, and finally, learners had to do something with the input by weighing their agreement against their disagreement.

Activity 3.2 Affective activity

- **Step 1**
  Read the following statements about the characteristics of George Bush and indicate whether you agree or disagree.

		Sono d'accordo	Non sono d'accordo
In generale:			
(1)	*È bello.*	☐	☐
(2)	*È basso.*	☐	☐
(3)	*È vivo.*	☐	☐
(4)	*È magro.*	☐	☐
(5)	*È ben vestito.*	☐	☐
(6)	*È artistico.*	☐	☐
(7)	*È delicato.*	☐	☐
(8)	*È aperto.*	☐	☐
(9)	*È arguto.*	☐	☐
(10)	*È caldo.*	☐	☐

- **Step 2**
  Compare with your partner. Do you have a negative or positive view about George Bush? Please tick!

- **Feedback**
  More than 50% *Non sono d'accordo* = You have a negative opinion about George Bush.
  More than 50% *Sono d'accordo* = You have a positive opinion about George Bush.

  Positive   Negative
  ☐   ☐

In the PI group subjects received only very limited feedback during the activities. the Instructor told the subjects whether their interpretations on the referential activities were correct or not but did not supply any other information. Specifically, the instructor did not re-explain noun–adjective agreement to someone who provided an incorrect answer. As Sanz (2004) demonstrated empirically, learners who performed structured input activities and who received explicit explanatory feedback did not outperform learners who performed the structured input activities and were informed only if their answer was correct or not.

Traditional Instruction (TI)

A second pack of materials also used in a previous study (Lee & Benati, 2007a) was used for the TI output-based group. These materials reflect one approach to the teaching of grammar that involves the paradigmatic presentation of the noun–adjective gender agreement in Italian and the subsequent practice in how to produce correct gender agreement in a sentence. All the activities used for the implementation of this approach were constructed to make learners produce gender agreement correctly at the sentence level. The TI treatment used for this experiment had the following characteristics: explanation and output practice. As seen in Figure 3.3, the materials presented all gender agreement forms in a paradigmatic way to include singular as well as plural. The TI group received explanation that included information about plural forms, as this is the usual way is to present the target form in traditional instruction. As exemplified in Activities 3.3 and 3.4, the practice activities require learners to practice producing correct forms in both oral and written modes.

Although the grammatical explanation was paradigmatic, we focused

---

Activity 3.3

- Complete the sentences making the right adjective agreement.

    (1) *La casa è (bello)* _____
    (2) *Marco è (brutto)* _____
    (3) *Lucia è (antipatico)* _____
    (4) *Paolo è (simpatico)* _____
    (5) *L'edificio è (alto)* _____
    (6) *Questa persona è (basso)* _____
    (7) *Lui è (grasso)* _____
    (8) *Claudia è (magro)* _____
    (9) *Londra è (cosmopolito)* _____
    (10) *È un uomo (dinamico)* _____

> **Activity 3.4**
>
> - Complete the sentences with the right adjective agreement.
>
>   (1) Questa macchina non è _____(bello)
>   (2) Questo film è_____ (bello)
>   (3) La persona è_____(Americano)
>   (4) Mia figlia è _____(Tedesca)
>   (5) Mi piace la donna _____(bruno)
>   (6) Mi piace l'uomo _____(biondo)
>   (7) La città è_____(vivo)
>   (8) George Bush è _____(antipatico)
>   (9) Clinton è _____(magro)
>   (10) Paolo_____ (alto)

the output practices on the singular forms so that TI learners would practice these forms to the same extent as the PI learners did.

Whereas in the input-based group, subjects were required to interpret and react to sentences that contained the target feature, in the TI group, subjects were required to produce the target item. Examples of the activities used in TI are Activities 3.3 and 3.4. For the TI treatment the types of activities used were mechanical completion and substitution activities in which learners have to complete a sentence by supplying the grammatically-correct form of the adjective provided.

The main emphasis of this type of instructional treatment was on form production from the beginning.

Control group (C)

Those learners who formed the control group were also enrolled in the beginning-level Italian course at the University of Greenwich. The control group received no instruction on the primary and secondary target linguistic features during the course of experimental treatment, but were subject to a comparable amount of exposure to the target language in their classroom for the same amount of time.

Tests

Pre- and post-tests were developed for measuring the primary effects of instruction on the first feature (noun–adjective gender agreement in Italian) and the secondary transfer-of-training effects on the second feature (future tense verb morphology in Italian).

The tests for the primary targeted feature comprised an interpretation task and a written production task. These are given in Figures 3.4 and 3.5.

Secondary Effects of Processing Instruction (Italian)

Interpretation activity

- Listen to each sentence in which a person is described and determine which person is described.

	[Pictures seen by learners]			[Sentences heard by learners]
(1)	Bill Clinton	Hilary Clinton	not sure	È stupido.
(2)	fat woman	fat man	not sure	È grassa.
(3)	slim man	slim woman	not sure	È magra.
(4)	famous actor	famous actress	not sure	È famoso.
(5)	male singer	female singer	not sure	È bravo.
(6)	train	car	not sure	È veloce.
(7)	woman	man	not sure	È interessante.
(8)	house	apartment	not sure	È ideale.
(9)	Sofia Loren	Pavarotti	not sure	È bello.
(10)	Brad Pitt	Uma Thurman	not sure	È intelligente.
(11)	Charles	Camilla	not sure	È reale.
(12)	a priest	a sister	not sure	È credente.
(13)	glass of beer	glass of wine	not sure	È buona.
(14)	comedian	female comedian	not sure	È divertente.
(15)	famous man	famous woman	not sure	È attraente.
(16)	tall man	tall woman	not sure	È alta.
(17)	woman	man	not sure	È favoloso.
(18)	big house	big apartment	not sure	È grande.
(19)	old woman	old man	not sure	È vecchia.
(20)	big woman	big man	I am not sure	È enorme.

Figure 3.4 Interpretation test (adjective)

The interpretation task consisted of 20 audio-taped sentences with 10 of these actual targets and the other 10 distracters. Specifically, the distracters were adjectives ending with -*e*. As in the treatment materials, the items on the pre- and post-tests described an object or a person represented by two different pictures. The learners' task was to determine which person or object was being described. They could chose between the two pictures or choose the 'I am not sure' option. Care was taken so that the tests were balanced in terms of difficulty and vocabulary. Because we examined beginning level learners we tended to use high-frequency vocabulary items. Correct responses were given a score of 1 and each incorrect response received a score of 0. The maximum possible score was 10 points whereas the minimum possible score was 0 points.

In the written production task, learners had to fill in the gaps in a short passage by producing the correct form of the adjective provided in brackets. There were 10 items, 5 of which required masculine agreement and 5 requiring feminine agreement. Again, students scored 1 point for each correct agreement and 0 for incorrect ones. The maximum possible score was 10 points and the minimum 0 points.

To assess the possible secondary transfer-of-training effects of instruction on the second linguistic item, two tasks were developed and used as pre-tests and post-tests. One task, provided in Figure 3.6, required learners to interpret the meaning of the target form and the other, provided in Figure 3.7, required them to produce it. For the interpretation task we created a set of simple sentences in which there were no adverbial indications of temporal reference. This test consisted of 20 aural sentences (10 in the present that served as distracters, and 10 targets in the future). The tests were recorded by a native speaker of Italian and presented to the subjects on a tape player. The verb, target or distracter, was never placed at the beginning of the sentence; it tended to occur in sentence-medial position. Additionally, temporal adverbs and subject nouns or pronouns were removed. The input was stripped in this way so that the learners could not

---

- Complete the following text with the right adjectives agreement.

  Milano è una città (bello) _____ ma (grigio) _____. Il centro di Milano è (caotico) _____ ma (suggestivo) _____.
  Milano non è (noioso) _____ come Genova ed è molto (organizzato). Non è (caro) _____ e la vita culturale è (vivo) _____.
  Il castello di Milano è (famoso) _____, (meraviglioso) _____ e (diverso) _____.

Figure 3.5 Production test (adjective)

- Indicate whether the speaker is relating information about the present or the future.

[Sentences heard by learners]

(1) present □ can't tell □ future □ *A casa tornerò insieme agli amici.*
(2) present □ can't tell □ future □ *Ad una amica compra un regalo molto bello.*
(3) present □ can't tell □ future □ *A casa di un amico caro ascolta la radio.*
(4) present □ can't tell □ future □ *Prima di partire saluterò tutti gli amici.*
(5) present □ can't tell □ future □ *Ad una compagna di scuola presto i libri di Italiano.*
(6) present □ can't tell □ future □ *In una scuola privata di Roma studia Italiano.*
(7) present □ can't tell □ future □ *Alla biblioteca dell'Università consulterò i libri.*
(8) present □ can't tell □ future □ *Al caffè dell'Università aspetta l'amico per andare al cinema.*
(9) present □ can't tell □ future □ *Con vari amici di scuola lavorerò in un bar..*
(10) present □ can't tell □ future □ *A tutti gli amici dell'Università manda una cartolina.*
(11) present □ can't tell □ future □ *La vacanze d'estate costerà molti soldi.*
(12) present □ can't tell □ future □ *A scuola studio la storia.*
(13) present □ can't tell □ future □ *Nel parco troverà una sua vecchia amica.*
(14) present □ can't tell □ future □ *In un ristorante cinese invita una amica a cenare.*
(15) present □ can't tell □ future □ *Dalla famiglia riceverà molti regali per il compleanno.*
(16) present □ can't tell □ future □ *In una festa cucinerò dei buonissimi spaghetti al pomodoro.*
(17) present □ can't tell □ future □ *In casa di un amico prenderà un caffè prima di tornare a casa.*
(18) present □ can't tell □ future □ *Nel campo da tennis gioca con un amico.*
(19) present □ can't tell □ future □ *In vari paesi d'europa compro un souvenir da portare a casa.*
(20) present □ cannot tell □ future □ *In compagnia di altri amici pranzerà in un ristorante francese.*

Figure 3.6 Interpretation task: Future tense

rely on those elements to assign tense but had to focus in on or attend to the verb morphology as the only indicator in the sentence as to when the action was taking place. This 20-item instrument was used as a pre-test/post-test measure of knowledge gained at interpreting future tense verb morphology at the sentence level. In addition to describing their performance as knowledge gained, we could also say that the test will measure if learners approach interpreting the future tense differently after they have practised processing noun–adjective agreement.

As was also the case with the interpretation task developed and used to measure interpretation of correct noun–adjective gender agreement, no repetition of any sentence was provided so that the test would measure real-time comprehension. Subjects had only a few seconds to establish whether the sentence was taking place in the present, in the future or if they could not tell. The reason why the interpretation task was time-limited is that it was developed to access spontaneous responses. Although the interpretation task consisted of 20 sentences, only performance on the future sentences was counted for the raw scores, giving a maximum score of 10. The raw scores were calculated as follows: incorrect response = 0 point, correct response = 1 point.

A written completion task (Figure 3.7) was developed and used to measure learners' ability to produce verb forms using the future tense (a modified cloze passage). The written production task consisted of a text with 10 sentences to complete. The students were required to complete the text by producing the future tense forms of the verbs provided in brackets. As is the case with this type of pedagogical activity, the verb in brackets was given in the infinitive form and all the verbs were morphologically regular in the future tense. Five minutes were allocated to complete this task. The two production tasks were, quite obviously, not developed to measure the impact of instruction on spontaneous communication. Our intent was to

- Complete the text with the future tense form of the verbs in brackets.

  L'anno prossimo (io) _____ (studiare) in una Universita` americana molto famosa. Anche Paola _____ (partire) per l'America per fare un Master a New York. Giovanna, invece_____ (restare) in Italia per finire gli studi. La mia ragazza mi _____ (raggiungere) in America per passare le vacanze insieme. Io _____ (passare) un anno meraviglioso e _____(girare) il mondo. (io)_____ (visitare) mia mamma e _____ (smettere) di fumare e _____ (cominciare) a fare sport. Giorgio mi ha detto che _____ (iniziare) a giocare a tennis e qualche volta mi _____ (chiamare) per fare una paertita.

Figure 3.7 Written production task (future tense)

measure formal accuracy. In the written task all 10 sentences contained a target form so that the raw scores were calculated as follows: fully correct future tense = 1 point; incorrect = 0 point.

Procedures

The purpose of this study was to measure primary and secondary transfer-of-training effects of instruction, in particular, by comparing different groups of students studying Italian. One group had been taught the target linguistic item of noun–adjective gender agreement through a TI treatment while another group was taught this item through a PI treatment. The main aim of the study was to determine whether at the end of an instructional period of two consecutive days, totalling four hours, we could also measure a transfer-of-training effect of instruction on a different linguistic feature albeit a feature affected by a similar processing principle. We aimed at establishing whether the group receiving PI would surpass the group of students receiving TI in an interpretation task and a written production task of both linguistic items.

The experiment was designed to make the results as objective as possible within the constraints of a University language programme. See Figure 3.1 for an overview of the experimental procedures. Pre-tests (interpretation and production) for both linguistic features were administered to all students one week before the beginning of the experimental treatment period. After the pre-tests, subjects were assigned to one of the three groups through a process of randomisation. The instructional period lasted for two days, with a total of four hours of instruction. Post-tests were administered immediately after the end of the instructional treatment, that is, at the end of the second day of instruction. After instruction, each learner took four tests: two interpretation tests and two production tests. The fact that both interpretation and production tasks were present in all the tests is clear evidence that neither instructional group was favoured. This possible task bias factor could invalidate the outcomes of the study, and was taken into account in designing the experiment. All the pre-tests and post-tests were balanced in terms of difficulty and vocabulary.

The interpretation task and the production tasks for both linguistic items were time-limited. While the interpretation task was measuring real-time comprehension, the production tasks were developed to elicit subjects' best performance. Therefore in the case of the production tasks it was decided to allow enough time for the subjects to accomplish the tasks – if too little time is made available, stress might affect subjects' performance. The TI group was familiar with the post-test production tasks, as a number of the activities in the TI materials were based on them. The TI group was not, however, familiar with the interpretation task. In contrast, the PI group was familiar with the interpretation task from having performed structured input activities, but not with the production tasks, as subjects from the PI group were not engaged in output activities. Both groups performed a task that their instructional treatment had incorporated. In this way, the groups were equally unfamiliar with each other's task.

The instructional materials used for this experiment had been previously piloted and subsequently used in an empirical study (Benati, 2004b). Many aspects of the research methodology had already been piloted in previous experiments and the final procedures for the experiment included the following:

(1) use of a randomisation procedure to make groups comparable;
(2) use of pre-test and post-test procedure;
(3) balanced materials in terms of difficulty and other items (vocabulary, verbs, adjectives and activities);
(4) balance between the tests in terms of difficulty and familiarity;
(5) balance in the amount of explicit instruction to which learners were exposed.

For the experimental treatments, all subjects across the three groups were taught by the same instructor (one of the researchers). This person was also the subjects' regular classroom instructor. In order to participate in the experiment, the subjects had to sign a consent form (Figure 3.8).

CONSENT FORM

This is a consent form for you to take part in an experiment in language instruction. You will be tested and with other students receive instruction and practice on a particular structure in Italian. Your answers will remain confidential. All the results will be reported through statistical representations and no individual results will be made available.

Your participation is only voluntary and you may choose to leave at any time and not complete the experiment. If you agree to participate, please indicate by signing below.

I agree to participate in this experiment. My participation is voluntary and I have read the above informed consent information.

_____
Name

_____
L1

_____ _____
Signature   Date

Figure 3.8 Consent form

To avoid the potential bias factor in a classroom experiment where the researcher is also the regular instructor, we took the following steps.

(1) The teacher acted as a facilitator during the experiment. He presented the linguistic feature under investigation by using the target language to explain how it works, and he followed the two instructional materials to the letter. For the control group, he continued with the normal topics and activities outlined in the teaching programme.

(2) The subjects were aware of the comparative nature of the study. This increased the possibility that the subjects' understanding of the nature of the experiment (in this particular case a pedagogical research involving a comparison of teaching methods) could produce a 'Hawthorne' effect (see Brown, 1988). The Hawthorne effect is the influence that the experimental conditions might have on a subject's performance; the fact that the subjects were aware of the nature of the experiment and that they were receiving special attention might have improved their performance. This potential bias and resultant effect exist in all comparative studies. In the present study the researcher made all possible efforts to pay the same amount of attention and show the same enthusiasm across the groups, which we hope removed or at least reduced any such effect. Ideal experiments require identical groups differing only in teaching methods. In real life, however, it is almost impossible to control everything fully. One-way ANOVAs were conducted on the raw scores for the interpretation and the production pre-test tasks to assess whether there were any statistically significant differences among the class means on any of the pre-test measures. Repeated measures ANOVAs were used on pre-test/post-tests measures to assess whether there were any relevant effects for Instruction and Time. In addition a *post hoc* Tukey's Honestly Significant Difference test was carried out to establish the contrasts between the effects of instruction in the three groups. The results of the statistical analyses carried out in this study are presented and analysed in the following section.

Results

Primary effects (on Italian noun–adjective gender agreement)

Pre-tests were administered to the students one week before the beginning of the instructional period. Two versions of the pre-test and the post-test were developed to form a split-block design. In the pre-test the PI group and the TI group received version A, while the control group received version B. In the post-testing phase the two versions were switched. The raw scores for each of the four pre-tests were subjected to a one-way

Table 3.5 Means and standard deviations (pre-test and post-test) for interpretation task (adjective gender agreement)

		Pre-test		Post-test 1	
Variable	n	Mean	SD	Mean	SD
Processing Instruction	9	0.6667	0.7071	5.777	1.301
Traditional Instruction	10	0.9000	0.5676	1.400	0.5164
Control	6	0.5000	0.5477	0.6657	0.6137

minimum score = 0, maximum score = 10

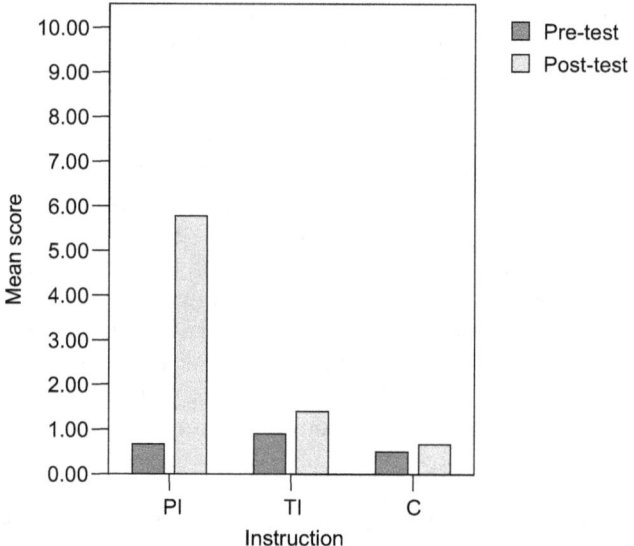

Figure 3.9 Results for interpretation task (adjective gender agreement)

ANOVA. The ANOVA conducted on the interpretation pre-test revealed no significant differences among the groups' means ($F_{2, 25} = 0.838$, $p = 0.446$) before the treatment period. This lack of difference means that any gains in the post-test are due to the instructional treatments and not to any previous knowledge. The means in Table 3.5 describing learners' scores on the interpretation pre-test and post-test suggest an improvement for the PI group after treatment. The descriptive analysis on the average scores of each group is displayed in Figure 3.9.

The repeated measures ANOVA revealed a significant main effect for Instruction ($F_{2,25} = 87.892$, $p = 0.000$) and for Time (pre-test vs. post-test) ($F_{2,25} = 119.839$, $p = 0.000$), and a significant interaction between Instruction and Time ($F_{4,25}$ = 39.138, p = 0.00). The *post hoc* Tukey's test showed that the PI group was significantly different from the TI group (p = 0.000), the PI group performed significantly better than the Control group (p = 0.000) and the scores of the TI group and the control group were not significantly different from each other (p = 0.215).

Learners in the PI group improved their performance on the interpretation task from the pre-test to the post-test, and their performance was greater and statistically better than the other two groups. This finding is the one that is echoed throughout the previous research on Processing Instruction.

The one-way ANOVA conducted on the written production task pre-test scores revealed no significant differences between the three groups ($F_{2,25}$ = 0.293, p = 0.749). As in the case of the interpretation task, we assume that any comparative effect found in the post-testing can therefore be attributed to the effects of the instructional treatments. A repeated measures ANOVA was conducted on the raw scores of the written production task. The results from the statistical analysis showed a significant main effect for Instruction ($F_{2,25}$ = 53.965, p = 0.000), a significant main effect for Time (pre-test vs. post-test) ($F_{2,25}$ = 273.343, p = 0.000) and significant interaction between Instruction and Time ($F_{4,25}$ = 36.680, p = 0.00). The Tukey's test on the post-test scores showed that both the PI and TI groups improved significantly, whereas the control group's apparent increase in scores on the post-test was not significant. These results are presented in Table 3.6 and graphically displayed in Figure 3.10. Specifically, the results indicated the following effects for instruction: both PI and TI groups made a significant improvement in production due to the treatments and that the PI group was not significantly different than the TI group (p = 0.178). Both groups performed significantly better than the control group (p = 0.001) which did not improve significantly. This finding is also echoed throughout the previous research on PI.

The performance of both the PI group and the TI group improved from pre-test to post-test, and was much greater than the control group. A

Table 3.6 Means and standard deviations (pre-test and post-test) for written production task (adjective gender agreement)

		Pre-test		Post-test 1	
Variable	n	Mean	SD	Mean	SD
Processing Instruction	9	0.3337	0.5061	4.756	0.8819
Traditional Instruction	10	0.5000	0.5270	5.300	0.9486
Control	6	0.4550	0.5467	0.6667	0.5164

minimum score = 0, maximum score = 10

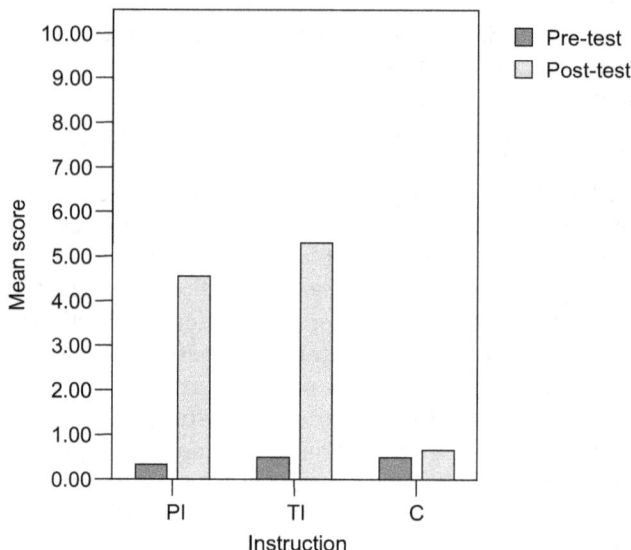

Figure 3.10 Results for written production task (adjective gender agreement)

summary of the repeated measures ANOVA testing for primary effects on both interpretation and production is shown later in Table 3.9.

Secondary transfer-of-training effects (on Italian future tense verb morphology)

We used a one-way ANOVA on the pre-test interpretation task scores of the three groups to ensure that there were no pre-existing differences between the groups. The result showed no significant differences among the means of the instructional treatment groups before instruction ($F_{2,25} = 0.393$, $p = 0.679$). They all went into the treatments and treatment period with equal and extremely limited knowledge of the secondary target item. Means and standard deviations for the interpretation tests are presented in Table 3.7 and displayed graphically in Figure 3.11. Perusing the means we note that the control group showed no change in performance from pre-test to post-test. The PI and TI groups do, by way of contrast, show improvement: about a 25% increase for the PI group and about a 4% increase for the TI group. We used a repeated measures ANOVA to compare the effects of Instruction and Time and the interaction between Instruction and Time. The statistical analysis revealed a significant main effect for Instruction ($F_{2,25} = 25.625$, $p = 0.000$), a significant main effect for Time ($F_{2,25} = 44.524$, $p = 0.000$); and a significant interaction between Instruction and Time ($F_{4,25} = 13.108$, $p = 0.00$). The *post hoc* analysis showed the following contrasts: the PI group's score is significantly better than the

Secondary Effects of Processing Instruction (Italian)

Table 3.7 Means and standard deviations (pre-test and post-test) for interpretation task (future tense)

		Pre-test		Post-test 1	
Variable	n	Mean	SD	Mean	SD
Processing Instruction	9	0.4446	0.5270	2.978	0.6676
Traditional Instruction	10	0.6000	0.6992	1.070	0.5664
Control	6	0.3345	0.5164	0.3357	0.5164

minimum score = 0, maximum score = 10

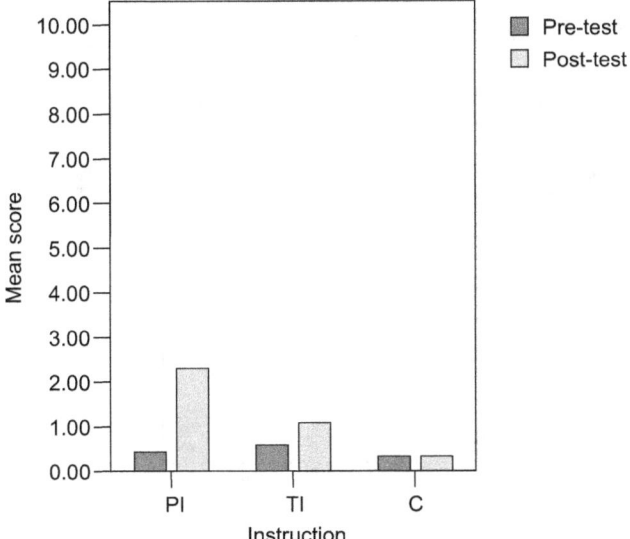

Figure 3.11 Results for interpretation task (future tense)

scores of both the TI group ($p = 0.004$) and the control group ($p = 0.000$). The scores for the TI and control groups are, however, not statistically significantly different from each other ($p = 0.124$).

What these results demonstrate is that the PI treatment is better than TI treatment and the control group in improving learners' interpretation of future tense morphology forms. As we can see from the means in Table 3.7, the PI group has slightly improved from pre-test to post-test compared with the other two groups and in particular with the control group. The improvement of the PI group from the pre-test to the post-test is 25% and some might

Table 3.8 Means and standard deviations (pre-test and post-test) for written production task (future tense)

Variable	n	Pre-test Mean	SD	Post-test 1 Mean	SD
Processing Instruction	9	0.6647	0.7071	1.4444	0.8833
Traditional Instruction	10	0.4000	0.5164	1.300	0.4830
Control	6	0.5050	0.5477	0.3333	0.5140

minimum score = 0, maximum score = 10

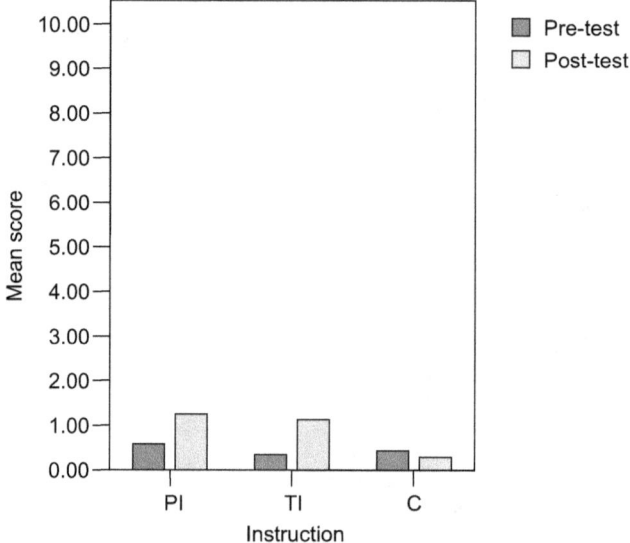

Figure 3.12 Results for written production task (future tense)

consider that only minimal improvement, but the difference is statistically significant. Furthermore, the difference came about in the absence of direct instruction on the target item. It is a transfer-of-training effect.

The means for the pre-test and post-test for production on Italian future tense are presented in Table 3.8 and presented graphically in Figure 3.12. A one-way ANOVA conducted on the pre-test production scores of the three groups revealed significant differences among the groups ($F_{2,25} = 0.629$), and hence no pre-existing differences between the groups. The subjects began the treatments and treatment period with equally limited knowl-

Secondary Effects of Processing Instruction (Italian)

Table 3.9 Summary of repeated measures ANOVA (adjective gender agreement)

Data	df	SS	MS	F	p
Interpretation					
Instruction	2	44.183	22.91	87.892	0.000*
Time	2	64.809	32.404	119.839	0.000*
Instruction x Time	4	65.542	16.3855	39.138	0.000*
Production					
Instruction	2	44.126	22.063	53.965	0.000*
Time	2	111.753	55.8765	273.343	0.000*
Instruction x Time	4	42.219	10.55475	36.680	0.000*

* = significant

Table 3.10 Summary of repeated measures ANOVA (future tense)

Data	df	SS	MS	F	p
Interpretation					
Instruction	2	12.230	6.115	25.625	0.000*
Time	2	20.625	10.3125	44.524	0.000*
Instruction x Time	4	12.506	3.1265	13.108	0.000*
Production					
Instruction	2	2.356	1.178	4.591	0.022*
Time	2	11.651	5.8255	4.468	0.024*
Instruction x Time	4	2.969	0.74225	4.128	0.030*

* = significant

edge of the forms of the future tense in Italian. We will, therefore, attribute any differences we find between the post-test scores to the effects of instruction on noun–adjective agreement. We carried out a repeated measures ANOVA on the raw scores for the production task in order to compare the effects of Instruction and Time (see Table 3.10). The statistical analysis revealed a significant main effect for Instruction ($F_{2,25} = 4.591$, $p = 0.022$), a significant main effect for Time ($F_{2,25} = 4.468$, $p = 0.24$) and a significant interaction between Instruction and Time ($F_{4,25} = 4.128$, $p = 0.30$). The Tukey's *post hoc* analysis showed the following significant contrasts: the PI group's score is significantly better than that of the control group ($p = 0.024$); the scores for PI and TI groups were not statistically different from each other ($p = 0.551$); and the scores for the TI and control groups were also not statistically different from each other ($p = 0.141$). These significant transfer-of-training effects are relatively modest. The PI group improved about 8% in producing future tense forms and the TI group improved about 9%. Again, this significant improvement took place in the absence of direct instruction on the target form, Italian future tense morphology.

Summaries of the two repeated measures ANOVAs for the secondary transfer-of-training effects are shown in Table 3.9 and Table 3.10.

Discussion and Conclusion

The two main objectives of this study were to investigate the primary and secondary transfer-of-training effects of PI. Primary effects on a linguistic form are those that result directly from instruction on that linguistic form. Transfer-of-training effects are those that result indirectly from instruction on another form. The forms under scrutiny here were the primary target of noun–adjective agreement and the secondary transfer-of-training target of the future tense morphology. The target language was Italian as learned by classroom-based native speakers of English. In order to accomplish these objectives a series of questions and hypotheses were formulated. The questions that guided our investigation are reiterated as follows:

(Q1) What are the primary effects of PI and TI on the acquisition of Italian noun–adjective agreement as measured by an interpretation task?

(Q2) What are the primary effects of PI and TI on the acquisition of Italian noun–adjective agreement as measured by a production task?

(Q3) Are there any secondary transfer-of-training effects of PI and TI from receiving instruction on noun–adjective agreement to the acquisition of Italian future tense morphology as measured by an interpretation task?

(Q4) Are there any secondary transfer-of-training effects of PI and TI from receiving instruction on noun–adjective agreement to the acquisition of Italian future tense morphology as measured by a production task?

These questions led us naturally to make a series of hypotheses based on previous research. They were the following:

(H1) PI will be a more effective type of instruction than TI and the control group in helping learners to interpret correctly and efficiently sentences containing noun–adjective gender agreement in Italian.

(H2) PI will be an equally effective type of instruction to TI in helping learners to produce correctly and efficiently sentences containing noun adjective gender agreement in Italian.

(H3) Learners receiving PI on noun–adjective agreement in Italian will transfer that training and process future tense morphology better than those receiving TI as measured by an interpretation task.

(H4) Learners receiving PI on noun–adjective agreement in Italian will transfer that training and process future tense morphology better than those receiving TI as measured by a production task.

As far as measuring primary effects is concerned, we compared two instructional treatments, PI and TI, and included a control group to help delineate these effects. We tested for effects on both interpretation and production tasks. Based on results of previous studies (Benati, 2004a; Lee & Benati, 2007a), we hypothesised that L2 learners receiving PI would outperform learners receiving TI and the control group in their ability to interpret efficiently and correctly sentences containing noun–adjective gender agreement forms in Italian (Hypothesis 1). In addition to that, we hypothesised that the PI group would be as effective as the TI group at producing accurately sentences containing noun–adjective gender agreement in Italian (Hypothesis 2).

The results of this study confirmed both hypotheses. In fact, the results show that the performance of the PI group on the interpretation tasks was statistically significantly superior to the performance of either the TI or control groups. The PI group gained about 50% on the interpretation task from pre- to post-testing whereas the TI grouped gained only about 5% and the control group gained only 1%. Both the PI group and the TI group significantly improved their performance from pre-test to post-test on the production task. The PI group gained about 44% from pre- to post-testing, while the TI group gained about 48%. As these percentages demonstrate, the two groups improved equally, in that there was no statistical difference in performance between the two groups. The control group gained only about 2%.

Learners in the TI group improved in the production task from pre-test to post-test, whereas the PI group improved in both interpretation and production tasks from pre-test to post-test. In TI learners are engaged in mechanical output practice (production-based), whereas in PI learners received structured input activities practice (interpretation-based). As pointed out by VanPatten:

> in processing instruction, learners are engaged in structured input activities, not output activities. Yet the processing group was able to perform as well if not better than the traditional group on a task with which the former had no familiarity but the latter did. Thus, task famil-

iarity can account for one set of results (those of the traditional group) but not the other (those of the processing group). (1996: 153)

Once again, these results have proved the important nature and purpose of Processing Instruction. PI is a form of instructional intervention that is very successful at helping learners to process forms that would otherwise not be processed, as they are redundant and non-meaningful. The results of PI instruction are that learners process the forms more efficiently and that they make the correct form–meaning connections necessary to advance their second language acquisition of Italian. PI achieves these results by altering inappropriate processing strategies such as, in this case, the Non-redundancy Principle and Non-meaningful Principle, and it is successful at helping learners to process input more efficiently and accurately. In the case of adjective gender agreement in Italian, the particular nature of PI practice seems to result in helping learners to make the proper form–meaning connections. The success of PI is in the structured input activities. In these activities, we manipulate the input. For noun–adjective agreement, we make the form of the adjective nonredundant and we make it more meaningful in that learners must use the form and connect it to a meaning. In a real sense, we place the form in a 'privileged position' in the activities so that learners must process it. As suggested by VanPatten (2002), Processing Instruction might be helping learners adjust their mechanisms for dealing with input and organising linguistic data when their processors, in the state they are prior to receiving PI, would fail to process an input sentence correctly. This failure would be due, in part, to their native language for, as Ellis (2007) notes, L2 learners come to the task of second language acquisition with their cognitive mechanisms fully committed and fully tuned to their native language. They must, through exposure and through Processing Instruction, recommit and retune those mechanisms to the L2.

We have defined transfer-of-training in terms of a primary and secondary linguistic target. We could also have defined transfer-of-training in terms of skill as in Skill Acquisition Theory (DeKeyser, 2007). Processing Instruction, as designed for research purposes, provides training in interpreting sentences. Learners who receive PI in research settings never produce the target form. Their training, then, is input-oriented and, according to Skill Acquisition Theory, this training should affect their performance only on input-oriented assessments (DeKeyser, 1997, 2007). Yet every PI study that has assessed both interpretation and production (as demonstrated in our review in Chapter 2), has found that PI practice significantly improves performance on production tasks. The fact that the PI group performed as well as the TI group on a production task does seem to prove that this type of instruction not only helped L2 learners to process noun–adjective gender agreement forms correctly, thus appropriately enriching their intake. It also had an impact on learners' developing linguistics system as learners were able to improve from pre-test to post-test in the production task and their performance was equivalent to the TI group. The TI group learners performed according to Skill Acquisition Theory in that they performed as trained. Their practices were output-oriented and they improved significantly on the production task. They did not improve significantly on the interpretation task.

The finding that PI improves both interpretation and production argues against the skill-specificity position of Skill Acquisition Theory. This double-benefit finding is remarkable if we consider that the PI group was exposed to an instructional treatment during which learners were involved only in activities aimed at interpreting input correctly and never produced the target feature. As argued by Lee and VanPatten (1995, 103), 'Processing Instruction has a significant impact on learners' developing linguistic system, and that impact is observable in both comprehension and production of target items'. PI seems to be essential and more successful than TI when we need to help learners to build their internal linguistics system.

We defined transfer-of-training effects as secondary and cumulative, and in this study investigated a secondary effect. That is, the second objective of the present study was to investigate whether learners would transfer or apply the primary effects of PI to another linguistic feature affected by the same or similar processing problems. Lee (2004: 319) raised the question as to whether 'learners who receive PI transfer that training to other forms' without any further instruction in PI. He hypothesised that learners receiving PI on a particular form or structure affected by a particular processing principle would be able to transfer that training to other forms or structures affected by the same or a similar processing problem. In this study we took up that challenge and measured possible secondary effects of instruction comparing/contrasting the effects of PI and TI. In measuring secondary transfer-of-training effects we addressed the question as to whether instruction on noun–adjective gender agreement instruction would eventually aid learners in processing future tense verb morphology. As we stated in Hypotheses 3 and 4, we hypothesised that we would find a positive secondary transfer-of-training effect for PI as measured by both interpretation and production tasks, and we did.

In fact, the results show that the performance of the PI group on the interpretation task was statistically significantly superior to the performance of either the TI or control groups. The PI group gained about 25% on the interpretation task from pre- to post-testing, whereas the TI grouped gained only about 4% and the control group gained nothing. Both the PI group and the TI group significantly improved their performance from pre-test to post-test on the production task. The PI group gained about 8% from pre- to post-testing while the TI group gained about 9%. As these percentages for production demonstrate, the two groups improved equally as much in that there was no statistical difference in performance between the two groups. The control group lost about 2%.

We have long advocated the superiority of Processing Instruction as an approach to grammar instruction over other form-focused output-oriented approaches based simply on the primary or direct effects of PI on the interpretation and production of a targeted linguistic item (e.g. Benati, 2001; Lee & VanPatten, 1995). We now advocate the superiority of PI over an output-oriented instruction based on the secondary transfer-of-training effects we see with PI, and especially because the transfer-of-training effects were found for both interpretation and production. These findings suggest that the previous training on PI that the L2 learners received has influenced the way these learners approach the target language. When confronted with a new context, that is, a new linguistic feature (future tense forms), the learners adopted to a limited degree a more appropriate target-language approach to processing. The Processing Instruction group improved 25% on interpreting future tense forms as a secondary effect of being taught to process noun–adjective agreement. We refer to this gain as modest. The group improved 8% on producing future tense forms as a secondary effect of being taught to interpret noun–adjective agreement. We will refer to this gain as small. Despite the fact that the improvement is minimal, the PI groups seems to have been able to transfer some of the training received on processing adjective gender agreement forms to the processing of future forms.

These small-to-modest gains suggest to us that these learners are developing a different intuition for processing Italian. PI is a successful intervention for enriching learners' intake and shaping their developing linguistic system. The results of this study showed that PI practice indeed has secondary transfer-of-training effects, as processing noun–adjective gender agreement effectively aided the processing of future forms.

Further research should continue to address the questions on transfer-of-training effects posed in the present study. Specifically, future research could explore Lee's (2004: 322) Hypothesis 11, 'The cumulative effects of PI will be greater than its isolated effects'. We recommend that research be carried out to compare two groups of learners receiving PI instruction on Italian future tense. One group of learners would receive the PI instruction as their first encounter with the future tense. The other group of leaners would be treated like the group we have investigated here; they would receive PI instruction on noun–adjective agreement first, and then would receive instruction on the future tense. This second group would be primed, in a sense, toward the future tense. One possible outcome is that the second primed group of PI learners would outperform the first group. Another possible outcome is that the second primed group would learn the future tense more quickly than the first group. but possibly not outperform them in the end.

While we underscore the positive outcomes in this study, we acknowledge certain limitations. Firstly, only a relatively small number of subjects participated in the study, 25 in total divided across three treatment groups. Further research could address this issue and replicate the experiment with a larger sample. Secondly, we have tested only for effects immediately following instruction. All previous PI research that has included a delayed post-test has found that the direct effects of PI are undiminished for at least a month; they do diminish but are still significant after eight months (VanPatten & Fernandez, 2004). We are confident that our primary effects would be durative, but we have not tested for any durative transfer-of-training effects. The present study could be replicated not only with a larger sample size but also using a delayed post-test to measure for any longer-term effects.

Chapter 4
From Processing Instruction on the Acquisition of English Past Tense to Secondary Transfer-of-Training Effects on English Third Person Singular Present Tense

WITH SCOTT DEAN HOUGHTON

Introduction

As our review of previous research presented in Chapter 2 documents, there has been a huge growth of research into the primary effects of PI over the last ten years. PI has caught the attention of a number of researchers focusing particularly on the acquisition of Romance languages but also, although to a lesser extent, on other languages such as Japanese and English. After much debate, scrutiny and some criticism of the theoretical underpinnings of PI, the research findings converge in their conclusions that PI is a highly effective form of grammar instruction that has powerful effects on acquisition.[1] Research on PI continues to develop and diversify, and there are still many areas that need to be investigated. The purpose of the present study is to further investigate transfer-of-training effects of PI, particularly secondary effects, in a classroom-based experiment. Importantly, the present study examines the acquisition of a non-Romance language (English) and targets as its primary linguistic feature one that has not yet been investigated. Of equal importance in the scheme of PI research is that the learners participating in the research are native speakers of Korean, a native language not yet explored in PI research. Based on the numerous convergent results of previous research, as well as on specific previous research on this target item (Benati, 2005), we can confidently hypothesise that PI will successfully alter the processing problems that L2 learners encounter when confronted with the primary target item. We have selected a secondary target item in English that is affected by the same processing principles. The primary target is the English past tense marker *-ed* and the secondary target is the English present tense marker, third person singular form *-s*. Both forms are verb final inflections and both signal temporality. As in the previous chapter, which examined noun–adjective agreement and future tense verb morphology, we want to determine if learners can transfer the training received with PI on past tense to processing present tense. We want to determine if the transfer to the secondary target item, affected as it is by the same processing problem as the primary target, can occur without any further instruction. To make this determination, we will compare the effects of PI with those of TI.

Target and Secondary Linguistic Items

To measure primary and secondary transfer-of-training effects two forms were selected that are affected by the same processing principle: simple past tense -*ed* and present tense third person singular -*s*. Both verbal morphemes are affected by the Lexical Preference Principle (P1b): 'learners will tend to rely on lexical items as opposed to grammatical form to get meaning when both encode the same semantic information' (VanPatten, 2004b: 14). In other words, 'Learners will ... seek out lexical forms of semantic notions in input before they seek out grammatical forms that encode the same semantic notions' (VanPatten, 2007: 118). It is, however, important to bear in mind that learners' processing strategies do not work in isolation (VanPatten, 2004b). Learners may be using several inefficient strategies to help them process input and some strategies may have more prominence than others (Lee, 1999). These factors must also be considered when determining processing difficulty. For both the primary and secondary target items, the presence of a lexical temporal indicator would make the grammatical forms redundant such that another Processing Principle could also be at play here. The Preference for Nonredundancy Principle (P1c) states: 'learners are more likely to process nonredundant meaningful grammatical form before they process redundant meaningful forms' (VanPatten, 2004b: 14). If L2 learners do not process a form in the input. then they cannot be acquiring it.

Primary target item

This form was selected for the instructional treatment for two reasons. Firstly, it is affected by the Lexical Preference Principle, which has been investigated in many other PI studies. As seen in Tables 2.1 to 2.5 (Chapter 2), the Lexical Preference Principle has been addressed by research covering all the different PI research foci. There is consistent and, in terms of number of findings, strong evidence that diverting learners' attention from a lexical item to a grammatical form with PI has a significant effect on learners' performance. This research has established positive primary effects on input processing as well as a positive effect on the output that learners produce. The effectiveness of PI in altering learners' inefficient or inappropriate processing strategies and instilling much more effective, target-language appropriate ones has also been generalised to different structures from a number of L2 languages and different native languages (Benati, 2005).

Let's examine the Lexical Preference Principle at work with the English past tense marker *-ed*. In the following sentences, both the lexical adverbial/adverbial phrases and the verb morphology convey pastness. For an L2 learner, the lexical indicators would take precedence over the grammatical form.

(1) Yesterday I played football.
(2) Last Tuesday we worked a 10 hour shift.
(3) A month ago, we visited Italy.

Additionally, in each of these examples, the past tense marker is a redundant form, made redundant by the adverbial phrases. VanPatten's input processing model states that, if a grammatical form is redundant, then a learner is not likely to attend to and/or process the form (VanPatten, 2002, 2004b, 2007). The learner's task is to make a form–meaning connection. But the task goes uncompleted in that the meaning that would be attached to the form has already been extracted from the utterance. The phrases 'yesterday', 'last Tuesday' and 'a month ago' give the L2 learners all they 'need to know' in this context. Their L2 system is sufficiently underdeveloped that it does not also detect and integrate the verbal morphology, in essence, matching the lexical item to a required formal feature. Also, from the L2 learners' perspective, it is more efficient to allow the lexical marker to exclusively supply the temporal framework. Why should two things do the work that one item alone can do?

Comprehension does not guarantee acquisition, but acquisition cannot take place in the absence of comprehension. For an early-stage L2 learner comprehension, can require quite a lot of effort. We noted in Chapter 1 when we discussed the Availability of Resources Principle that comprehension difficulties may prevent L2 learners from processing forms in the input. If they do not process the form, they will not make a form–meaning connection. The example we provided from Lee (1999: 50) showed how a learner had difficulty interpreting the initial phrase in a sentence; so much so, that he abandoned any attempt at interpreting the part of the sentence that contained the targeted past tense form. The effort required to process the lexical items may exhaust attentional capacity such that L2 learners would not be able to process and store subsequent linguistic information. Learners certainly could not process and store the same amount as native speakers would be able to during real-time comprehension.

Word order in English with respect to adverb placement is flexible. In the three sentences above, the adverb may occur in either sentence initial or sentence final position. When in initial position, the adverb gains more processing saliency. As noted in Chapter 1 when we discussed the Sentence Location Principle, initial position is the most salient position and is the most favourable position from a processing perspective. The grammatical marker is, on the other hand, commonly found in sentence medial position, the least salient or favoured processing position. The location of the form makes it more likely that the target form will not be processed. The aim of PI is to push learners to process these grammatical markers that they might well have otherwise missed.

The second reason that we selected English past tense -ed marker for investigation is that it has previously been examined in PI research. Benati (2005) compared the effects of different instructional types, including PI, on this linguistic feature. Whereas he examined beginning- level adult native speakers of Greek and Chinese, the present study will add another dimension to the research base. We focus our present study on adolescent native speakers of Korean.

Secondary target item

The present tense third person singular morpheme -s was selected as the secondary target item for two reasons. First, this morpheme and the primary target morpheme are equally affected by the Lexical Preference Principle and the Preference for Nonredundancy Principle. The secondary target item means 'someone other than the speaker or person being spoken to'. We are, therefore, examining secondary transfer-of-training effects. Second, the rule governing the use of this morpheme is a relatively simple subject-verb agreement rule but assigning the form -s its correct meaning is a processing challenge. The grammatical rule seems straightforward: to form the simple present tense third person singular, add -s.^{2}

(4) I like chocolate but Mary likes vanilla more.
(5) I prefer hiking whereas Phillip prefers swimming.
(6) Phillip swims three times a week but I hike only on weekends.

Ellis (2007) describes the processing challenge facing L2 learners with respect to processing -s in the input. The one form has many functions that the processor must account for or categorise and then distribute. As illustrated above our secondary target form functions as a subject-verb agreement marker. It also functions as a possessive form, a contracted copula, and a plural marker.

(7) Do you know its exact location?
(8) It's too late.
(9) I have three great kids.

Pienemann (2007) also discusses the processing difficulties that L2 learners encounter with this morpheme in terms of feature unification.

Processing in Pienemann's framework refers to mental processes that lead to language production. The noun phrase in subject position is marked as third person singular. The verb in the verb phrase should also be marked as third person singular in English simple present tense. The mental processor must unify these two features or marking and it must do so across the two constituents, i.e. across the noun phrase to the verb phrase. Learners must reach a developmental stage at which cross-constituent feature unification can take place. Until then, they will not produce the concordance. Pienemann (2007: 143) posits a processability hierarchy: in stage 1, no grammatical information is exchanged across parts of a sentence; in stage 2, grammatical information is exchanged within a phrase, that is, within a noun phrase or within a verb phrase; in stage 3, grammatical information is exchanged across the noun and verb phrases in the sentence. Our secondary target item requires a sentence-level procedure to take place.

Within VanPatten's theory of Input Processing, our secondary target item is affected by several processing principles (VanPatten, 2004b: 14: see also Table 1.2 in Chapter 1). They are:

- (P1b) *Lexical Preference Principle*: learners will tend to rely on lexical items as opposed to grammatical form to get meaning when both encode the same semantic information.
- (P1c) *Preference for Nonredundancy Principle*: learners are more likely to process nonredundant meaningful grammatical form before they process redundant meaningful forms.
- (P1f) *Sentence Location Principle*: learners tend to process items in sentence initial position before those in final position and those in medial position.

The present tense third person -*s* is a grammatical marker that carries the semantic meaning of 'someone other than the speaker or person being spoken to' but, in reality, it has very little communicative value. The form is always made redundant because English requires an overt subject (noun or pronoun) in the surface form of the sentence. That is, the 'someone other than the speaker or person being spoken' to is obligatorily stated in the sentence. In sentence (11) below, the word *he* and the form -*s* both inform us that someone else is being spoken about. Without the word *he*, the sentence would be ungrammatical, as in sentence (12).

(10) What does he want?
(11) He wants tea.
(12) Wants tea.

Once L2 learners have processed the lexical item, they need not also process the grammatical form. The grammatical form does not give them new information.

Verb morphology in general may also be subject to the additional processing problem of sentence position. Most grammatical forms, like the third person singular, are in sentence medial position, which is the most difficult in terms of processing saliency (Sentence Location Principle, P1f). Learners will perceive items in initial and sentence-final positions more easily. Our example sentences are all short and simple, but the input to which learners are exposed during communicative exchanges may not always consist only of short, simple sentences. VanPatten and Cadierno (1993) included target items embedded in discourse. Several other PI studies have used these same materials (e.g. Morgan-Short & Bowden, 2006; Sanz, 1997; VanPatten & Oikennon, 1996)

Review of Previous PI Research on the Target Linguistic Items

As previously described in Chapter 2, all PI-based studies that have examined the Lexical Preference Principle converge on the finding that L2 learners can be taught (instructed/directed/trained) not to rely on a lexical item to the detriment of processing grammatical form. They are taught to use grammatical form to make a form–meaning connection. Directing learners to the form and instructing them how to use the form to make meaning is a more appropriate target-language-based processing strategy. The target languages investigated include the Romance languages of Italian, French and Spanish as well as the typologically distinct languages of English and Japanese. Whereas the majority of studies have examined the effects of PI on native speakers of English learning Romance languages, the results also include native speakers of Italian (studying Japanese), Greek (studying English) and Chinese (studying English). In all these studies, the direct/primary effects of PI are found in increasing significantly the ability of learners to process and interpret the meaning of forms in the input. Amazingly, the results of PI are 100% consistent; PI also increases significantly learners' ability to produce the target form accurately. By teaching learners to process input, the form–meaning connections they make are also available to the developing system to aid it in producing correct output. So, learning to process input correctly is fundamental to aiding second language development.

To date, only one other investigation on the effects of PI has measured the direct effects of the primary target form used in the present study. Benati (2005) was the first to target the English simple past tense morpheme -*ed*. He designed a study that compared the relative effects of three instructional types: Processing Instruction (PI), Traditional Instruction (TI) and meaning-based output instruction (MOI). The important contributions of this particular study are that it moved the research base away from the Romance languages and, of even greater importance, it examined the effects of PI on native speakers of languages other than English. The participants were native speakers of Greek and Chinese. Additionally, Benati (2005) was only the second PI-based study to examine adolescents (the first being VanPatten and Oikennon, 1996). Both groups were high-school-aged students studying English as an academic subject in their home countries. They had no previous knowledge of the target form as verified by a pre-test and a background questionnaire. The instruction they received, no matter the type, represented their initial exposure to the target item.

Learners in all three instructional groupings received explicit information about the form and use of the targeted linguistic item. The PI learners also received information about employing appropriate processing strategies for connecting a form with its meaning. The activities the learners engaged in are classified as structured input activities (SIA). To structure the input so that learners focus on the form and use it to make a form–meaning connection, Benati removed all temporal adverbs from the input. Only the target form, occurring in word final position, was available to learners to correctly interpret the temporal reference of the sentence. For research purposes, learners interpreted the meaning only of the target form. As is the case in all PI research, the learners in the PI group, during the treatment period, did not receive an activity that required them to produce the target form.

After the MOI learners received explicit information about the target form, they immediately set about practising the form by producing it as they carried out a set of meaning-based activities; these were all form-production practices. The MOI learners never used the target form to interpret the temporal reference of a sentence during the treatment period. The TI learners also engaged exclusively in form-production practices. Their practices were of two types, balanced equally in the materials, mechanical and meaningful practices. The mechanical practices require learners to manipulate form, but do not require that the learners comprehend the meaning of the sentence. The correct or incorrect answer is simply whether or not the target form was produced accurately. The meaningful activities for the TI group matched those from the MOI group. The difference between the groups then is in the presence or absence of mechanical activities.

Feedback to the learners was tightly controlled across the three groups, and was limited to telling learners whether their answers were correct or incorrect. No other information was elaborated. They did not, for example, receive explicit information about forming or using the target form if their answer was wrong. To measure the effects of the three treatments Benati (2005) used a pre-test with an immediate post-test design that followed two days of instruction. Time and curriculum constraints prevented delayed post-testing.

From pre-test to post-test, only the learners in the PI group significantly improved their performance on the form-interpretation task. Neither the MOI nor TI group improved significantly on the interpretation task, though the MOI group's score did improve somewhat. From pre-test to post-test, all three instructional groups improved significantly on the form production task. The three groups improved equally, an important finding in that the PI group never produced the target form during the instructional treatment. Because the PI group improved in two areas not just one, we assert that PI is a better instructional intervention than either MOI or TI. The learners who are taught to work with the input are the ones who take in form–meaning connections that they can access for making output. The learners who are taught to produce output do not make form–meaning connections that are useful for working with input.

Research Questions

In Lee (2004) the then-extant PI research was summarised and evaluated and future directions for research were suggested in the form of various hypotheses. Of relevance here is Hypothesis 9, as Lee explains ' ... PI researchers might move one step away from assessing direct/primary effects and determine whether secondary effects develop in learners as a result of receiving PI. Do learners who receive PI transfer that training to other forms?' (Lee, 2004: 319). The present study was designed to examine the primary and possible transfer-of-training effects of PI. To do so, we compared PI with traditional instructional treatments (TI) of output instruction on the target linguistic feature. The research questions that guide this study are framed in terms of this comparison:

(Q1) What are the primary effects of PI and TI on the acquisition of English simple past tense marker -*ed* as measured by an interpretation task?

(Q2) What are the primary effects of PI and TI on the acquisition of English simple past tense marker -*ed* as measured by a form production task?

(Q3) Are there any secondary transfer-of-training effects of PI and TI from receiving instruction on English simple past tense marker -*ed* to the acquisition of English present tense third person singular marker -*s* as measured by an interpretation task?

(Q4) Are there any secondary transfer-of-training effects of PI and TI from receiving instruction on English simple past tense marker -*ed* to the acquisition of English present tense third person singular marker -*s* as measured by a production task?

Based on the previous empirical findings presented in Chapter 2, the results we found for Italian noun–adjective agreement and future tense morphology and the research reviewed in this section on the primary effects of PI, TI and MOI on second language acquisition, the following hypotheses related to research questions (Q1) and (Q2) on can be formulated as follows:

(H1) PI will be a more effective type of instruction than TI in helping learners to interpret correctly and efficiently sentences containing English simple past tense maker -ed.

(H2) PI will be an equally effective type of instruction to TI in helping learners to produce correctly and efficiently sentences containing English simple past tense maker -ed.

The main objective of the present study was, however, to discover whether the positive and primary effects of PI can be transferred/applied by L2 learners to other features affected by the same processing problem. Previous research has clearly and consistently demonstrated that PI has direct and primary effects on learners as it helps them to alter inappropriate processing strategies. Our research in Chapter 3 established a secondary transfer-of-training effect on two linguistic features of Italian. Based on these findings, we will hypothesise that we will uncover a secondary transfer-of-training effect for English. We are, in essence hypothesising that after PI instruction on English simple past tense marker -ed, learners will use the more appropriate L2-based processing strategy in a novel situation. That is, we hypothesise that they will develop an L2-driven intuition about processing. PI instruction will, to paraphrase Ellis (2007), help the learners not be so committed and tuned to their first language. Our hypotheses regarding transfer of training are as follows.

(H3) Learners receiving PI on the simple past tense marker -ed in English will transfer that training and process the third person singular present tense marker -s better than those receiving TI as measured by an interpretation task.

(H4) Learners receiving PI on the simple past tense marker -ed in English will transfer that training and process the third person singular present tense marker -s better than those receiving TI as measured by a production task.

Methods and Procedures

Participants

Two groups of subjects, numbering 26 in the final data pool, participated in this investigation. They were all native speakers of Korean who were learning English as part of their middle school curriculum in Korea. All subjects were enrolled in the beginning-level class. The initial subject pool, numbering 81, was reduced to 26 subjects, as only subjects who scored less than 50% of the maximum score on the pre-tests (both the interpretation

Secondary Effects of Processing Instruction (English)

and production tests) were included in the final data pool. In addition to the elimination score on the pre-tests, we used the following set of criteria to select the population of this study:

(1) all participants had to be native speakers of Korean;
(2) they all had to be beginning-level learners of English;
(3) they should not have been taught or should not have have been previously exposed to the primary and secondary target linguistic targets (English simple past tense marker *-ed* and English third person singular present tense *-s*) through instructional materials or through contact with English outside the classroom.

After administering a pre-test two weeks prior to the treatment, a randomisation procedure was adopted to assign learners to one of the two groups. The two instructional groups consisted of the PI group and the TI group – whose eventual numbers, through attrition, were 12 and 14, respectively. These students participated in the two-day instructional treatment period, which was then followed immediately by the post-test. No control group was used in this experimental study. We provide an overview of the experiment in Figure 4.1.

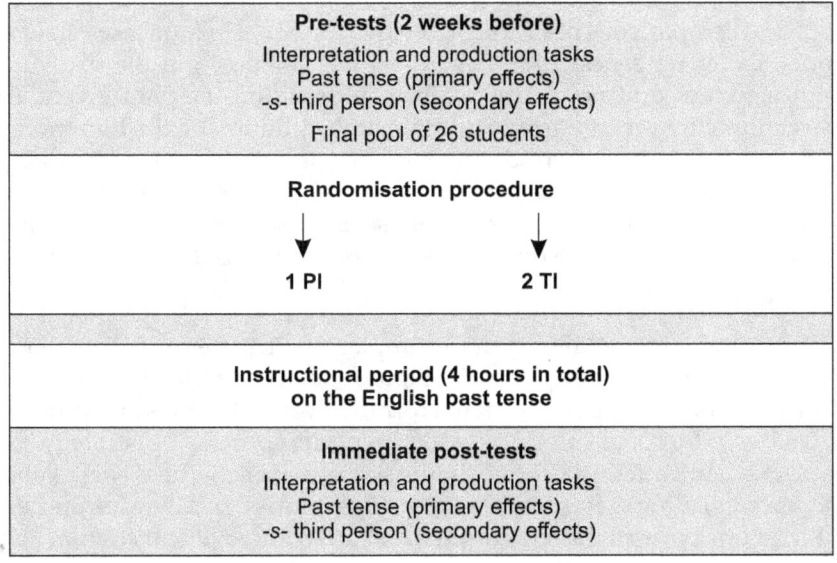

Figure 4.1 Overview of the experiment

Materials

Two separate sets of instructional materials were developed for this study. The processing group received PI treatment, and thus received materials that were input-based and processing-oriented. The traditional group received TI treatment, and thus received materials that were output-based and production-oriented. The two sets of materials were balanced in terms of number of activities. Each group carried out 10 activities so that learners would have equivalent exposure to either processing practice or output practice. The instructional materials consisted of highly frequent lexical items because the learners are beginning level, and the vocabulary used in the different sets of instructional materials was roughly the same. In Figures 4.2 and 4.3 we provide the explicit information about the primary target item that the PI and TI groups received. They were given the same explicit information about how to form the simple past tense in English, and both groups engaged in a brainstorming activity to generate lexical temporal markers associated with the past. The explicit information stops there for the TI group, but continues for the PI group. The PI group received additional information about the specific processing problem addressed in this investigation. Supplying processing information is part of the explicit information supplied to PI groups (Lee & VanPatten, 1995, 2003; VanPatten, 1996; Wong, 2004a). Yet, as presented in Table 2.3 in Chapter 2, in the five empirical comparisons of PI and SI, the two are equal in four cases. In other words, the effectiveness of PI lies in learners carrying out the structured input activities and not in the explicit information they are given. The instructional treatment lasted approximately 4 hours for the two groups. During the treatment period, feedback on performance was limited to telling participants whether an answer was right or wrong. No further explanation was offered and students seemed satisfied with the limited feedback. Limiting the feedback was consistent across the two groups.

PI treatment

The Appendix contains many examples of PI materials. PI materials consist of explanation, as seen in Figure 4.2. The explanation contains explicit information about the target form, its formal features and function, as well as additional information on a specific processing strategy that learners should attempt to apply in the subsequent activities. These subsequent activities are the structured input (SI) activities, and they are the heart of PI. As one peruses the structured input activities, one will see that at no point did learners in the PI group ever produce the target form in any of the activities. The structured input activities were constructed following PI guidelines from a number of sources (Farley, 2005; Lee & VanPatten, 2003; Wong, 2004a). As pointed out already in Chapter 2, there are six main guidelines that must be adhered to when developing SI activities. This point cannot be underscored enough, as there have been previous studies where the tenets of PI were not followed and results were adversely affected. If guidelines are not followed carefully, the question arises as to whether the activities are really SI activities at all. VanPatten and Wong (2004) discuss Allen's (2000) materials and learners' potential reliance on event probabilities to derive a correct answer rather than relying on making a form–meaning connection. Farley (2001a) addressed Collentine's (1999) materials. VanPatten and Sanz replied to Salaberry's materials. For these studies, the issue centred on the nature of structured input as opposed to comprehension practices. We have already provided in Chapter 2 a more thorough analysis of these guidelines. They can help instructors and researchers alike to construct effective SI activities to help learners to overcome certain L2-based processing problems. Looking at the materials for

Teacher's instructions

- The past simple tense is one of the tenses used to talk about events in the past. It refers to finished actions and events. Very often the English past simple tense ends in *-ed*. This is the regular past tense.

    For example [*write on board*]:

    I played tennis with Paula.

- When you talk about a finished time in the past, the English past simple tense is often accompanied by a temporal adverb or time expression.
    For example [write on board]:

    Yesterday, I smoked 20 cigarettes

- Can anybody tell me some other adverbs?
    [*brainstorm temporal adverbs and write on board*]

	night		morning		afternoon
	Saturday	yesterday>	afternoon	this >	morning
last >	week		evening		evening
	month				
	year				

VERY IMPORTANT!

- Do not rely on the temporal adverb to understand when the action takes place as sometimes you can hear a sentence without the temporal adverb.

- You must pay attention to the tense ending to understand when the action takes place.

- In the case of describing past events, pay attention to the ending of the verb: *-ed*. [*teacher circle and underline -ed in the examples*]

Figure 4.2 Explicit information for PI treatment

this study alone, it can be seen that only one form was kept in focus (past tense -*ed*) to ensure maximum efficiency, and a brief, to-the-point, rather than lengthy, grammar explanation was used. We had, after all, focused on one thing as per the guidelines for creating structured input activities. The explanation does not matter, as much as doing the activities.

There are two kinds of SI activities: referential and affective (Farley, 2005; Lee & VanPatten, 1995; Wong, 2005), and both require learners to attend to form to get meaning or to work with meaning. The difference is that for referential activities there is only one correct answer, and that answer requires learners to have processed the target form correctly. The learner would have had to have processed the past tense marker in order to finish a sentence with either 'yesterday' or 'tomorrow'. With referential activities, the instructor can check item-by-item that the learner has made the right form–meaning connection. Affective activities differ in that there is no right or wrong answer. Instead, learners process communicative, meaning-bearing input and express an 'an opinion, a belief or some other affective response ... ' (Wong, 2004a: 42). Most research on PI has offered learners a mixture of affective and referential activities. Each type of activity exposes learners to the target form.

Learners respond to the items in an activity by understanding what they hear or read. In affective activities, for example, in order to complete the activity learners must understand the meaning of each utterance (each

---

Teacher's instructions

- The past simple tense is one of the tenses used to talk about events in the past. It refers to finished actions and events. Very often the English past simple tense ends in **-ed.** This is the regular past tense.

  For example [*write on board*]:

  I played tennis with Paula.

- When you talk about a finished time in the past, the English past simple tense is often accompanied by a temporal adverb or time expression.
  For example [write on board]:

  Yesterday, I smoked 20 cigarettes

- Can anybody tell me some other adverbs?
  [*brainstorm temporal adverbs and write on board*]

	night		morning		afternoon
	Saturday	yesterday>	afternoon	this >	morning
last >	week		evening		evening
	month				
	year				

Figure 4.3 Explicit information for the TI treatment

utterance contains the target linguistic item) to relate the sentences to their own lives or to the world as they know it. In referential activities learners must connect form to meaning in order to correctly interpret the time reference. Referential activities can be made even more communicative/meaningful when a further affectively-oriented step encourages learners to relate the sentence to their own lives. Farley (2005: 87) advises that referential activities should precede affective ones because ' ... with referential activities coercing form–meaning mappings first, the effects of the activities that follow are likely heightened and processing becomes more likely to occur'. Farley also suggests that there should be more referential activities then affective ones. In the PI materials used in the present study there are six referential activities and four affective ones.

Activity 4.1 is an example of a referential activity. The learners must indicate the time frame encoded in each verb form they read. The answer is right or wrong based on the form of the verb in the sentence. Each of the sentences refers to the students' teacher and so all the past tense items were designed to contain true information. The activity includes an affectively-oriented second step in which the learners refer to the past tense items from the first step and evaluate their content as a whole. To conclude that the teacher had an interesting or boring weekend does not require the learner, especially a beginning-level learner, to produce the target form on his or her own. The learner might read off a sentence on the page, but that is hardly producing the form in a communicative context.

Activity 4.2 is an example of an affective activity. The activity begins with listening to a short piece of connected discourse, a story about someone's

---

Activity 4.1 Sample referential activity

Your teacher's life!

- **Step 1**
  Read the following statements about things your teacher does and decide whether he/she does them now or did them last weekend:

He/She		Now	Last weekend
(1)	... played tennis.	☐	☐
(2)	... talks to the class.	☐	☐
(3)	... talked to his mother.	☐	☐
(4)	... argued with a friend.	☐	☐

  [*followed by 6 more items of identical structure*]

- **Step 2**
  Now decide in pairs whether your teacher's weekend was an interesting or a boring weekend.

first day in London. All the items to which the learners must respond are in the past tense. They know the temporal reference but are working with the information or content. After responding, in step 2 they are given the text in written form so they can check their answers. Finally, to complete the activity and to encourage the learners to relate to the content, they are asked if they knew the places mentioned and if they would like to visit them.

When learners are first exposed to input, lengthier discourse can overload working memory, therefore sentences are kept short at first so that learners do not struggle with comprehension. Once learners have had an opportunity to notice and process a form, they are then exposed to longer utterances, and finally to connected discourse. The PI materials that participants received in this study contained short sentences in the initial activities. Later, the treatment moved to connected discourse, as shown in Activity 4.2. Activities also provided learners with both aural and written input to account for different learner preferences and also to provide a

---

Activity 4.2 Sample affective activity

My first day in London

- **Step 1**
  Listen to the following story that a student told about his first day in London and decide which statements accurately describe what happened:

  [*Instructor's script:*]
  I really wanted to see Madame Tussaud's, so early in the morning I took a quick shower and washed myself, and travelled by train to Baker Street station. I had my picture taken with David Beckham, well the wax model that is. I also visited Trafalgar square and saw Nelson's Column. There were so many pigeons there that I thought they owned the place! ... [*discourse continues*]

  TRUE OR FALSE   THE STUDENT ...
  _____   (1) ... wanted to see Buckingham Palace.
  _____   (2) ... showed pictures of Hyde Park to his parents.
  _____   (3) ... stayed in bed most of the morning.

  [*followed by 7 more items of identical structure*]

- **Step 2**
  Now read the text you have just listened to and check your answers. Would you like to change any of your answers? Then ask your teacher to give you the answers.

- **Step 3**
  Read the text again. Do you know any of the famous places mentioned above? Would you like to visit any of them?

certain variety in the materials. In this way some activities (as in Activity 4.2) might have a first step that required learners to listen to input and in the next step they would read the input they had just heard. Alternatively, an activity that provided aural input might be followed by another that provided written input.

Following the tenets of communicative language teaching as described by Lee and VanPatten (1995, 2003), learners were pushed to do something with meaning-bearing input rather than just receiving input. Learners had to make different kinds of decisions based on form and meaning. For example, a typical SI activity, such as Activity 4.1, may contain a binary option from which learners choose the correct temporal adverbs such as 'yesterday' or 'right now'.

The guideline that is of fundamental importance states that an SI activity must keep learners' processing strategies in mind and so must address at least one of the processing principles outlined in Chapter 1 (Table 1.1). As Wong (2004b: 42) states rather categorically, 'If the activity is not constructed to pre-empt an inefficient processing strategy, then it is not an SI activity'. All 10 PI activities used in this study have been designed to address the Lexical Preference Principle (P1b). To that end, all temporal adverbs were removed from the input so that learners would be pushed to process the simple past tense form to get meaning. Learners could not rely on lexical items to determine the correct time reference as they normally would because we did not give them any.

VanPatten (2004a, 2007) reminds us that the Processing Principles do not operate in isolation. In addition to working with the Lexical Preference Principle we also worked with the Sentence Location Principle (P1f), which states that learners may have difficulty processing a form that is in the middle of a sentence. Keeping this strategy in mind, in all our SI activities we moved the target form into the beginning of a sentence. This position is the most privileged and most salient position. The learners are, therefore, more likely to process a form they encounter early in the sentence. For example, in Activity 4,1 we structured the target items by removing the 'he/she' from the sentences and placing it in a header as a lead in to the input items. 'He/She' is the grammatical subject of all the sentences and could, therefore, easily be placed as a header. In doing this, we succeeded in placing the past tense *-ed* consistently in the initial position of the input items to which learners were exposed. In Activity 4.2, all the target sentences have the same grammatical subject, the student. We could easily remove this phrase from the input items and use it as a header. The result is that each input item began with a verb marked for simple past tense. Initial position is a privileged processing position and so we structured the input to take advantage of this processing position.

TI treatment

The first empirical investigations of PI compared its effects with those of a traditional type of output-focused instruction, termed TI for Traditional Instruction (VanPatten & Cadierno, 1993). Several subsequent investigations also compared these two instruction types as can be seen in our review in Chapter 2. TI consists of two classes of output-focused practices, mechanical and meaningful. At the time, the blend of mechanical and meaningful output practice or more precisely, the move in classroom instruction from beginning with mechanical practices to following up with meaningful practices, represented the instruction that was prevalent in North America, as well as elsewhere in the world. Many teachers' classrooms were typified by these practices and they were addressed in teacher training courses. Mechanical form-production activities still prevail in some parts of the world, and in others they have either disappeared or their importance has been minimised.

In the research, TI consists of three components. The first is a paradigmatic presentation of grammatical forms. Following explanation comes practice. Learners first practise mechanical activities in which they are producing correct forms. If the form is correct, then the answer is correct. That is, for these activities, the correct answer is to supply the correct form. From mechanical practices learners proceed to meaningful activities. The meaningful activities are also form-focused, but the learners are freer to contribute real world information. Previous investigations that have used TI as the comparative treatment differ with regard to the number of these types of activities. In her investigation of Spanish preterite tense, for example, Cadierno (1995) used more mechanical activities in her TI treatment than she did meaningful ones. Benati (2005), on the other hand, used an equal balance of mechanical and meaningful activities for his TI treatment. Additionally, he developed a third treatment group (MOI) that received only meaning-based activities that required learners to practice making output after receiving explicit information (see Table 2.1). The change in balance may well reflect a decade of reorienting teaching practices.

The TI materials used in the present study can be found in the Appendix. The first component of the materials was the explicit information that learners received about the target form. They were given a brief explanation about how to form the past tense in English. They were not, however, given any information about processing strategies, nor over-reliance on adverbials nor directions to pay attention to the ends of verbs. The explanation was followed immediately by activities that required the learners to produce the target form in their output.

Activities 4.3 and 4.4 serve as examples of how TI requires learners to produce the form in order to complete the activity. For Activity 4.3, the

Activity 4.3 Sample TI activity

- Put the following verbs in the sentences below.
  Put them in the past simple tense.

  stay phone check watch talk

(1) Yesterday morning I _____ with my teacher about my essay mark.
(2) This morning, John _____ in bed for a few hours
(3) Last night I _____ my homework before handing it in
(4) Last weekend I _____ a really exciting film

[*followed by 6 more items of identical structure*]

Activity 4.4 Sample TI activity

- Complete the sentences below by changing the infinitive of the verbs in brackets to the past tense.
- For example:
  Yesterday, I met my friends and ... (play)
  You could write down and <u>played football with them</u>

(1) Last Christmas I ... (to receive)
    _____

(2) Last month it was my birthday and I ... (to celebrate)
    _____

(3) London was great, I really ... (like)
    _____

---

learners fill in the blank with the correct form of the verb supplied. Adverbials signal to them the appropriate tense. Other mechanical activities may involve making substitutions or transformations of the sentence to incorporate the target form. A more meaningful but still guided output practice is found in Activity 4.4, in which learners must complete the sentences with the target form.

One of the main criticisms of traditional practice, from a communicative perspective, is that learners need not attend to meaning in order to complete the activity. Lee and VanPatten (1995, 2003) questioned what value a purely mechanical practice could offer to second language development. Wong and VanPatten (2003) answered the question empirically; mechanical practices are not effective. As can be seen in our sample output-focused activities, we use temporal adverbs to cue the appropriate time frame. In other words, the output practices are not 'structured' as structured input practices are. The language of the output practices has not been manipulated to address the Lexical Preference Principle because output practices do not do that. Whatever the learners in the TI group are doing, they are practicing past tense -*ed* forms mediated by lexical temporal adverbs.

Tests

To assess primary and secondary transfer-of-training effects of the two instructional treatments, PI and TI, we used a pre-test and immediate post-test design. The tests consisted of both interpretation and production measures for both the target and secondary linguistic items (the simple past tense -*ed* morpheme and the third person singular, present tense marker -*s*). The use of interpretation and production measures has always been to ensure that neither instructional treatment is favoured in the assessments. The PI group should improve on interpretation. The PI group should improve on production. But, does performance improve across the tests? In creating the assessment tasks, we took learners' beginning-level knowledge of the target language into account and so, accordingly, used high-frequency lexical items and balanced these across the various assessment tasks.

The interpretation task for the primary linguistic target is provided in Figure 4.4. As the figure shows, the interpretation tasks consisted of 20 items for which learners indicated temporal reference or were offered the option of not knowing ('can't tell'). Ten of the items were distracters in that they used a present tense form for which the correct answer would be 'right now'. The ten target items on which learners were scored contained the targeted linguistic item, past tense -*ed*. In the interpretation task, learners were required to listen to sentences from which temporal adverbs had been removed, so that learners could not rely on these to assign tense. Instead, they would have to rely on verbal morphology to indicate when the action took place (present or past temporal reference). As far as possible, we designed the interpretation tasks to tap real-time comprehension. To that end, we allowed only a short gap of 5 seconds between questions for learners to mark their answers. For interpretation measures raw scores were calculated so that a correct answer received 1 point and any incorrect answer would receive no points. The maximum score possible would, therefore, be 10 points for the interpretation tests (either pre-test or post-test)

We also utilised a production task for pre- and post-testing that required learners to produce the target forms in an extended written discourse that relatedto what two people did together. The production task for the primary linguistic target is provided in Figure 4.5. As the figure shows, the production tasks consisted of 10 items structured as a modified cloze test. Each target item, in its citation or dictionary entry form, was given to the

Secondary Effects of Processing Instruction (English) 107

> - Listen to the sentences and decide whether the action occurred last week or right now in the present.
>
> | | last week | can't tell | right now | [*Sentences heard by the students*] |
> |------|-----------|------------|-----------|--------------------------------------|
> | (1) | x | | | I cleaned the kitchen. |
> | (2) | | | | I hate mathematics. |
> | (3) | | | | I walk to college. |
> | (4) | | | | I talked with my mum. |
> | (5) | | | | I posted letters. |
> | (6) | | | | I dress in smart clothes for an interview. |
> | (7) | | | | I typed my essay. |
> | (8) | | | | I fixed my light. |
> | (9) | | | | I played chess with my teacher. |
> | (10) | | | | I hate English food. |
> | (11) | | | | I arrive in London. |
> | (12) | | | | I listen to music on my ipod. |
> | (13) | | | | I called Tom. |
> | (14) | | | | I use my phone on the train. |
> | (15) | | | | I need more time to study. |
> | (16) | | | | I celebrated my birthday with all my friends. |
> | (17) | | | | I liked pop music. |
> | (18) | | | | I visit my uncle in Japan. |
> | (19) | | | | I smoked a cigarette. |
> | (20) | | | | I changed into my suit. |

Figure 4.4 Interpretation task

learners in parentheses after a blank. Such production tests assess learners' ability to produce the correct form of the past tense of the indicated verb. All verbs were, of course, regular in that their past tense forms were inflected with the -*ed* morpheme. We included no examples such as 'speak/spoke' or 'take/took'. The written task allowed learners to monitor and edit their performance and was therefore not assessing spontaneous production. Once again, the scoring procedure we followed was to assign 1 point for a correct form and no points for an incorrect form.

Tests for secondary effects followed the same design as those we used to assess primary effects. We present the interpretation task for third person present tense -*s* in Figure 4.6. The learners listened to sentences from which subject nouns and pronouns had been removed because the pedagogical task was to identify the correct subject. Learners were required to listen for

- Learners must fill in the gap with the right verb (10 gaps).

  Yesterday, John **1**_____ (phone) his girlfriend Mary and they **2**_____ (talk) together for about an hour. Mary **3**_____ (want) to play tennis later that day. So John quickly **4**_____(brush) his teeth and **5**_____(dress) in his white t-shirt and shorts. At 1pm he **6**_____ **(walk)** to the tennis courts to meet Mary. They **7**_____(play) together for about two hours and **8**_____(enjoy) themselves a lot. Afterwards, they **9** _____(watch) a movie together. Later at John's house he 10 _____(cook) a meal for Mary. Unfortunately, the food was terrible and Mary was sick!

Figure 4.5 Production task

- Listen to the sentences and decide whether or not each sentence is referring to Simon or his class mates:

	Simon	class mates	not sure	[Sentences heard by the students]
(1)	___	___	___	likes English food.
(2)	___	___	___	play football every day.
(3)	___	___	___	travel around the world.
(4)	___	___	___	wants more free time.
(5)	___	___	___	believes in God.
(6)	___	___	___	loves the English weather.
(7)	___	___	___	hate exams.
(8)	___	___	___	celebrate Christmas.
(9)	___	___	___	walk to university every day.
(10)	___	___	___	forgets to do homework
(11)	___	___	___	arrives late for classes.
(12)	___	___	___	needs a big breakfast in the morning.
(13)	___	___	___	sleep at midnight.
(14)	___	___	___	jogs in a local park.
(15)	___	___	___	wake up at 6am in the morning.
(16)	___	___	___	works part time in a supermarket.
(17)	___	___	___	think English trains are terrible.
(18)	___	___	___	knows many English people.
(19)	___	___	___	drink a lot of coffee in the morning.
(20)	___	___	___	read a lot of English newspapers.

Figure 4.6 Interpretation task

the inclusion or omission of third person -s on the verb and subsequently select the person or persons who were the agents of these sentences. The learners had three options to choose from: Simon, his classmates or 'not sure'. This third option was provided to discourage guessing and so that learners were not forced into a binary option. We followed the same procedure as in the interpretation test for the primary linguistic target. Specifically, the sentences were read only once. No repetition was provided so that learners had to mark their answers immediately after hearing the sentences to measure spontaneous comprehension. The test consisted of 20 items altogether; 10 for the third person singular marker -s (Simon) and 10 distracters that consisted of the general present tense form of the verb (his classmates). Raw scores were calculated on the target items, with a possible maximum score of 10 points for correct responses. That is, we assigned one point per correct response and no points for an incorrect response.

We also utilised a production task for pre- and post-testing that required learners to produce the target forms in extended written discourse. The paragraph relates the daily routine of an individual from waking through working and reading to fall asleep. The production task for the secondary linguistic target is provided in Figure 4.7. As seen in Figure 4.7, the production tasks consisted of 10 items structured as a modified cloze test. Each target item, in its citation or dictionary entry form, was provided to the learners in parentheses after a blank. The production tests assess learners' ability to produce the correct form of the present tense of the indicated verb. Learners are not under pressure on this task to supply their answers immediately or in the order presented. The written task allows learners to monitor and edit their performance and is therefore not assessing spontaneous production. The scoring procedure we followed was to assign 1 point for a correct form and no points to an incorrect form, yielding a possible maximum score of 10.

- Fill in the gap with the correct form of the verb.

    Every day John **1**_____(wake) up at 6am. At 7am he **2**_____ (travel) to university by train. The trains are usually slow and so John **3**_____(arrive) late to university, which annoys both John and his teacher. He **4**_____ (like) the drinks at starbucks café so, after his lectures, he always **5**_____(meet) his friends for a chat and a coffee. He usually **6**_____(stay) for a few hours. On the way home, he **7**_____(buy) food and vegetables and **8**_____(prepare) a big meal for himself. He **9**_____(read) in his bed for about an hour and usually **10**_____(sleep) around 11pm.

Figure 4.7 Production task

Procedures

This classroom-based experiment follows other PI studies by keeping the same basic design tenets as the original PI study by VanPatten and Cadierno (1993), specifically, a pre-test/post-test repeated measures design. This study is the second in a new branch of PI research: the investigation of transfer-of-training effects. Learners in one group will be taught the English simple past tense marker -*ed* using a PI treatment in order to help them alter their reliance on lexical items (Lexical Preference Principle, P1b). Another group will be taught the English simple past tense marker -*ed* using a TI treatment for which they will be practicing producing the target in mechanical and meaningful output activities. Our goal is to determine if learners can transfer that training by applying it to a novel form. For this research we selected a secondary target that is also affected by the Lexical Preference Principle, the English third person singular present tense marker -*s*.

The learners who participated in the study were native speakers of Korean whose study of English was only in its initial stage. The same instructor delivered both the PI and TI treatments. This instructor, who was not one of the researchers, understood the design tenets of PI and acted as a facilitator during the treatment phases. The instructor would intervene only in order to inform the learners that their answers were correct or incorrect. The instructor displayed the same enthusiasm when delivering both sets of materials. To examine the short-term effects of instruction, we used a pre-test and an immediate post-test. We were unable to examine more durative effects owing to curriculum constraints. The pre-testing pack contained four tests: two interpretation tests and two production tests. The post-testing packet contained a version of the four pre-tests. During post-testing, then, the interpretation tests would have been familiar to the learners from the PI group whereas the production tests would have been familiar to those in the TI group. Each group performs a familiar and an unfamiliar task.

Only those who scored below 60% on the pre-tests were included in the final pool for the instructional treatment phase. Using this score is an attempt to account for possible previous knowledge of the target forms, which would then allow the researcher to make claims regarding the effects of instruction on improving performance. Once the final pool was identified, the students were randomly assigned to an instructional treatment. Randomisation should lessen or eliminate any confounding influence of extraneous variables and helps promote group comparability across instructional treatment. Pre-testing and post-testing combined lasted approximately 30 minutes. The instructional treatments lasted four hours each and were delivered across two days of instruction. An immediate post-test was then carried out at the end of the second day of instruction.

Results

Primary effects (simple past tense -ed marker)

Pre-tests were administered to the students two weeks before the beginning of the instructional treatment period. It is important to establish that there were no pre-existing differences between the PI and TI groups so that we can attribute any post-treatment differences to the effects of instruction. The one-way ANOVA conducted on the interpretation pre-test for the simple past tense revealed, as hoped, no significant differences among the groups' means, $(F_{1,26} = 0.081, p = 0.887)$ before the treatment period. The means for the learners' scores on the interpretation test for simple past tense, both pre- and post-tests, are given in Table 4.1. The means indicate an improvement for the PI group but not the TI group. The descriptive analysis is presented graphically in Figure 4.8.

Table 4.1 Means and standard deviation (English past tense) for interpretation task pre-test and post-test

		Pre-test		Post-test 1	
Variable	n	Mean	SD	Mean	SD
Processing Instruction	12	3.41	1.50504	8.08	1.72986
Traditional Instruction	14	3.50	1.45444	3.38	1.40055

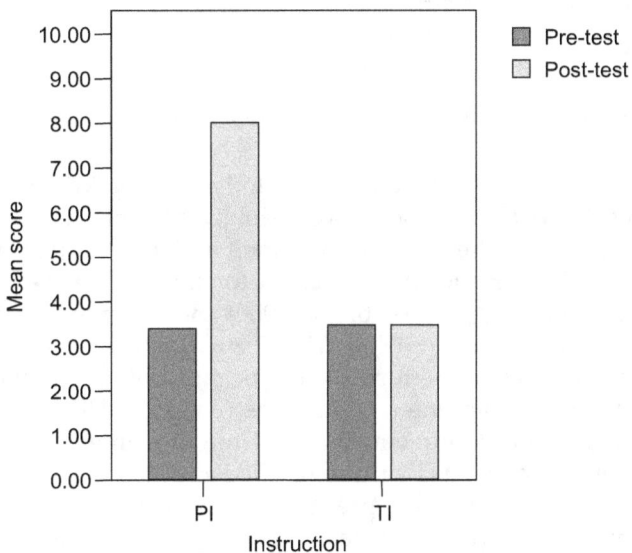

Figure 4.8 Results for interpretation task (simple English past tense)

Table 4.2 Means and standard deviation (English past tense) for production task pre-test and post-test

		Pre-test		Post-test 1	
Variable	n	Mean	SD	Mean	SD
Processing Instruction	12	2.41	1.83196	6.66	1.61433
Traditional Instruction	14	2.21	2.35922	7.00	1.70970

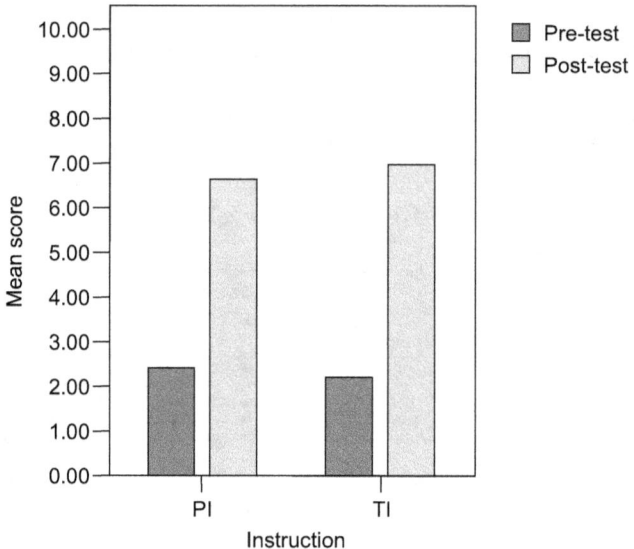

Figure 4.9 Results for production task (simple English past tense)

These scores were submitted to a repeated measures ANOVA for which Instruction (PI and TI) was the between-subjects factor and Time was the within-subject factor. The pre-test was Time 1 and the post-test Time 2. The analysis yielded a significant main effect for Instruction ($F_{1,26}$ = 299.859, p = 0.000), for Time ($F_{1,26}$ = 75.610, p = 0.000) and a significant interaction between Instruction and Time ($F_{1,26}$ = 17.742, p = 0.000). A follow-up analysis showed that the PI group performed significantly better than the TI group (t = 0.000). The significant interaction of Instruction and Time is due to the PI group's significant improvement from Time 1 to Time 2, whereas the TI group did not improve. The PI group reached an 80% accuracy level which is a 46% improvement from the pre-test to the post-test.

The mean scores on the pre-test and post-test for learners' written production of English simple past tense are given in Table 4.2 and presented graphically in Figure 4.9. A one-way ANOVA on the written production

Table 4.3 Summary of repeated measures ANOVA (English past tense)

Data	df	SS	MS	F	p
Interpretation					
Time	1	35.179	70.359	75.610	0.000*
Instruction	1	552.8655	1105.731	299.859	0.000*
Time x Instruction	1	6.80	13.600	17.742	0.000*
Production					
Time	1	118.651	237.302	169.704	0.000*
Instruction	1	94.632	189.264	187.252	0.923
Time x Instruction	1	33.8885	67.777	15.597	0.447

* = significant

task pre-test scores for English simple past tense showed no significant difference between the PI and TI groups ($F_{1,26} = 0.058$, $p = 0.812$) prior to instruction. No pre-existing differences were found so that we will attribute any differences in post-test scores to the effects of instruction. A repeated measures ANOVA was carried out on the raw scores of the written production task. The results from the statistical analysis revealed no significant main effect for Instruction ($F_{1,26} = 187.252$, $p = 0.923$), a significant main effect for Time (pre-test vs. post-test) ($F_{1,26} = 169.704$, $p = 0.000$) and no significant interaction between Time and Instruction ($F_{1,26} = 15.597$, $p = 0.447$). The *t*-test conducted on the post-test scores showed no significant difference between the PI and TI groups ($t = 0.614$). In other words, both groups improved significantly as a result of instruction, and both groups improved equally. The PI group improved 42% and the TI group improved 48% on the written production task from pre-test to post-test. A summary of the repeated measures ANOVAs for primary effects is provided in Table 4.3.

Secondary effects (third person singular present tense -s)

Means and standard deviations for the interpretation tests are presented in Table 4.4 and displayed graphically in Figure 4.10. We used a one-way ANOVA on the pre-test interpretation task scores of the two groups to ensure that there were no pre-existing differences between the groups. The result showed no significant differences between the means of the two instructional treatment groups before instruction ($F_{1,26} = 0.085$, $p = 0.985$). The groups possessed equivalent knowledge of English third person singular present tense -s before receiving instruction on the English past tense marker. We used an ANOVA with repeated measures to compare the

Table 4.4 Means and standard deviation (English -s third person) for interpretation task pre-test and post-test

		Pre-test		Post-test 1	
Variable	n	Mean	SD	Mean	SD
Processing Instruction	12	3.21	1.83196	5.41	1.08362
Traditional Instruction	14	3.42	1.39859	2.71	1.89852

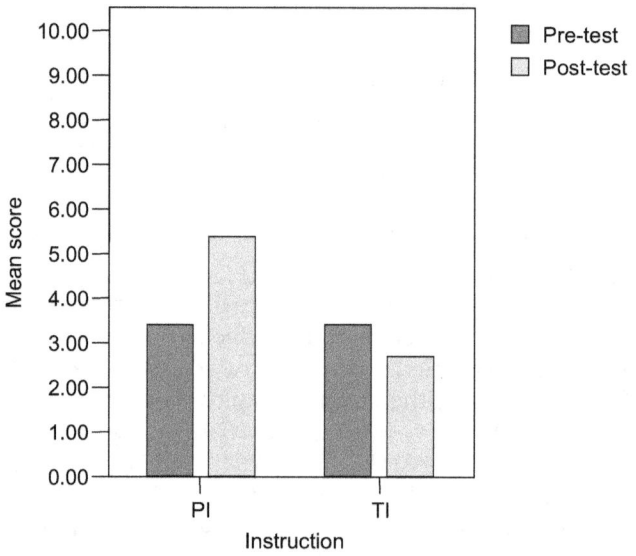

Figure 4.10 Results for interpretation task (English -s third person)

effects of Instruction and Time and the interaction between Instruction and Time. The statistical analysis revealed a significant main effect for Instruction ($F_{1,26}$ = 193.898, p = 0.000), a significant main effect for Time ($F_{1,26}$ = 17.616, p = 0.000), and a significant interaction between Time and Instruction ($F_{1,26}$ = 6.258, p = 0.020). The t-test carried out on the post-test scores for Instruction showed that the PI group's performance was statistically higher than TI group's (t = 0.000). The significant interaction is due to the fact that only the PI group improved. As the means in Table 4.4 show, the PI group improved 22% from pre-test to post-test on the secondary target item.

The means for the written production scores on the secondary target item are given in Table 4.5 and presented graphically in Figure 4.11. In the one-way ANOVA of the pre-test production scores of the two groups, we found no pre-existing differences between the groups ($F_{1,26}$ = 0.089,

Table 4.5 Means and standard deviation (English -s third person) for production task pre-test and post-test

		Pre-test		Post-test 1	
Variable	n	Mean	SD	Mean	SD
Processing Instruction	12	3.31	1.31137	4.41	1.72486
Traditional Instruction	14	3.21	2.00686	2.50	1.95133

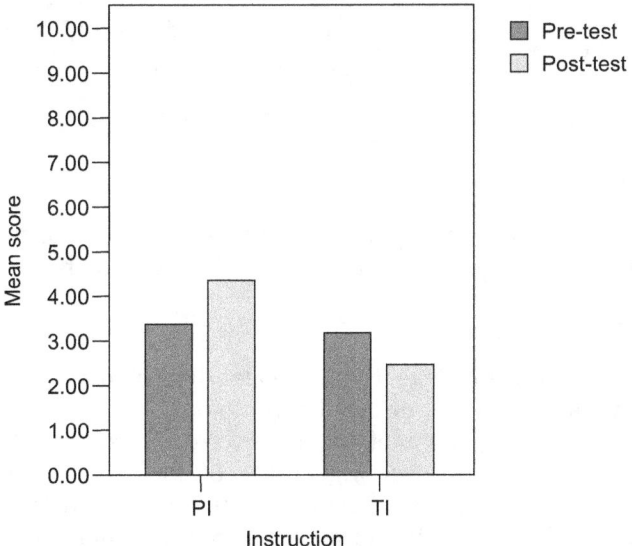

Figure 4.11 Results for production task (English -s third person)

$p = 0.768$). The groups had equivalent knowledge of the secondary target item before the beginning of the treatment period. We conducted an ANOVA with repeated measures on the raw scores for the production task, which revealed significant effects for Instruction ($F_{1,26} = 105.213$, $p = 0.000$), significant effects for Time ($F_{1,26} = 12.365$, $p = 0.002$) and significant interaction between Instruction and Time ($F_{1,26} = 2.574$, $p = 0.022$). The t-test conducted on the post-test scores revealed that the PI group significantly outperformed the TI group ($t = 0.015$). This unequal improvement accounts for the significant interaction between Instruction and Time. Only one group improved with time; the other did not. The PI group demonstrates an 11% increase from pre-test to post-test; students in the PI group can produce more third person singular present tense -s markers after receiving instruc-

Table 4.6 Summary of repeated measures ANOVA (English -s third person)

Data	df	SS	MS	F	p
Interpretation					
Time	1	11.901	23.802	17.616	0.000*
Instruction	1	362.3085	724.617	193.898	0.000*
Time x Instruction	1	11.693	23.386	6.258	0.020*
Production					
Time	1	4.7475	9.495	12.365	0.000*
Instruction	1	296.4845	592.969	105.213	0.000*
Time x Instruction	1	7.2535	14.507	2.574	0.022*

* = significant

tion on the English simple past tense marker -*ed*. A summary of the repeated measures ANOVA for secondary effects is shown on Table 4.6.

Discussion and Conclusion

As we discuss our findings it will be clear that the results of this study support VanPatten's model of input processing (VanPatten, 2002, 2004b, 2007). The two main objectives of this study were to investigate the primary and secondary transfer-of-training effects of PI. Primary effects on a linguistic form are those that result directly from instruction on that linguistic form. Transfer-of training effects are those that result indirectly from instruction on another form. The forms under scrutiny here were the primary target of English past tense -*ed* marker and the secondary transfer-of-training target of the English third person singular present tense -*s* marker. Both forms are affected by the Lexical Preference Principle (P1b) primarily, and the Sentence Location Principle (P1f) to a lesser degree. The target language was English as learned by classroom-based native speakers of Korean who were learning English in Korea – the first PI study to address this group of native speakers. In order to accomplish these objectives a series of questions and hypotheses were formulated. The questions that guided our investigation are here reiterated.

(Q1) What are the primary effects of PI and TI on the acquisition of English simple past tense marker -*ed* as measured by an interpretation task?
(Q2) What are the primary effects of PI and TI on the acquisition of English simple past tense marker -*ed* as measured by a form production task?
(Q3) Are there any secondary transfer-of-training effects of PI and TI from

receiving instruction on English simple past tense marker -*ed* to the acquisition of English present tense third person singular marker -*s* as measured by an interpretation task?

(Q4) Are there any secondary transfer-of-training effects of PI and TI from receiving instruction on English simple past tense marker -*ed* to the acquisition of English present tense third person singular marker -*s* as measured by a production task?

The following hypotheses were formulated:

(H1) PI will be a more effective type of instruction than TI in helping learners to interpret correctly and efficiently sentences containing English simple past tense maker -*ed*.

(H2) PI will be an equally effective type of instruction to TI in helping learners to produce correctly and efficiently sentences containing English simple past tense maker -*ed*.

(H3) Learners receiving PI on the simple past tense marker -*ed* in English will transfer that training and process the third person singular present tense marker -*s* better than those receiving TI as measured by an interpretation task.

(H4) Learners receiving PI on the simple past tense marker -*ed* in English will transfer that training and process the third person singular present tense marker -*s* better than those receiving TI as measured by a production task.

To measure primary effects, we compared two instructional treatments, PI and TI. We tested for effects on both interpretation and production tasks. Based on results of previous studies, specifically, Benati (2005) as well as others reviewed in Chapter 2, we hypothesised that L2 learners receiving PI would outperform learners receiving TI on the ability to interpret efficiently and accurately sentences containing the English simple past tense marker -*ed* (Hypothesis 1). Additionally, we hypothesised that the PI group would be as effective as the TI group at producing accurately the English simple past tense marker -*ed* in sentences (Hypothesis 2).

The results of this study confirmed both hypotheses. In fact, the results show that the performance of the PI group on the interpretation tasks was statistically significantly superior to the performance of the TI group. The PI group gained about 44% on the interpretation task from pre- to post-testing whereas the TI grouped lost about 2%. Both the PI group and the TI group significantly improved their performance from pre-test to post-test on the production task. The PI group gained about 42% from pre- to post-testing while the TI group gained about 48%. As these percentages demonstrate the two groups improved equally, in so far as there was no statistical difference in performance between the two groups.

In measuring secondary transfer-of-training effects, we addressed the question of whether instruction on the English simple past tense marker *-ed* would eventually aid learners in processing the English third person singular present tense marker *-s*. As we stated in Hypotheses 3 and 4, we hypothesised that we would find a positive secondary transfer-of-training effect for PI as measured by both interpretation and production tasks, and we did. These results support those found for Italian noun–adjective agreement and future tense morphology presented in Chapter 3.

In fact, the results show that the performance of the PI group on the interpretation task was statistically significantly superior to the performance of the TI group. The PI group gained about 22% on the interpretation task from pre- to post-testing whereas the TI group lost about 7%. Only the PI group significantly improved their performance from pre-test to post-test on the production task. The PI group gained about 11% from pre- to post-testing while the TI group lost about 7%. The results for PI found for English verb markers converge with those presented in Chapter 3 for Italian, but those found for TI diverge. The TI learners of Italian also showed secondary transfer-of-training effects in form production.

To what do we attribute the success of PI as an intervention that yields significant results in form processing and form production on primary as well as secondary transfer-of-training linguistic targets? The answer is deceptively simple. PI is effective in all these areas because it alters the way learners process, work with, and/or otherwise approach the primary linguistic data in the input. In a sense, learners are taught to reassess they way make meaning from the input. They are taught to use a form and to connect that form to a meaning. This account surely addresses the reason underlying the primary effects. The reason underlying the secondary transfer-of-training effect is that PI has effectively altered the internal processing mechanisms that work with primary linguistic data. In the context of the present study, learners were taught to use verb final morphology and could do so successfully after training. We hypothesise that their internal linguistics system has restructured, or at least has begun to be restructured, such that it now includes a processing slot on the ends of verbs. Their internal systems now have information that morphology in verb final position might be meaningful. Importantly, the learners' production mechanisms have access to this new information about the verb final slot. This cannot be said for TI. TI practice only makes the form available for production; it cannot make it available to processing mechanisms. If one of the goals of language instruction is to help students to become better, more efficient, learners then PI is invaluable in that it makes learners better and more efficient.

The results of the previous chapter, which also demonstrated positive, secondary transfer-of-training effects, in combination with the positive transfer-of-training effects we have presented in this chapter lead us to propose the Strengthening Hypothesis. Our research has now presented two empirical findings that support Lee's (2004) hypothesis on the transfer-of-training effects of PI. We have found transfer-of-training effects within the same processing principle (i.e. lexically co-referenced verb final morphology, *-ed*, to lexically co-referenced verb final morphology, *-s*), as well as across processing principles (i.e. non-meaningful, redundant nominal morphology, gender agreement, to lexically co-referenced verbal morphology, future tense). Given these results, we propose the Strengthening Hypothesis, a hypothesis formulated to stimulate further research into the effects of PI on second language acquisition.

- *The Strengthening Hypothesis:* second language learners who receive multiple PI treatments that address the same processing principle will increasingly strengthen their use of the more optimal processing strategy until it becomes their default strategy for processing second language input.

This hypothesis essentially states that, the more PI learners receive, the greater the expected secondary effects will be. Only future research on the effects of PI can confirm or not the Strengthening Hypothesis.

Along with the Strengthening Hypothesis we would also propose the Optimal Hypothesis. The Lexical Preference Principle (P1b) states, 'Learners will tend to rely on lexical items as opposed to grammatical from to get meaning when both encode the same semantic information' (VanPatten, 2004b: 14). Optimally we would want learners to abandon their reliance on lexical items when this is detrimental to processing grammatical form. We propose, then, the Optimal Hypothesis with an eye to stimulating further research on the effects of PI.

- *The Optimal Hypothesis*: when learners transfer their PI training, they will be more likely to process new grammatical forms as opposed to relying on lexical items to get meaning, when both encode the same semantic information.

As with all empirical research, the present study is limited in several ways.

While we underscore the positive outcomes in this study, we acknowledge certain limitations. The size of the final data pool is small. Future research could replicate our study, but with a larger sample size. We were unable to include a control group in the present study, but in light of the research presented in Chapter 3, the control group might have given us information related only to TI rather than to PI. Also, we know that the primary effects of PI hold over time (e.g. VanPatten & Fernandez, 2004). We do not know whether the secondary effects of PI will hold over time. We were unable to include delayed post-testing in the present study, but future research could address this important issue.

Note

1. Detailing the criticisms and concerns surrounding PI is beyond the scope of our present work. VanPatten, the theory's originator, addresses these issues in his 2004b essay and in his 2007 presentation of the theory. In particular, the reader is directed to the section of the 2007 chapter titled 'Common Misunderstandings' (VanPatten, 2007: 127)
2. The grammatical morpheme -*es* is the phonetically distributed allomorph of the third person singular. For the purposes of the present study we have isolated and targeted only -*s*. This allomorph occurs in the phonetic context of following a voiceless consonant.

Chapter 5

From Processing Instruction on the Acquisition of French Imparfait to Secondary Transfer-of-Training Effects on French Subjunctive and to Cumulative Transfer-of-Training Effects with French Causative Constructions

WITH CECILE LAVAL

Introduction

In this chapter we present the results of our third classroom experimental study designed to investigate transfer-of-training effects of PI on the acquisition of French. The present study examined secondary effects by measuring whether learners receiving PI on the French imperfect tense, our primary linguistic target, can transfer the instructional training they receive to the acquisition of other forms of French. More specifically, we sought to measure secondary transfer-of-training effects on the acquisition of French subjunctive used for expression of doubt and cumulative transfer-of-training effects on French causative constructions with *faire*. Both French imperfect and French subjunctive present second language learners with a morphological processing problem captured in the Lexical Preference Principle (VanPatten, 2004b). Because the processing problem is the same for the two forms, we refer to the transfer-of-training effects as secondary ones. From French imperfect to French causatives with *faire* is a move from morphology to syntax and involves two extremely different processing problems; the Lexical Preference Principle and the First Noun Principle (VanPatten, 2004b). Because we are addressing different processing problems we refer to the transfer-of-training effects as cumulative.

We will present the findings of an experiment that investigated the possible transfer-of-training effects of two types of form-focused instruction on the acquisition of past imperfective aspect, subjunctive mood and causative constructions in French. PI (input-based) will be compared to traditional (output-based) instruction. Three groups were used. One receiving PI, one receiving TI and the third, serving as a control group, that did not receive instruction on the three target linguistic items over the duration of the investigation.

Primary, Secondary and Cumulative Target Linguistic Items

Primary target item: French imperfect tense

The past tense with imperfective aspect in French was chosen as the primary linguistic target as it has never been investigated in previous PI research, although Spanish past tense imperfective aspect has (Lee *et al.*, 2007). The acquisition of this form is affected by the Lexical Preference Principle Principle (P1b), which states that learners tend to process lexical items as opposed to grammatical form when both encode the same semantic information. The processing problem facing second language learners of French is that they may not attend to the verbal inflections in the input if they were co-referenced with lexical temporal/aspectual adverbials. Learners prefer to process the lexical items over the grammatical forms. They do not need to process both, because they both encode the same information.

A potential consequence of this processing problem is that learners might come to rely exclusively on the lexical forms in the input. If they were to do so, then they would not process the grammatical markers. If they do not process the grammatical marker, then they could not possibly acquire it (Lee, 1999). The following sentence serves as an example. The temporal/aspectual adverbial is underlined and the temporal aspectual morphology is in bold.

(1) <u>Pendant les vacances d'été</u>, Paul dorm**ait** toute le journée.
 (During the summer vacation, Paul would sleep all day long.)

Second language learners might come to rely on the lexical phrase that indicates a past time frame for the aspectual information, and fail to process the grammatical marker (*-ait*). The primary linguistic target is also affected by a second processing problem captured as the Sentence Location Principle (VanPatten, 2004b). From an input processing perspective, it matters whether a form occurs in sentence initial, medial or final position with sentence initial position being the most favoured processing position of the three. As seen in both the sentence above and the following sentence, the imperfect form frequently occurs in sentence medial position, the least salient processing position. In the speech stream, learners are not likely to detect it.

(2) *La semaine dernière Marie ne voul**ait** plus partir.*
 (Last week Marie did not wish/want to leave any more.)

Secondary target item: French subjunctive

The subjunctive mood morphology in French was chosen as a secondary target item for the principal reason that it is affected by the same processing principles as the French past tense imperfective aspect: specifically, the Lexical Preference Principle and the Sentence Location Principle. In the following sentence, the lexical expression of doubt that triggers subjunctive use is underlined, and the subjunctive morphology is in bold type.

(3) *Je <u>doute</u> que Paul vienne souvent à la maison.*
(I doubt that Paul will come quickly to the house.)

This particular structure is often termed difficult, if not extremely difficult, for native speakers of English learning a romance language. Collentine (1998) discusses this difficulty at length. The subjunctive, with the exception of a few fixed expressions and certain constructions, occurs in clauses introduced by *que* or by conjunctions ending in *que* (e.g. *quoique,* 'although'). We have chosen to investigate the acquisition of the present subjunctive mood morphology in dependent nominal clauses introduced by *que* after expressions of doubt because this form has been investigated in previous PI research (Farley, 2001a; Lee & Benati, 2007a, 2007b). The French subjunctive of doubt functions in a very similar way as the subjunctive of doubt in Spanish and Italian. It occurs in nominal dependent clauses after expressions of doubt in the main clause. Such expressions include *Je doute que* (I doubt that) and *Je ne crois pas que* (I don't believe that). It also occurs in interrogatives whose semantics express doubt from the speaker perspective. For example, in French, but not Spanish, *Penses-tu que* ... ? (Do you think that ...?) would be followed by a nominal dependent clause in which the verb form would be present subjunctive mood. By way of contrast, expression of certainty would not trigger the use of the subjunctive mood but would use the present indicative in the dependent clause. Such expressions include, *Je crois que* ... (I believe that) and *Je suis sûr(e) que* ... '(I am sure that).

The acquisition of French subjunctive, as in the case of French imperfect , is affected by the Lexical Preference Principle (P1b). In French the mood in the subordinate clause is indicated as a verb final morphological marker. This morphology is triggered by the meaning of a verb or verb phrase in the main clause. The subjunctive form in the dependent clause is, then redundant and non-meaningful. In addition to the Lexical Preference Principle, this use of the subjunctive is also affected by two other principles.

- (P1c) *Preference for Nonredundancy Principle*: learners are more likely to process nonredundant meaningful grammatical form before they process redundant meaningful forms.

- (P1d) *Meaning-Before-Nonmeaning Principle*: learners are more likely to process meaningful grammatical forms before non-meaningful forms, irrespective of redundancy. (VanPatten, 2004b: 11)

In sentence (4) the word *doute* exclusively expresses the idea of doubt:

(4) *Je doute qu'il vienne.*
 (I doubt that he will come.)

The form of the verb *vienne* lacks meaning and is redundant. All the learners needs to extract from *vienne* is its meaning, not its form. As Lee (1987, 1998) showed with the Spanish subjunctive, learners do not need to attend to the subjunctive form of the verb in the nominal clause in order to get the meaning of either the verb or the sentence.

Additionally, the subjunctive may be affected by an additional processing problem captured by the Sentence Location Principle (P1f). In the majority of French utterances of the type discussed here, the subjunctive form tends to occur in medial position in the dependent clause. This positioning contributes to the likelihood that second language learners would not process it. For example, in utterance (5) the subjunctive inflection (the *-enne* of *comprenne*) is found in the middle of the clause. Perceiving the form in the speech stream would be challenging for second language learners.

(5) *Je ne crois pas qu'elle comprenne la situation.*
 (I do not believe she understands the situation.)

Cumulative target item: French causative construction with *faire*

The French causative was chosen in this study because it was our intention to measure possible cumulative transfer-of-training effects for PI. To do so requires us to use a form affected by a different processing principle, in this case the First Noun Principle (P2). We also chose to investigate this structure because it has been investigated previously in PI research (VanPatten & Wong, 2004).

According to the First Noun Principle, 'learners tend to process the first noun or pronoun they encounter in a sentence as the subject/agent' (VanPatten, 2004b: 18). Learners assign the role of agent/subject to the first noun or pronoun they encounter in a sentence, even if this noun or pronoun is not the agent nor the subject. While French is considered an SVO language (i.e. its canonical word order is subject verb object), other word orders are possible. At issue for second language acquisition is that, when learners misassign the role of the first noun or pronoun, they are delivering erroneous intake to their developing linguistic system.

Research has also shown that the First Noun Principle accounts for the way learners initially process the French causative. The causative generally takes the form seen in examples (6) and (7). What appears on the surface to be a compound verb with one subject is not. It is a complex verbal construction for which there are two agents.

(6) *Charles fait promener le chien à Emma.*
Charles-makes-to-walk-the-dog-to-Emma
Charles makes Emma walk the dog.

(7) *Mes professeurs me font travailler beaucoup.*
My-teachers-me-make-work-hard.
My teachers make me work hard.

The first verb is *fait*, with its obligatorily pre-posed subject/agent *Charles*. The second verb is *promener* with its subject/agent, *Emma*, obligatorily placed after the verb and marked by the preposition *-à*. At the surface level this noun appears as the object of the preposition *-à*. It is assigning the subject/agent to the second verb that presents the processing problem to second language learners of French. When asked 'Who walks the dog?' learners overwhelmingly respond that 'Charles' does, since he is the first noun in the sentence. When asked to give a rough translation, learners will indicate that the sentence means something like 'Charles walks the dog for Emma' or 'Charles walks Emma's dog'. In sentence (6), taken from VanPatten and Wong (2004: 99), the causative structure is somewhat different because the underlying agent of the second verb appears before the verb – not as a subject pronoun but as an object pronoun. When asked 'Who works hard?' learners will tend to say 'My professors', once again demonstrating reliance on the first-noun processing strategy. Their overall interpretation of the sentence is something like 'My teachers work hard for me'. Very problematic for acquisition is that learners are apparently not processing the verb *faire* in these constructions. They hold the first noun as the subject and then find the next meaningful element, the second verb, to link with the subject. They then misinterpret *à* in a variety of ways.

Note that learners may make correct interpretations even though they may not be able to process all the sentence constituents correctly. According to VanPatten and Wong (2004: 101), learners may rely on the lexical semantics and event probabilities instead of word order to interpret causative sentences correctly. Lexical semantics refers to what verbs require as agents for the action to occur (e.g. +/- animacy) while event probability refers to the likelihood of events in the real world. Event probability would affect how learners would process French causatives with *faire*. Thus, if learners heard a French causative sentence such as (8), event probabilities would help them to a correct interpretation.

(8) *Le professeur fait faire les devoirs à ses élèves.*
The-professor-makes-to-do-the-homework-to-his/her-students.
The professor makes his/her students do homework.

In the real world, learners are more likely to think that the students are doing homework for the professor and not that the professor is doing homework for the students. The real world delineates clearly prototypical professor/student roles.

Review of Previous PI Research on the Target Linguistic Items

Previous PI research on aspect

Lee *et al.* (2007) examined the effects of PI delivered in a classroom to the entire group, PI delivered individually on a computer, and PI delivered individually in a classroom. For the latter treatment they downloaded the computer screens of the PI-computer treatment and used them as individualised work packets in a classroom. They investigated both negative informal commands and past tense preterite/imperfect aspectual distinction in Spanish. The preterite is used to express perfective aspect whereas the imperfect is used to express imperfective aspect. In their study, the subjects had already been taught the preterite and were receiving for the first time instruction on aspectual distinction. For both target linguistic items, Lee *et al.* found no significant differences across the three different PI treatments. They concluded that PI could be delivered effectively in classrooms to a group, on computers to individuals, or in classrooms to individuals.

Previous PI research on the subjunctive

Previous investigations of the effects of PI on the acquisition of subjunctive verb morphology have all demonstrated that PI brings about significant improvement on learners' performance on interpretation and production tasks (Farley, 2001a, 2004a, 2004b; Lee & Benati, 2007b). Farley (2001a) compared the effects of PI and MOI (meaning-based output instruction) on Spanish subjunctive. He found that the PI group significantly outperformed the MOI group on the interpretation test, but that the two groups performed equally well on the production test. Later Farley (2004a) replicated his 2001 study but with a greater number of participants, 67 instead of 29. This time he found no differences between the effects of the PI and MOI groups on either the interpretation or production task. Both groups improved significantly and performed equally well. Farley (2004b) examined the relative effects of full PI and SI on the acquisition of Spanish subjunctive. Both groups made significant improvement on the interpretation and production tasks, but the full PI group made greater gains than the SI group.

Lee and Benati (2007a) investigated the effects of PI and MOI, delivered either in classrooms or on computers, on the acquisition of Italian and French subjunctive of doubt/opinion. The findings for the two languages were identical. Those learners who received PI performed better on the interpretation test than those who received MOI. Both groups performed equally well on the production test. There was no significant difference in interpretation and production scores between those who received classroom instruction and those who received individualised computer instruction. We concluded that PI was a more effective instructional treatment than MOI, given the differences on the interpretation test, and also that computers can effectively deliver PI. They can deliver it as effectively as classroom instructors.

Lee and Benati (2007b) investigated the effects of PI and textually enhanced PI that was delivered either in a classroom or via computer on the acquisition of Italian subjunctive of doubt/opinion. In the enhanced PI treatments, the target forms received acoustic enhancement (louder and with greater tension in the vocal muscles) if the input was aural or textual enhancement (bold) if the input was written. We found no statistically significant differences across the three treatments on either production or interpretation tests. All three types of PI were effective at improving learners' interpretation and production of Italian subjunctive forms. We concluded that structured input could not effectively be enhanced any more than it is. Structuring input makes the form as salient to the learner as it can be. Additionally, we concluded that computers can deliver PI just as effectively as classroom teachers can.

PI research on French causative

VanPatten and Wong (2004) investigated the effects of PI, TI and neither (a control group) on the acquisition of French causative constructions with *faire*. Their aim was to replicate Allen (2000), but with the idea of controlling the input for event probabilities as discussed above and to clean up other items in the post-tests (VanPatten & Wong, 2004: 111). They used a pre-test/post-test design. The results on the interpretation task showed that both the PI and TI groups improved significantly more than the control group, and that the PI group improved significantly more than the TI group. This study is unique in finding that a TI group improved on the interpretation task. For the production task, they found that both PI and TI groups improved equally and that both improved significantly more than the control group. Their results differ quite a bit from Allen's. VanPatten and Wong concluded that replication studies are important in second language acquisition research. Differences in assessments and treatments may well yield differences in outcomes.

Research Questions

The present study was designed to examine the primary and possible transfer-of-training effects of PI. The transfer-of-training effects we sought to investigate were both secondary and cumulative. To do so, we compared PI with a traditional instructional treatment (TI) of the primary target linguistic item and for comparison purposes included a control group who did not receive instruction. The research questions that guide this study are framed in terms of this comparison. The questions are as follows.

(Q1) What are the primary effects of PI and TI on the acquisition of French past tense imperfective aspect as measured by an interpretation task?

(Q2) What are the primary effects of PI and TI on the acquisition of French past tense imperfective aspect as measured by a form production task?

(Q3) Are there any secondary transfer-of-training effects of PI and TI from receiving instruction on French past tense imperfective aspect to French subjunctive mood morphology as measured by an interpretation task?

(Q4) Are there any secondary transfer-of-training effects of PI and TI from receiving instruction on French past tense imperfective aspect to French subjunctive mood morphology as measured by a production task?

Based on previous empirical findings presented above and in Chapter 2 on the primary effects of PI and TI in second language acquisition the following hypotheses related to research questions 1 and 2 on can be formulated:

(H1) PI will be a more effective type of instruction than TI and the control group in helping learners to interpret correctly and efficiently sentences containing French past tense imperfective aspect.

(H2) PI will be an equally effective type of instruction to TI in helping learners to produce correctly and efficiently sentences containing French past tense imperfective aspect.

One of the principal objectives of the present study was, however, to discover whether the positive and primary effects of PI can be transferred/applied by L2 learners to other features affected by the same processing problem. Previous research has clearly and consistently demonstrated that PI has direct and primary effects on learners as it helps them to alter inappropriate processing strategies. The research presented in the two previous chapters has supported our hypotheses regarding secondary transfer-of-training effects. Consequently, we will hypothesise that we will uncover transfer-of-training effects. We are, in essence hypothesising that after PI instruction on French past tense imperfective aspect, learners will use a more appropriate L2-based processing strategy in a novel situation. That is, we hypothesise that they will develop an L2-driven intuition about processing. PI instruction will, to paraphrase Ellis (2007), help the learners not be so committed and tuned to their first language. We hypothesise that

(H3) Learners receiving PI on French past tense imperfective aspect will transfer that training and process subjunctive mood morphology better than those receiving TI as measured by an interpretation task.

(H4) Learners receiving PI on French past tense imperfective aspect will transfer that training and process subjunctive mood morphology better than those receiving TI as measured by a production task.

The other principal objective of the present study was to discover whether the positive and primary effects of PI can be transferred/applied by L2 learners to other features affected by a completely different processing problem. That is, we sought to address whether or not there were cumulative transfer-of-training effects for PI.

(Q5) Are there any cumulative transfer-of-training effects of PI and TI from receiving instruction on French past tense imperfective aspect to French causative constructions with *faire* as measured by an interpretation task?

(Q6) Are there any secondary transfer-of-training effects of PI and TI from receiving instruction on French past tense imperfective aspect to French causative constructions with *faire* as measured by a production task?

The research presented in the two previous chapters has supported our hypotheses regarding secondary transfer-of-training effects. Consequently, we will hypothesise that we will uncover cumulative transfer-of-training effects. After PI instruction on French past tense imperfective aspect, learners will develop an L2-driven intuition about processing. They will approach L2 input differently than the TI learners will. Will PI instruction help the learners not be so committed and tuned to their first language? We hypothesise that it wil.

(H5) Learners receiving PI on French past tense imperfective aspect will transfer that training and process French causative constructions with *faire* better than those receiving TI as measured by an interpretation task.

(H6) Learners receiving PI on French past tense imperfective aspect will transfer that training and process French causative constructions with *faire* better than those receiving TI as measured by a production task.

Methods and Procedures

Participants

The present study was carried out at the University of Greenwich with a final sample size of 30 undergraduate students who were enrolled in intermediate-level French course (level 2), as part of their undergraduate degree. Participants completed an informational/consent form and were given the six pre-tests (two per target linguistic item) two weeks before the instructional treatments took place. The instructional treatment lasted for one class period of two hours and post-tests were administered immediately after the end of the instructional treatment. The activities in both treatments were delivered in the classroom by one of the researchers. The initial subject pool (45) was reduced to 30 subjects as, for the validity of the study, only English native speakers of English were included. Additionally, the subjects should not have been exposed in the classroom to any of the three targeted linguistic items before the treatment. Subjects who scored more than 50% in the pre-tests (interpretation and production tests) were not included in the final pool. The three immediate post-tests on the three grammatical features were administered to the three groups after the end of instruction. Only participants who had participated in each stage of the experiment (pre-tests, instructional treatment, and post-tests) were included in the final data collection.

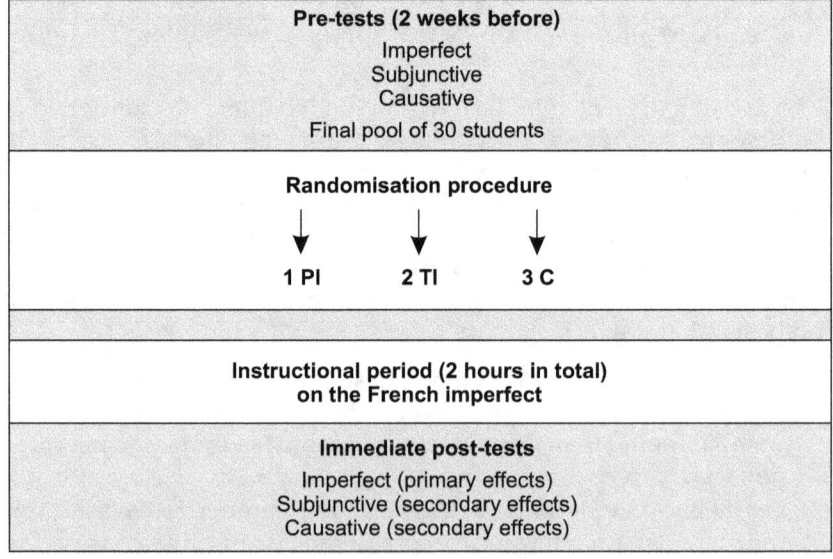

Figure 5.1 Overview of the experiment

The final pool (reduced from 45 to 30 subjects) consisted of 9 males and 21 females ranging in age from 18 to 25 years old. A randomisation procedure (see Figure 5.1) was adopted (L2 learners were randomised before the administration of pre-tests) to form three groups. The two instructional groups consisted of the PI group ($n = 13$) and the TI group ($n = 10$). A control group ($n = 7$) was also used in this experimental study. Participants were tested on their ability to interpret and to produce the three linguistics target features (imperfect, subjunctive of doubt, and causative construction with *faire*) at sentence level.

Materials

Two separate instructional packets were designed for this study, one for the group receiving PI instructional treatment and one for the group receiving TI treatment. The materials addressed the French past tense called *'imparfait'*. The materials developed for the PI group consisted of explicit information about the forms and function of the imperfective past tense, information about processing strategies, and structured input activities as practices. During the PI treatment, learners were taught how to process input sentences and assign meaning to the target form. The TI group received a type of instruction that consisted of a more traditional grammar explanation of rules and forms and mechanical and meaningful practices that required learners to produce the target form. Both sets of instructional materials were balanced for vocabulary, activity types, number of activities and practice time. The vocabulary used and the verbs targeted were roughly the same in both treatments. The choice of vocabulary and verbs consisted in familiar and frequent items for intermediate L2 learners of French.

As in VanPatten and Cadierno (1993), the first page of both packs contained explicit grammar explanation about the *imparfait*. The two groups received the same amount of information about how to form and use the imperfect in French. The explicit information differed, however, in the way it was practised. In the PI treatment practice focused on comprehension/interpretation activities, whereas in the TI treatment practice focused on production activities. The difference between the activities in the processing and traditional group can be summarised as follows. The structured input activities in the processing group required participants to attend to both meaning and form to successfully complete the activities, but the learners were never required to produce the target forms. The activities in the traditional pack required learners to produce the target forms. These production activities moved from mechanical to meaningful. Mechanical activities do not require participants to attend to meaning in order to successfully complete the activity, whereas meaningful activities do.

Although the explicit information was different in the two instructional treatments, the time allocated to grammatical explanation was exactly the same in the two treatments. In both treatments, 10 activities followed the presentation of the explicit information. The first five activities focused on the third person singular (-*ait*). After completing these activities, participants again received explicit information about the target form, but this time focusing on the ending of the 1st and 2nd person of the singular (-*ais*). These two endings are homophonous in French. This explicit information was followed by five more activities; structured input activities in the processing group and mechanical and communicative activities in the traditional group.

Processing Instruction (PI)

The material for the PI treatment reflects one approach to the teaching of grammar which encourages L2 learners to focus their attention on the French imperfect forms in the input. In the presentation of the target item the relation between form and meaning was always in focus. In addition to the explicit information regarding forms and functions of the past imperfective tense, the PI group received information about the processing problems. Lexical items such as *l'année dernière* (last year), which communicate past time frame, encourage learners to leave past tense markers undetected in the input, as learners tend to rely on lexical cues over grammatical forms to encode semantic information. In the PI materials all lexical cues to past time and imperfective aspect were removed. At no point during instruction were students in the PI group asked to produce the correct verb inflection in the French imperfect. Rather they were engaged in processing input sentences so that they could make better form–morning connections.

In the material pack for the PI group, the activities comprised of structured input activities as described by Lee and VanPatten (1995, 2003) that consisted of both referential and affective activities. Referential activities are those meaning-based activities with right or wrong answers as in Activity 5.1. For this activity, the subjects heard a series of sentences, each of which had Zinédine Zidane as the grammatical subject. The learners were asked to tick boxes to indicate whether the statement they heard about Zinédine Zidane was referring to his past life as a professional football player or his current life as a retired football player. The only way to correctly decide to which part of his life the sentence referred was to process the verbal inflection and use it. It was either past or present. To add another layer of meaningfulness we had learners do something with the input, one of the six guidelines for creating structured input activities (Lee & VanPatten, 1995, 2003). Learners were asked to indicate if Zinédine Zidane was busier as a professional football player than he is as a retired football player.

Activity 5.1 Referential activity

- **Step 1**
  Listen to the following statements made by a journalist about the life of Zinédine Zidane and decide whether each statement is referring to his past life as a professional football player or to his life now as a retired football player.

	professional football player	retired football player	[Sentences heard] *Zinédine Zidane ...*
(1)	☐	☐	... *jouait au football dans le monde entier.*
(2)	☐	☐	... *gagnait beaucoup de coupes.*
(3)	☐	☐	... *passe du temps avec sa famille.*
(4)	☐	☐	... *participait à beaucoup de diners officiels.*
(5)	☐	☐	... *s'entrainait avec Ronaldo.*
(6)	☐	☐	... *s'occupe de ses enfants.*
(7)	☐	☐	... *est directeur de l'association ELA.*
(8)	☐	☐	... *téléphone à Thierry Henry pour discuter.*
(9)	☐	☐	... *marquait beaucoup de buts.*
(10)	☐	☐	... *était le meilleur joueur de football au monde.*

- **Step 2**
  Now decide if Zinédine Zidane was busier when he was a professional football player or now that he is retired.

In affective activities students offer a personal reaction to a statement or sentence by indicating, among other things, whether or not it's true for them or some other reference group with which they are familiar or who in their family does that. In Activity 5.2, for example, learners read a series of statements about teenagers' actions. All the items use the target form. The learners were asked to tick boxes to indicate whether a parent, a relative, and/or their instructor would have carried out any of the statements they read. Meaning is kept in focus because the learners are relating the information to the people they know. Another layer of meaningfulness is included in this activity in that the learners get to find out if they were accurate about their instructor's teenage years. Processing strategies are kept in mind because none of the sentences contains a lexical adverbial to cue tense and aspect.

Feedback during the instructional treatment was quite limited and restricted. On the referential activities, the instructor told the learners whether or not their interpretations were correct, but did not offer any further information on the item or any further explanation. As can be seen in both Activities 5.1 and 5.2, learners never have to produce the target form

> **Activity 5.2 Affective activity**
> (Adapted from Farley, 2004)
>
> **In their teens ...**
>
> - **Step 1**
>   Imagine what your parent's life was like as a teenager many years ago. What about another relative, or your instructor? Can you imagine who partied too much? Who argued with his/her teacher a lot? Read over each statement and decide whether each individual (parent, relative or instructor) did these things or not.
>
> | Il/Elle ... | Parent | Relative | Instructor |
> |---|---|---|---|
> | (1) ... se disputait avec son professeur. | ☐ | ☐ | ☐ |
> | (2) ... ne passait pas son baccalauréat. | ☐ | ☐ | ☐ |
> | (3) ... trichait aux examens. | ☐ | ☐ | ☐ |
> | (4) ... avait de très bonnes notes. | ☐ | ☐ | ☐ |
> | (5) ... buvait de l'alcool à 15 ans. | ☐ | ☐ | ☐ |
> | (6) ... faisait la fête toute la nuit. | ☐ | ☐ | ☐ |
> | (7) ... visitait beaucoup de pays. | ☐ | ☐ | ☐ |
> | (8) ... organisait des soirées étudiantes. | ☐ | ☐ | ☐ |
>
> - **Step 2**
>   Find out if your instructor did any of the above. Are you surprised?

in order to activities is that the target form is presented in as salient a position as possible. By removing the subject noun or pronoun we are able to place the target form in initial position, the most favoured processing position. This is in order to help L2 learners to make correct form–morning connections.

Traditional Instruction (TI)

The instructional pack used for the TI treatment reflects a different approach to the teaching of grammar. More traditional approaches involve the paradigmatic presentation of the French imperfect, all persons, all forms, regular and irregular. The TI group was not given any information about processing problems, the tendency to rely on lexical items or information about listening for the forms in the input because such information is not part of traditional approaches to grammar instruction. An instructor not versed in PI would not deal with processing problems during a grammar explanation. After the learners had been given explicit information on the French past imperfective tense, all practice was oriented to producing the correct verbal inflection. All the activities used for the implementation of this approach were constructed to make learners produce the

> **Activity 5.3**
>
> **What's Appropriate?**
>
> - **Step 1**
>   Use the indicated verbs in brackets to describe the typical day of one of your lecturers.
>
>   *Mon professeur ...*
>
>   (1) ... *(préparer)* _____ sa classe.
>   (2) ... *(venir)* _____ à l'université en voiture.
>   (3) ... *(noter)* _____ les examens.
>   (4) ... *(porter)* _____ des vêtements chics.
>   (5) ... *(lire)* _____ le journal tous les jours.
>
> - **Step 2**
>   Now use the indicated verbs in brackets to describe a typical student's day during the last holidays.
>
>   *Pendant les vacances d'été, Paul ...*
>
>   (1) ... *(dormir)* _____ toute la journée.
>   (2) ... *(travailler)* _____ chez MacDonald.
>   (3) ... *(faire)* _____ la fête tous les soirs.
>   (4) ... *(se coucher)* _____ à 5 heures du matin.
>   (5) ... *(écouter)* _____ de la musique «garage».

target form in either oral or written mode. The activities included the following types of practice: fill-in-the-blank tasks, sentence completion tasks, traditional substitution drills and transformation tasks.

As in VanPatten and Cadierno's original PI study (1993), activities in the traditional pack followed the pattern of moving from mechanical to meaningful and then to communicative practice. Activity 5.3, for example, is a mechanical output practice. The learners begin by conjugating a set of verbs to describe their instructor's activities. The truth of the statements is not addressed. The correct answer is the correct form of the verb. The activity moves to conjugating a set of verbs that describe what someone did during the last summer vacation. Again, the truth of the statements is never at issue. The sentence is correct if the form of the verb is correct.

For Activity 5.4, learners have to transform a series of sentences that refer to the present activities of a fictitious person into a series of sentences that refer to what the person used to do before. Most of the items are meaningful in that the information contained in the sentence would have to change somewhat to accommodate the different life circumstances of the person's past. Feedback during the instructional treatment was quite limited and restricted. The instructor told the learners only whether or not the forms they produced were correct, and did not offer any further information on the item or any further explanation of the French past imperfective tense.

Activity 5.4

- Here are some things Caroline is doing today.
  Follow the model and what she used to do.

MAINTENANT	AVANT
(1) Elle pèse 55 kilos.	Elle pesait 105 kilos.
(2) Elle fait une taille 38.	_____
(3) Elle ne fume pas.	_____
(4) Elle travaille beaucoup.	_____
(5) Elle a besoin de 1500 calories par jour.	_____
(6) Elle fait du sport.	_____
(7) Elle vient au travail en vélo.	_____
(8) Elle se relaxe au yoga.	_____
(9) Elle a besoin de manger peu.	_____
(10) Elle parle de se marier.	_____

Control group (C)

Learners in the control group received no instruction on the primary, secondary or cumulative target features during the treatment period, but were exposed to a comparable amount of the target language for the same amount of time.

Tests

Pre- and post-tests were developed for measuring the primary effects of instruction on the first feature (French past tense imperfective aspect), the secondary transfer-of-training effects on the second feature (French subjunctive mood morphology), and the cumulative transfer-or-training effects on the third feature (French causative constructions with *faire*). These tests are given in Figures 5.2 to 5.7. Pre-tests and post-tests consisted of a sentence level interpretation task and a sentence level production task for each of the three linguistic features.

An example of an interpretation test for the primary linguistic target is

Interpretation test

- You will hear 20 sentences and you must decide whether the action is referring to an action in the present, in the past, or if you are not sure.
  You have 8 seconds after hearing the sentence to tick your answer.
  You must tick ☑ either Present, Past or Not sure.

Sample of the student's score table:

	Present	Past	Not sure
1	❑	❑	❑
2	❑	❑	❑
3	❑	❑	❑

Transcript of the tape
[with past tense in **bold** and correctly ticked on the score table]:

		Present	Past	Not sure
1	Je parle à mon père au téléphone.	❑	❑	❑
2	**Tu chantais sous la douche.**	❑	☑	❑
3	**Il discutait avec son frère.**	❑	☑	❑
4	Elle travaille dans sa chambre.	❑	❑	❑
5	**Tu habitais aux Etats-Unis.**	❑	☑	❑
6	**J'aimais le tennis et le football.**	❑	☑	❑
7	**Il rêvait de l'Australie et de ses kangourous.**	❑	☑	❑
8	Je pense à ma mère en France.	❑	❑	❑
9	**Il parlait très bien le français, l'italien et le chinois.**	❑	☑	❑
10	Tu manges trop de chocolat.	❑	❑	❑
11	Je voyage beaucoup surtout en Europe.	❑	❑	❑
12	Tu danses très bien.	❑	❑	❑
13	Elle joue au tennis et au badminton.	❑	❑	❑
14	**Je cuisinais beaucoup de desserts au chocolat.**	❑	☑	❑
15	Il aide son frère avec ses exercices de français.	❑	❑	❑
16	**Tu envoyais des lettres à ta mère.**	❑	☑	❑
17	Je regarde la télévision jusqu'à 22 heures.	❑	❑	❑
18	**Tu donnais des cours de français et d'espagnol.**	❑	☑	❑
19	**Elle arrivait en retard à l'école une fois par semaine**	❑	☑	❑
20	J'adore les croissants, les pains au chocolat et les brioches.	❑	❑	❑

Figure 5.2 Interpretation test

given in Figure 5.2. It consisted of 20 recorded sentences; 10 of these contained targets and the other 10, written with present tense, served as distracters. The items were recorded by a native speaker of French and presented to the subjects on a CD player. The interpretation task required participants to listen to a series of sentences about people doing various activities and to determine whether the action was in the present or in the past. For example, participants heard the sentence *Emma parlait au téléphone* (Emma was speaking on the phone) and then had to decide whether the sentence expressed 'Present', 'Past' or if they were 'Not Sure'. They were given the option of indicating whether they were 'not sure' to discourage guessing. The different versions of the tests were balanced in terms of difficulty and vocabulary used with a tendency to favour the use of high-frequency items. Subjects received 1 point if the target sentence was interpreted correctly and no points if they were wrong or they were not sure how to interpret the sentence correctly. The maximum score possible was 10 points with a minimum possible score of 0 points. Only target items were scored, not the distracters. Each item was read only once.

In the production task (Figure 5.3), learners had to fill the blanks in a short passage by producing the correct form of the verb. Scoring for the production task consists of a 2, 1, 0 point system for a possible maximum score of 20 points. A participant received 2 points if the sentence completion contained a verb in the correct past tense form. If the verb was in the past tense but was the wrong person or if the learner had switched verb category endings, a score of 1 point was allocated to the answer. Any other response received a score of 0 points. This scoring procedure was adapted from Cadierno's (1995) study of the Spanish preterite tense (a past tense of perfective aspect) in which she gave partial credit for forms.

To assess the possible secondary transfer-of-training effects of instruc-

---

- Put the verbs in brackets in the correct form.

    Hier j'_____ (être) au supermarché avec mon ami Charles. A côté de moi, à ma droite, une jeune femme grande et blonde _____(porter) des lunettes de soleil noires. Bizarre dans un supermarché, non?

    Je _____(montrer) donc discrètement cette femme blonde à Charles. Elle _____ (marcher) dans notre direction puis quelques secondes plus tard, elle _____ (enlever) ses lunettes de soleil et nous _____ (faire) un sourire tout en parlant sur son portable. Je _____ (rester) paralysée, je ne _____ (pouvoir) plus parler et je _____(penser) «oh mon Dieu, je rêve!». Charles me dit alors: «cette femme blonde aux lunettes de soleil: c'est Madonna!» et deux minutes plus tard Charles _____ (avoir) son autographe.

Figure 5.3 Production test

Interpretation test

- You will hear the end of 20 sentences. Tick the appropriate beginning for each sentence you hear in the table below.
If you are not sure, please tick ☑*Je ne suis pas sûr(e)*. You will have 8 seconds after hearing the end of the sentence to tick your answer.

Sample of the student's score table:

Transcript of the tape
[with appropriate beginnings
in **bold** and correctly ticked]:

1	❏ *Je pense qu'elle* ❏ *Je ne suis pas sûr qu'elle* ❏ *Je ne suis pas sûr(e)*

1	☑ **Je doute qu'il** ❏ *Je sais qu'il*	*vienne avec nous.*
2	❏ *Je ne pense pas qu'elle* ❏ *Je suis persuadée qu'elle*	*va en vacances à Milan.*
3	☑ **Je doute qu'il** ❏ *Je crois qu'il*	*sache la réponse.*
4	❏ *Je pense qu'elle* ❏ *Je ne suis pas sûr qu'elle*	*lit souvent le journal.*
5	❏ *Je crois qu'elle* ☑ **Je doute qu'elle**	*aille régulièrement à la piscine.*
6	❏ *Je sais qu'elle* ☑ **Je ne crois pas qu'elle**	*prenne de la drogue.*
7	❏ *Je pense qu'il* ☑ **Je ne crois pas qu'il**	*ait beaucoup de travail*
8	❏ *Je ne pense pas qu'il* ❏ *Je crois qu'il*	*conduit une moto.*
9	❏ *Je pense qu'il* ❏ *Je ne crois pas qu'il*	*s'entend bien avec ses parents.*
10	❏ *Je crois qu'il* ❏ *Je doute qu'il*	*fait une fête.*
11	❏ *Je sais qu'elle* ❏ *Je ne crois pas qu'elle*	*dort beaucoup.*
12	☑ **Je ne crois pas que mon chien** ❏ *Je pense que mon chien*	*puisse nager.*
13	☑ **Je ne crois pas qu'il** ❏ *Je pense qu'il*	*sache chanter.*
14	❏ *Je sais qu'il* ❏ *Je doute qu'il*	*écrit des poèmes.*
15	❏ *Je pense qu'elle* ❏ *Je ne pense pas qu'elle*	*fait beaucoup de sport.*
16	☑ **Je doute qu'elle** ❏ *Je sais qu'elle*	*réussisse ses examens.*
17	❏ *Je crois qu'elle* ❏ *Je doute qu'elle*	*peint.*
18	❏ *Je ne crois pas qu'il* ❏ *Je pense qu'il*	*ment.*
19	❏ *Je crois qu'il* ☑ **Je ne pense pas qu'il**	*veuille un nouvel ordinateur.*
20	❏ *Je suis sûr qu'elle* ☑ **Je ne suis pas certain qu'elle**	*fasse bien la cuisine.*

Figure 5.4 Interpretation test

tion on the second targeted linguistic item (the French subjunctive in nominal clauses after expressions of doubts), an interpretation task and a production task were developed and used as a pre-test/post-test measure of knowledge gained at interpreting the French subjunctive of doubt. The interpretation task consisted of 20 recorded sentences; 10 of these contained the targeted linguistic forms and the other 10 used the present tense of the indicative mood. The latter were distracters and were not scored. The items were recorded by a native speaker of French and played to the subjects on a CD player. The interpretation task required the learners to listen to the nominal dependent clause of each sentence and then to select the appropriate beginning for the sentence. In essence, we separated the lexical indicator of subjunctive mood *Je doute que* (I doubt that) from the subjunctive mood morphology. Learners could not rely on the lexical indicator, but rather had to process the subjunctive form to link it to the lexical indicator. By dividing and restructuring the sentences in this way, we were able to move the target form into a more salient processing position. Note that this is the secondary target item, and these learners have never been exposed to it in an instructional setting. They listened to these sentences without knowing anything about subjunctive morphology.

As in the case of the interpretation task developed to measure correct interpretation of the primary linguistic target, no repetition was provided. Subjects heard each clause once and then had only 5 seconds to decide which beginning was appropriate. Again, they were given the option to indicate if they were not sure. We wanted to discourage guessing.

Scoring of the 10 target items on the interpretation task consisted of 1 versus 0 point system per item for a possible maximum score of 10 points. A subject received 1 point if the target sentence was assigned its correct beginning and received 0 points if the selection was incorrect.

The written production task consisted of 10 sentences with blanks

---

- Put the verbs in brackets in the correct form.

(1) *Je ne pense pas que le français* _____ *(être) facile.*
(2) *Je pense qu'elle* _____ *(suivre) des cours de danse.*
(3) *Je pense qu'il* _____ *(vouloir) se remarier.*
(4) *Je doute que Marie* _____ *(prendre) l'avion seule.*
(5) *Je ne suis pas sûr qu'il* _____ *(avoir) envie d'aller au cinéma.*
(6) *Je sais que Paul* _____ *(venir) souvent à la maison.*
(7) *Je ne suis pas certain qu'elle me* _____ *(rejoindre) en Italie.*
(8) *Je ne crois pas qu'elle* _____ *(conduire) bien.*
(9) *Je pense que Jean* _____ *(réussir) bien dans son travail.*
(10) *Je crois qu'il* _____ *(savoir) jouer du piano.*

Figure 5.5 Production test

Secondary and Cumulative Effects of PI (French) 141

Interpretation test

- You will hear 20 sentences. For each sentence you hear, answer the question that accompanies it and determine who is doing the activity.
  You have 8 seconds after hearing the sentence to answer the question.
  You only need to write someone's name to answer the question.
  You may also tick *Je ne suis pas sûr(e)* (I am not sure) if appropriate.

  Sample of the student's score table:

		Je ne suis pas sur(e)
1	Who watches the film?	❑
2	Who eats the soup?	❑

Transcript of the tape [with *faire* causative sentences in **bold**:

#	Sentence	Question	pas sur(e)
1	**Claire fait regarder le film à Charles.**	Who watches the film?	❑
2	Mark *mange la soupe d'Emma*.	Who eats the soup?	❑
3	Tom *prend la voiture de Léo*.	Who takes the car?	❑
4	Louis *fait la vaisselle de Sandra*.	Who does the dishes?	❑
5	**Paul fait faire le ménage à Sophie.**	Who does the housework?	❑
6	**Marie fait voir les photos à Louise.**	Who watches the photos?	❑
7	**Bob fait les devoirs de Simon.**	Who does the homework?	❑
8	**Sarah fait promener le chien à Zoë.**	Who walks the dog?	❑
9	**Je fais prendre un bain à Théo.**	Who is having a bath?	❑
10	Nathalie *fait la cuisine pour Juliette*.	Who does the cooking?	❑
11	Mark *joue sur l'ordinateur de Laura*.	Who plays on the computer?	❑
12	**Charlotte fait manger Olivia.**	Who is eating?	❑
13	**Mon professeur nous fait aller au centre de langue une fois par semaine.**	Who goes to the language centre?	❑
14	**Charles me fait rendre un livre à la bibliothèque.**	Who brings the book back to the library?	❑
15	Il *fait le repassage pour son père*.	Who does the ironing?	❑
16	**Ma mère me fait écrire une lettre à mon grand-père.**	Who writes the letter?	❑
17	La soeur *fait un dessin pour mon père*.	Who draws?	❑
18	Caroline *nettoie la voiture de Alison*.	Who washes the car?	❑
19	**Mon père fait boire du lait à Théo chaque matin.**	Who drinks milk every morning?	❑
20	Ma tante *mange le gâteau de mon oncle*.	Who eats the cake?	❑

Figure 5.6 Interpretation test

followed by the infinitive form of a verb. The participants were directed to complete the sentences with the correct form of the verb. Of these sentences five require the use of the indicative present tense (distracters) and five items require the use of the subjunctive. Five minutes were allocated to complete this task. Scoring for the production task consists of a 2, 1, 0 point system for a possible maximum score of 10 points. A participant received 2 points if the sentence completion contained a verb in the correct subjunctive form. If the verb was in the subjunctive but was the wrong person, a score of 1 point was allocated to the answer. Any other response received a score of 0 points.

To assess the possible cumulative transfer-of-training effects of instruction on the third linguistic item (the French causative with *faire*) an interpretation task and a production task were developed and used as a pre-test/post-test measure of knowledge gained at interpreting the French causative at the sentence level. The interpretation task consisted of 20 recorded sentences. Of these sentences, 10 (distracters) did not use the causative and 10 of the items did. These were the target items we scored. The tests were recorded by a native speaker of French and played to the subjects on a CD player. The interpretation task required participants to listen to the 20 sentences and then indicate who was performing the action by answering the questions or by ticking *Je ne suis pas sûr(e)* (I am not sure) if they did not know. Participants had 5 seconds to answer the question and no repetition of the item was provided so that we could measure real-time comprehension. Scoring for the interpretation task consisted of a 1 versus 0 point system per item for a possible maximum score of 10 points. A participant received 1 point if the person performing the action was identified correctly and received 0 points if the person performing the action was wrong or the participant indicated an inability to determine who performed the action.

The written production task consisted of 10 written items with blanks in which participants had to complete the sentence to describe who was doing what on the each of the 10 pictures shown to them using an overhead projector. Each sentence was begun for the learners. These beginnings contained a grammatical subject and the verb form *fait*. Of the 10 pictures/sentences five used the French causative and five did not. These latter items served as distracters and were not scored. Participants had 10 seconds to complete each sentence. Scoring for the production task consisted of a 2, 1, 0 point system for a possible maximum score of 10 points. A participant received 2 points if the sentence completion contained a verb in the correct form using the causative. If the causative was used but the wrong person is indicated, a score of 1 point was allocated to the participant. Any other response received a score of 0 points.

- For each picture that is shown on the overhead, complete the sentence to describe it and determine who is doing the activity. You will have 10 seconds to complete each sentence.
  (1) *Jean fait* _____
  (2) *Luc fait* _____
  (3) *Claudine fait* _____
  (4) *Marc fait* _____
  (5) *Diane fait* _____
  (6) *Marie fait* _____
  (7) *Paul fait* _____
  (8) *Philippe fait*_____
  (9) *Laura fait* _____
  (10) *Sara fait*_____

Figure 5.7 Production test

Procedures

The main purpose of this study was to measure secondary and cumulative transfer-of-training effects of instruction by comparing the performance of second language learners of French who had been taught a specific linguistic item (imperfect past tense) via one of two treatments. These treatments were a traditional focus-on-forms approach (TI) and a psycholinguistically derived intervention focused on teaching learners to process input (PI). We aimed to establish whether the processing group receiving PI would surpass the traditional group receiving TI on an interpretation task and a written form-completion production task on the primary target item (on which they received instruction), as well as on two other targeted items (on which they did not receive instruction). The experiment was designed to make the results as objective as possible within the constraints of a University language programme. An overview of the experiment was given in Figure 5.1. Pre-tests assessing interpretation and production for the three linguistics features were administered to all students two weeks before the beginning of the instructional period. The total number of tests administered was six. After pre-testing, the subjects were randomly assigned to one of the two treatment groups or to the control group. The instructional treatment period lasted for one class period, a two-hour block of time. The post-tests were administered immediately after completing the instructional treatment. The total number of post-tests administered was six. The fact that both interpretation and production tasks were present in all the tests is clear evidence of the fact that neither instructional group was favoured. This possible task bias factor could invalidate the outcomes of the study, and was taken into account in the design of the experiment. All the pre-tests and post-tests were balanced in terms of overall difficulty and the use of high frequency vocabulary.

Subjects were given a limited time to complete the interpretation tasks and the production tasks. The interpretation task was designed to measure real-time comprehension and so the items were not repeated. The production tasks were developed to elicit subjects' best performance. We decided to allow enough time for the subjects to accomplish the tasks comfortably. The TI group was familiar with the format and requirements of the production tasks as a number of instructional activities were based on them. This group was not, however, familiar with the interpretation tasks. They performed no such activity during the instructional treatment. On the other hand, the PI group was familiar with the format and requirements of the interpretation tasks as they had carried out similar activities during the instructional treatment. The PI group had not performed any production tasks during instruction but only as part of pre- and post-testing. Each treatment group was equally unfamiliar with half of the assessment tasks. All three groups were taught by the same instructor (a researcher) during the period of instruction. She was not, however, the participants regular classroom instructor. In the end, the experiment included the following features:

(1) the use of a randomisation procedure to make groups comparable;
(2) the use of a pre-test/post-test procedure;
(3) balance in the materials in terms of difficulty and vocabulary (verbs, adjectives);
(4) balance across the assessment tasks in terms of difficulty and familiarity;
(5) balance in the amount of explicit instruction to which learners were exposed.

Results

To address the research questions that guided this study, we conducted a one-way ANOVA on the pre-test scores for the interpretation and the production tasks in order to determine whether there were any statistically-significant differences between the three groups before the beginning of the experimental period. The desired situation was that we would find no pre-existing differences. We used a repeated measure ANOVA to assess whether there were any significant effects for Instruction and Time and whether there was a significant Interaction between Instruction and Time. Where effects were found, we then carried out a *post hoc* Tukey's test to establish where statistical differences were between the three groups. The results of the statistical analyses carried out in this study will now be presented and analysed for each of the three linguistic targets.

Primary effects (on French imperfect)

The pre-test for the interpretation task was administered to the participants two weeks before the beginning of the instructional period. All three groups received the same version of the pre-test. The raw scores were submitted to a one-way ANOVA that revealed no significant differences among the groups' mean scores, ($F_{2,28} = 0.778, p = 0.470$). This means that we will attribute any gains in the post-test scores to the instructional treatments and not to any previous knowledge of the learners. The means in Table 5.1 are for the learners' scores on the interpretation test, both pre-test and post-test. These numbers suggest that the PI group improved as a result of instruction. The means are displayed in Figure 5.8.

Table 5.1 Means and standard deviation (French *imparfait*) for interpretation task pre-test and post-test

		Pre-test		Post-test 1	
Variable	*n*	*Mean*	*SD*	*Mean*	*SD*
Processing Instruction	13	2.38	0.86972	8.15	1.46322
Traditional Instruction	9	3.00	1.32288	3.55	1.58990
Control	6	2.66	1.36626	2.83	1.16905

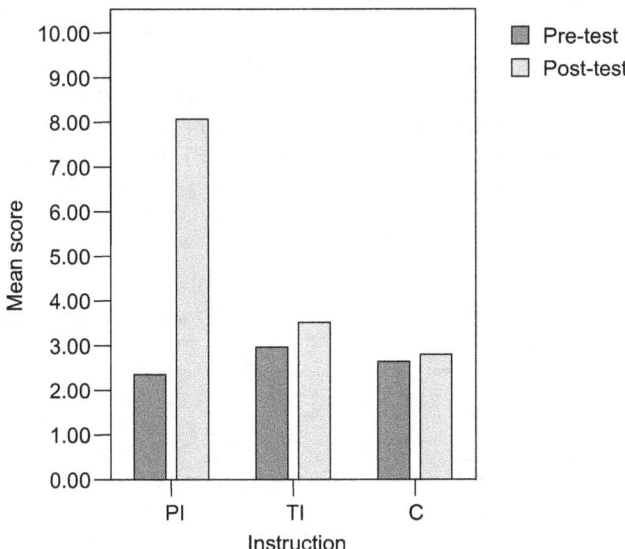

Figure 5.8 Results for interpretation task (French *imparfait*)

The mean scores were submitted to a repeated measures ANOVA for which Instruction was the between-group variable and Time the repeated measure. The results of the ANOVA indicated significant main effects for Instruction ($F_{2,28} = 58.032, p = 0.000$) and Time ($F_{2,28} = 13.701, p = 0.000$, as well as a significant interaction between Instruction and Time ($F_{4,28} = 8.424, p = 0.000$). The *post hoc* Tukey's test showed that the PI group performed significantly better than the TI group ($p = 0.002$); that the PI group performed significantly better than the control group ($p = 0.001$); and that the scores of TI group and the control group were not significantly different from each other ($p = 0.678$). A significant interaction is typical of situations in which only one group improves over time and the others do not.

The means for the three groups' pre-test and post-test scores on the written production task for the primary linguistic target are given in Table 5.2 and are displayed graphically in Figure 5.9. The one-way ANOVA conducted on the written production task pre-test scores for the primary linguistic target showed no significant difference between groups prior to instruction ($F_{2,28} = 1.098, p = 0.349$). As was the case of the interpretation task, we will attribute any differences after instruction to the effects of the instructional treatments themselves. The means in Table 5.2 suggest improvement for both instructional treatments. The raw scores of the written production task were submitted to a repeated measures ANOVA. The results from the statistical analysis showed significant main effects for Instruction ($F_{2,28} = 21.882, p = 0.000$) and Time ($F_{2,28} = 13.642, p = 0.000$), as well as a significant interaction between Instruction and Time ($F_{4,28} = 10.844, p = 0.000$). The Tukey's test on the interaction showed that both the processing group and the traditional group improved significantly from pre-test to post-test. Additionally, there was no significant difference between the scores for the two groups ($p = 0.814$) and both groups significantly outperformed the control group ($p = 0.000$). The control group, on the other hand, did not show a significant difference in pre-test and post-test scores.

Table 5.2 Means and standard deviation (French *imparfait*) for production task pre-test and post-test

		Pre-test		Post-test 1	
Variable	n	Mean	SD	Mean	SD
Processing Instruction	13	0.1538	0.37553	14.15	3.91250
Traditional Instruction	9	0.6667	2.0000	15.11	6.73507
Control	6	1.1667	1.83485	1.1667	2.04124

Secondary and Cumulative Effects of PI (French)

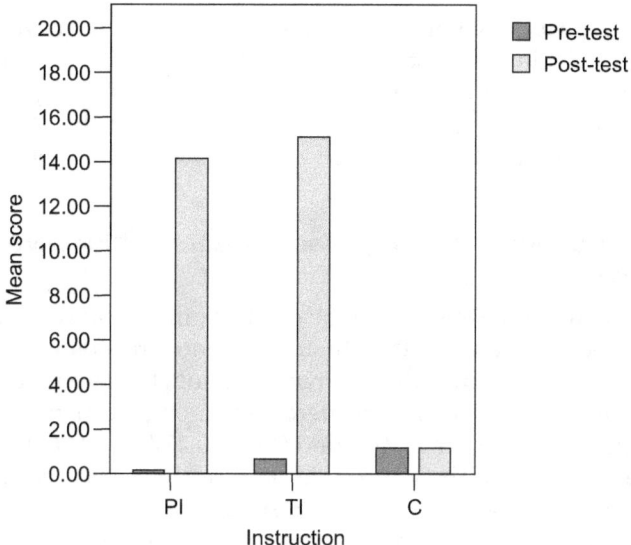

Figure 5.9 Results for production task (French *imparfait*)

Table 5.3 Summary of repeated measures ANOVA (French *imparfait*)

Data	df	SS	MS	F	p
Interpretation					
Time	2	100.658	50.329	58.032	0.000*
Treatment	2	69.577	34.789	13.701	0.000*
Time x Treatment	4	54.401	13.600	8.414	0.000*
Production					
Time	2	474.603	237.302	21.882	0.000*
Treatment	2	378.528	189.264	13.642	0.000*
Time x Treatment	4	271.111	67.777	10.844	0.000*

* = significant

A summary of the two repeated measures ANOVAs for primary effects is shown on Table 5.3. In sum, learners in the processing group improved their performance in the interpretation task from the pre-test to the post-test, and their performance was greater and statistically better than the other two groups. The PI group learned to process the primary linguistic target, French past tense with imperfective aspect. The TI group who practised making output did not learn to process input. These learners did, however, successfully perform on a production test. The TI group learned to produce the primary linguistic target, but not better than the PI group. The PI group also learned, as a consequence of working with input, to produce the target form.

Secondary transfer-of-training effects (French subjunctive mood morphology)

We used a one-way ANOVA on the pre-test interpretation task scores of the three groups to ensure that there were no pre-existing differences between the groups' knowledge of French subjunctive mood morphology. The results showed no significant differences among the instructional treatment groups' means before instruction ($F_{2,28} = 0.277$, $p = 0.760$). Means and standard deviations for the interpretation tests are presented in Table 5.4 and displayed graphically in Figure 5.10. These means show a modest increase in score for the PI group but a decrease in scores for the TI and control groups. We used an ANOVA with repeated measures to analyse the effects of Instruction and Time and the interaction between Instruction and Time. The statistical analysis revealed significant main effects for Instruction ($F_{2,28} = 14.528$, $p = 0.000$) and Time ($F_{2,28} = 2.559$, $p = 0.047$) as well as a statistically significant interaction between Instruction and Time ($F_{4,28} = 0.582$, $p = 0.021$). The *post hoc* analyses showed that the effect for instruction was due to the scores of the processing group being significantly higher than those of the traditional group ($p = 0.016$) and the control group ($p = 0.022$). There was no difference in scores between the TI and control groups ($p = 0.727$).

As we can see from the means in Table 5.4, the processing group has slightly improved from pre- to post-test compared with the other two groups, and in particular with the control group. Although the improvement of the PI group from the pre-test to the post-test is only about 20%, it is statistically significant. What these results demonstrate is that there are secondary effects in the interpretation test for the processing group. The PI

Table 5.4 Means and standard deviation (French subjunctive) for interpretation task pre-test and post-test

		Pre-test		Post-test 1	
Variable	n	Mean	SD	Mean	SD
Processing Instruction	13	1.76	1.09193	3.69	1.65250
Traditional Instruction	9	2.11	1.53659	1.77	1.39443
Control	6	1.66	1.21106	1.16	0.98319

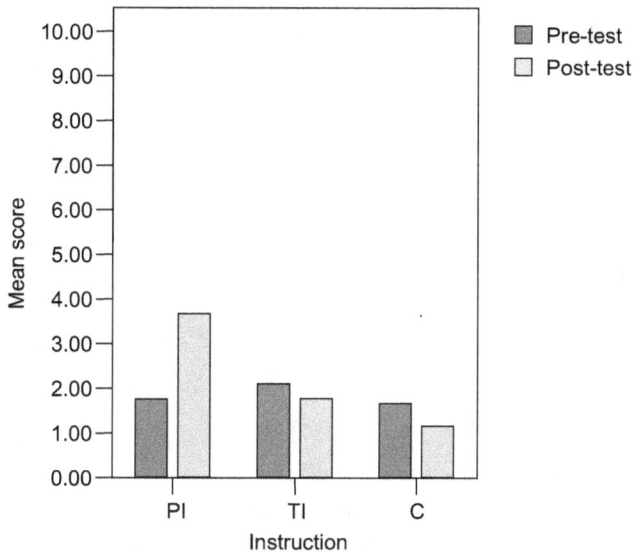

Figure 5.10 Results for interpretation task (French subjunctive)

Table 5.5 Means and standard deviation (French subjunctive) for production task pre-test and post-test

Variable	n	Pre-test		Post-test 1	
		Mean	SD	Mean	SD
Processing Instruction	13	0.000	0.00000	1.00	0.57735
Traditional Instruction	9	0.000	0.00000	0.222	0.44096
Control	6	0.000	0.00000	0.000	0.00000

treatment is more effective than the TI treatment and the control group in affecting learners' interpretation of subjunctive forms.

We continued to investigate the secondary transfer-of-training effects by analysing the production data. The means for the pre-test and post-test production scores are given in Table 5.5 and displayed in Figure 5.11. The one-way ANOVA conducted on the pre-test production scores of the three groups showed no significant differences between the three groups; this was not so surprising, given that all learners scored zero on the production pre-test. We then conducted an ANOVA with repeated measures on the raw scores for the production task.

The statistical analysis revealed significant main effects for Instruction ($F_{2,28} = 12.170$, $p = 0.000$) and for Time ($F_{2,25} = 11.912$, $p = 002$) as well as a significant interaction between Instruction and Time ($F_{4,28} = 8.952$, $p = 0.000$).

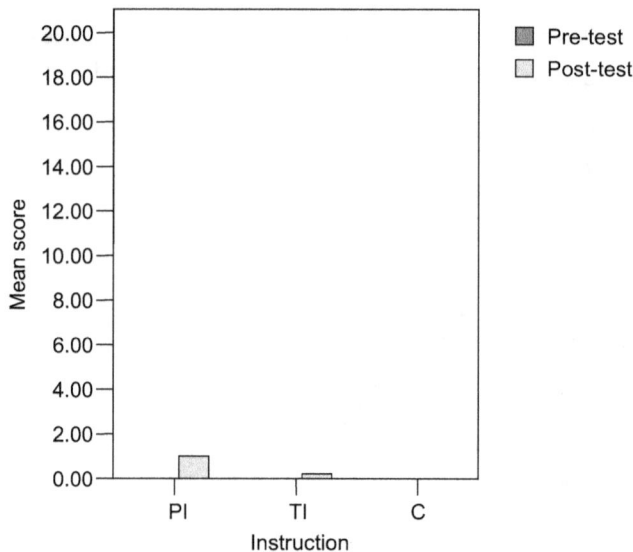

Figure 5.11 Results for production task (French subjunctive)

Table 5.6 Summary of repeated measures ANOVA (French subjunctive)

Data	df	SS	MS	F	p
Interpretation					
Time	2	18.842	9.421	14.528	0.000*
Treatment	2	15.863	7.931	2.559	0.047*
Time x Treatment	4	1.674	0.4185	0.582	0.021*
Production					
Treatment	2	2.704	1.352	12.170	0.000*
Time	2	2.778	1.389	11.912	0.000*
Time x Treatment	4	2.106	0.5265	0.5265	0.000*

* = significant

The *post hoc* analysis showed the following contrasts. First, the PI group's scores were higher than those of the control group ($p = 0.000$). Second, the PI group's scores were also higher than the TI group's ($p = 0.037$). And, third, there was no significant difference in scores between the TI and control groups ($p = 0.437$).

A summary of the ANOVA repeated measures for secondary effects is shown on Table 5.6. The PI group made a modest but significant 10% improvement from pre-testing to post-testing on producing the secondary linguistic target. The TI group improved only 2%, and this change in performance was not statistically significant. These findings are very consistent with the findings of the other two studies presented in this book. It is the third set of findings demonstrating secondary transfer-of-training effects for PI.

Cumulative transfer-of-training effects (French causative construction with *faire*)

The means for the interpretation pre-test and post-test results for the French causative construction with *faire* are given in Table 5.7 and graphically displayed in Figure 5.12. The means suggest that the PI group

Table 5.7 Means and standard deviation (French causative) for interpretation task pre-test and post-test

		Pre-test		Post-test 1	
Variable	*n*	*Mean*	*SD*	*Mean*	*SD*
Processing Instruction	13	1.23	1.30089	4.61	2.66266
Traditional Instruction	9	0.8889	0.60093	0.3333	0.500433

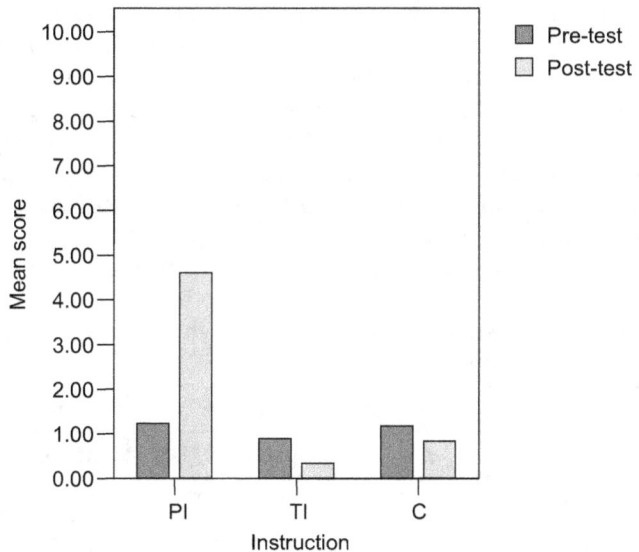

Figure 5.12 Results for interpretation test (French causative)

improved their interpretation whereas the other two groups means decreased from pre-test to post-test. We again used a one-way ANOVA on the pre-test interpretation task scores of the three groups to determine that there were no pre-existing differences between the groups. The result showed no significant differences among the instructional treatment groups' means before instruction ($F_{2,28} = 0.337$, $p = 0.717$). We then conducted a repeated measures ANOVA to compare the effects of Instruction and Time. The statistical analysis revealed significant main effects for Instruction ($F_{2,28} = 18.312$, $p = 0.000$) and for Time ($F_{2,28} = 10.211$, $p = 0.001$), as well as a significant interaction between Instruction and Time ($F_{4,28} = 6.215$, $p = 0.020$). The post hoc analysis showed the following contrasts. The PI group's scores are better than both the TI group's ($p = 0.001$) and the control group's ($p = 0.018$). There was no difference between the scores of TI and control groups ($p = 0.846$). As we can see from the means in Table 5.7, the PI group improved 34% from pre-test to post-test in interpreting correctly the underlying structure of French causative constructions.

We now present our final analysis. The means for the production tests on French causative constructions with *faire* are given in Table 5.8 and are displayed graphically in Figure 5.13. The one-way ANOVA conducted on the pre-test production scores of the three groups showed no pre-existing differences between the groups. This finding was not surprising in that all learners scored a zero on the production pre-test. We then carried out an ANOVA with repeated measures on the raw scores for the production task. The statistical analysis revealed significant main effects for Instruction ($F_{2,28} = 17.803$, $p = 000$) and for Time ($F_{2,28} = 26.561$, $p = 000$) as well as a significant interaction between Instruction and Time ($F_{4,28} = 6.561$, $p = 000$). The post hoc analysis showed the following contrasts. The PI group's scores are better than both the TI group's ($p = 0.013$) and the control group's ($p = 0.038$). There was no difference between the scores of TI and control groups ($p = 0.673$). The PI group's 10% improvement again proved significant whereas the TI group's 2.7% improvement did not.

A summary of the two repeated measures ANOVAs conducted to reveal

Table 5.8 Means and standard deviation (French causative) for production task pre-test and post-test

		Pre-test		Post-test 1	
Variable	n	Mean	SD	Mean	SD
Processing Instruction	13	0.000	0.00000	1.079	0.49355
Traditional Instruction	9	0.000	0.00000	0.272	0.35094
Control	6	0.000	0.00000	0.000	0.00000

Secondary and Cumulative Effects of PI (French)

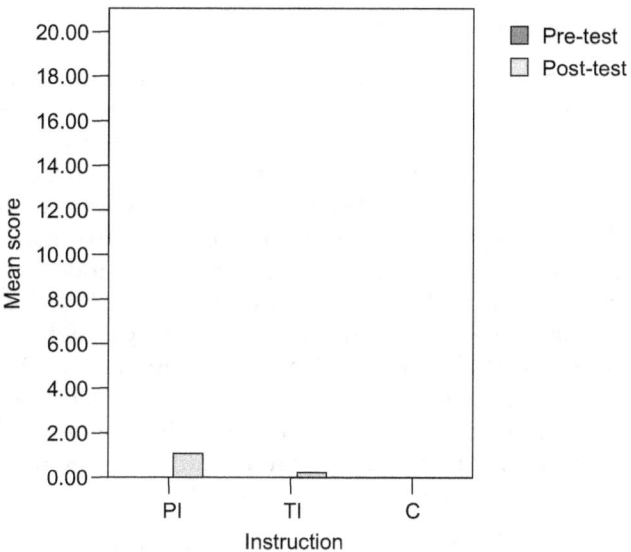

Figure 5.13 Results for production task (French causative)

Table 5.9 Summary of repeated measures ANOVA (French causative)

Data	df	SS	MS	F	p
Interpretation					
Treatment	2	51.737	25.869	18.312	0.000*
Time	2	65.858	32.929	10.211	0.001*
Time x Treatment	4	8.780	2.195	6.215	0.020*
Production					
Treatment	2	3.189	1.595	17.803	0.000*
Time	2	5.379	2.689	26.561	0.000*
Time x Treatment	4	2.379	0.5947	6.561	0.000*

cumulative transfer-of-training effects is given in Table 5.9. The present study is the first to demonstrate that Processing Instruction not only has primary or direct effects on learners' interpretation and production, but also has secondary and cumulative transfer-of-training effects on both interpretation and production.

Discussion and Conclusion

The three main objectives of this study were to investigate the primary, secondary transfer-of-training and cumulative transfer-of-training effects of PI. Primary effects on a linguistic form are those that result directly from instruction on that linguistic form. Transfer-of training effects are those that result indirectly from instruction on another form. The forms under scrutiny here were the primary target of past tense imperfective aspect and the secondary transfer-of-training target of the subjunctive mood morphology. In both, verb final morphological markings are affected by the same processing problems. The cumulative transfer-of-training target was causative constructions whose underlying subject–verb relations are misinterpreted by learners. The target language was French as learned by classroom-based native speakers of English. In order to accomplish these three objectives a series of questions and hypotheses were formulated. The questions that guided our investigation are reiterated as follows.

(Q1) What are the primary effects of PI and TI on the acquisition of French past tense imperfective aspect as measured by an interpretation task?

(Q2) What are the primary effects of PI and TI on the acquisition of French past tense imperfective aspect as measured by a form production task?

(Q3) Are there any secondary transfer-of-training effects of PI and TI from receiving instruction on French past tense imperfective aspect to French subjunctive mood morphology as measured by an interpretation task?

(Q4) Are there any secondary transfer-of-training effects of PI and TI from receiving instruction on French past tense imperfective aspect to French subjunctive mood morphology as measured by a production task?

(Q5) Are there any cumulative transfer-of-training effects of PI and TI from receiving instruction on French past tense imperfective aspect to French causative constructions with *faire* as measured by an interpretation task?

(Q6) Are there any secondary transfer-of-training effects of PI and TI from receiving instruction on French past tense imperfective aspect to French causative constructions with *faire* as measured by a production task?

Based on previous empirical findings presented in Chapter 2, the review of findings of previous PI research on our target linguistic items, and the research findings reported in Chapters 3 and 4, we made a series of hypotheses related to the research questions.

(H1) PI will be a more effective type of instruction than TI and the control group in helping learners to interpret correctly and efficiently sentences containing French past tense imperfective aspect.
(H2) PI will be an equally effective type of instruction to TI in helping learners to produce correctly and efficiently sentences containing French past tense imperfective aspect.
(H3) Learners receiving PI on French past tense imperfective aspect will transfer that training and process subjunctive mood morphology better than those receiving TI as measured by an interpretation task.
(H4) Learners receiving PI on French past tense imperfective aspect will transfer that training and process subjunctive mood morphology better than those receiving TI as measured by a production task.
(H5) Learners receiving PI on French past tense imperfective aspect will transfer that training and process French causative constructions with *faire* better than those receiving TI as measured by an interpretation task.
(H6) Learners receiving PI on French past tense imperfective aspect will transfer that training and process French causative constructions with *faire* better than those receiving TI as measured by a production task.

The results of our investigation confirm all six hypotheses. To illustrate the primary, secondary transfer-of-training effects and the cumulative transfer-of training effects, we have summarised in Table 5.10 the percentage change in scores from pre-test to post-test on both the interpretation and production tasks. Processing Instruction demonstrates these effects because it fundamentally alters the way second language learners work with input. Doing so brings about changes in the processors that work with input and that convert that input into intake for the developing system. PI changes the way learners interact with primary linguistic data, a claim made especially salient by the significant cumulative effects (see Table 5.10).

Based on the results reported in Chapter 4 in which we found secondary transfer-of-training effects from one verb morpheme to another verb morpheme, we hypothesised that learners' internal systems had restructured or at least had begun to restructure such that their systems now included a verb final slot. This account also describes what happened in the present study with French verb morphology for the primary and second effects. An important and utterly consistent PI finding is that the learners' language production mechanisms have access to this new information about the verb final slot. TI practice only makes the form available for production. TI can not make a form available to processing mechanisms. Extrapolating from our cumulative transfer-of-training findings we assert that PI learners are more efficient language learners.

Table 5.10 Summary of results

		Primary	*Secondary*	*Cumulative*
Processing InstructionI	intepretation	58%	20%	34%
	production	69%	10%	11%
Traditional Instruction	intepretation	5%	-5%	-5%
	production	71%	2%	3%
Control	intepretation	2%	-5%	-5%
	production	0%	0%	0%

We now have three sets of findings that demonstrate secondary transfer-of-training effects for PI in support of Lee's (2004) hypothesis regarding transfer-of-training.

The results of the previous chapter, that also demonstrated positive, secondary transfer-of-training effects, in combination with the positive transfer-of-training effects we have presented in this chapter lead us to reiterate and underscore the Strengthening Hypothesis. Only future research on the effects of PI can confirm or not the Strengthening Hypothesis. In essence we hypothesise that multiple PI treatments on different linguistic targets that all pose the same processing problem to learners will have a profound effect on learners' underlying systems. We hypothesise that the L2-driven processing strategy learned will eventually become the learners' default strategy for working with primary linguistic data. For example, if learners received PI instruction on French past tense imperfective apsect, followed by PI on subjunctive mood morphology, followed by PI on future tense morphology, then they would adopt the L2 appropriate (word final) processing strategy to process imperative or conditional forms. We would not see just a secondary effect of 10%–20% as we did in the present study, but an even greater effect.

The most important finding of the present study, arguably, is that PI offers learners cumulative transfer-of-training effects. PI learners trained on verbal morphology gained 11% in form production and 34% in form interpretation on a syntactic construction. When we combine this finding with that presented in Chapter 3, we hypothesise that PI learners develop better intuitions about working with L2 input. Remember from Chapter 3 that we taught learners how to process nonmeaningful and redundant nominal morphology. They then transferred that training to process meaningful verbal morphology. They gained 8% in form production and 25% in form interpretation. Given these findings we also propose the Intuition Hypothesis, developed in part from Lee's (2004: 320) hypothesis.

Intuition Hypothesis: learners who receive PI on one form will, as a result, extrapolate from that training and develop L2-appropriate intuitions for working with L2 input.

As with all empirical research, the present study is limited in several ways. While we underscore the positive outcomes in this study, we acknowledge certain limitations. The size of the final data pool could be more robust so that we could have included multiple groups of learners in each instructional treatment and we could have magnified the size of the control group. Future research could replicate our study but with a larger sample size. Also, we know that the primary effects of PI hold over time (e.g. VanPatten & Fernandez, 2004), but we do not know whether the secondary and cumulative transfer-of-training effects of PI will also hold over time. We were unable to include delayed post-testing in the present study, but future research could address this important issue.

The findings of this investigation (primary effects) led to the following conclusions:

- PI is a more effective instructional treatment than TI in helping L2 learners at interpreting sentences containing French imperfect form;
- PI is as successful as TI in helping learners at producing sentences containing French imperfect forms;
- PI is successful at altering processing problems that affect the French imperfect forms (the Lexical Preference Principle and the Sentence Location principle).

The findings of this investigation (secondary) led to the following conclusions:

- Subjects in the processing group were able to transfer the PI training received for the French imperfect to another linguistic form in French (subjunctive) affected by similar processing problems;
- Subjects in the processing group were able to transfer the PI training received for the French imperfect to another linguistic form in French (causative) affected by different processing problems.

Chapter 6
Final Comments

Processing Principles

The three empirical investigations that we have presented in Chapters 3, 4 and 5 all shared the same overarching goal, which was to move Processing Instruction research into a new area or strand of investigation. Our work explored previously uncharted territory with respect to what we know about the effects of Processing Instruction on second language acquisition. We have demonstrated in the three experiments that Processing Instruction not only gives learners the direct or primary benefit of learning to process and produce the morphological form on which they received instruction, but also a secondary benefit in that they transferred that training to processing and producing another morphological form on which they had received no instruction. Additionally, our third experiment presented in Chapter 5 showed a cumulative benefit of Processing Instruction in that learners transferred their training processing morphology to processing and producing a syntactic construction.

Our research on Processing Instruction is framed by VanPatten's work (empirical and theoretical) on input processing (VanPatten, 1996, 2004a, 2007b). We presented the Processing Principles associated with his theoretical framework in Chapter 1. We also presented some of the empirical work from which VanPatten developed the principles, as well as other empirical work that supports the principles. In Table 6.1, we provide a summary of the Processing Principles that framed our investigations.

In Chapter 4 we presented research on the acquisition of English verb morphology by native speakers of Korean learning English in a Korean middle school. The two target linguistic items were the simple past tense marker *-ed* and the third person singular, present tense marker *-s*. The acquisition of both morphemes is affected by the Lexical Preference Principle: 'learners will tend to rely on lexical items as opposed to grammatical form to get meaning when both encode the same semantic information' (VanPatten, 2004b: 9). Tense or time is often signalled in ways other than morphological inflection. Real world context often signals when the event expressed took place, takes place or will take place. More importantly from a processing perspective, a lexical item might co-occur with the morphological marker such that they both encode the same semantic information. The adverbial expression 'last night' tells us the same thing that *-ed* does.

Table 6.1 Summary of the processing principles investigated

Targeted linguistic item	Processing principle(s)	Transfer-of-training linguistic item	Processing Principle(s)
Italian noun–adjective agreement	P1c. *Preference for Nonredundancy*: learners are more likely to process nonredundant meaningful grammatical form before they process redundant meaningful forms. P1d. *Meaning before Nonmeaning*: learners are more likely to process meaningful grammatical forms before non-meaningful forms irrespective of redundancy.	Italian future tense	P1b. *Lexical Preference*: learners will tend to rely on lexical items as opposed to grammatical form to get meaning when both encode the same semantic information.
English past tense *-ed*	P1b. *Lexical Preference*: learners will tend to rely on lexical items as opposed to grammatical form to get meaning when both encode the same semantic information.	English 3rd person singular, present tense *-s*	P1b. *Lexical Preference*: learners will tend to rely on lexical items as opposed to grammatical form to get meaning when both encode the same semantic information.
French past tense, imperfective aspect	P1b. *Lexical Preference*: learners will tend to rely on lexical items as opposed to grammatical form to get meaning when both encode the same semantic information.	French subjunctive mood	P1b. *Lexical Preference*: learners will tend to rely on lexical items as opposed to grammatical form to get meaning when both encode the same semantic information. P1d. *Meaning before Nonmeaning*: learners are more likely to process meaningful grammatical forms before non-meaningful forms irrespective of redundancy. P1f. *Sentence Location*: learners tend to process items in sentence initial position before those in final position and those in medial position.
French past tense, imperfective aspect	P1b. *Lexical Preference*: learners will tend to rely on lexical items as opposed to grammatical form to get meaning when both encode the same semantic information.	French causative constructions with *faire*	P2: *First Noun Principle*: Learners tend to process the first noun or pronoun they encounter in a sentence as the subject or agent. P1a: *Primacy of Content Words* Learners process content words in the input before anything else.

The adverb 'today' tells us some of the same thing that -s does; it tells us the time frame. The obligatory subject in English tells us some of what -s does; it indicates third person. Processing Instruction structures the input that learners receive so that it does not contain lexical items that encode the same semantic information as the morphological inflection does. Learners are forced to process the morphology and connect it with the meaning of past time.

In Chapter 3 we presented research on the acquisition of Italian nominal and verbal morphology by native speakers of English learning Italian in university-level classrooms. The two target linguistic items were adjective noun gender agreement markers and future tense morphology. The acquisition of these morphemes is affected by different but related processing principles. The processing problem that learners encounter with noun–adjective gender agreement is that of meaningfulness. The agreement markers on adjectives do not carry semantic information, only grammatical information about the gender of the noun. Additionally the adjectival gender marking is redundant in that the noun is also marked for gender as would be an article preceding the adjective. VanPatten (2004b) referred specifically to adjective agreement in Romance languages when he formulated two principles of input processing. They are the Preference for Nonredundancy Principle: 'learners are more likely to process nonredundant meaningful grammatical form before they process redundant meaningful forms' (VanPatten, 2004b: 11) and, the Meaning-before-Nonmeaning Principle: 'learners are more likely to process meaningful grammatical forms before nonmeaningful forms irrespective of redundancy' (VanPatten, 2004b: 11). Processing Instruction structures the input that learners receive so that it eliminates (or severely reduces) redundancy and it makes the grammatical marker on the adjective the only element available for assigning reference. Learners are forced to process the morphological marker on the adjective and connect it to gender. The future tense in Italian is affected by a different processing principle, the Lexical Preference Principle. As we stated with English tense morphology, a lexical item will give the same semantic information as the future tense marker. The adverbial *domani* tells us some of the same thing that *-rà* does; it tells us when something will take place.

In Chapter 5 we presented research on the acquisition of French verb morphology and syntax by native speakers of English learning French in university-level classrooms. We examined two verbal morphemes and one syntactic construction. As can be seen in Table 6.1, these three linguistic targets present learners very different processing problems. The verb form on which learners received instruction was the past tense imperfective aspect marker. As is the case with all tense morphemes, they can be made redundant by a lexical item (the Lexical Preference Principle). Processing

Instruction on this verb form consisted of isolating the form by removing all other indicators of time. Learners were forced to use the verb form to assign tense. The other targeted verb form was subjunctive mood morphology, which presents learners with several processing problems. These verbal markers occur in subordinate (dependent) clauses, and the form is triggered by the semantics of the verb phrase in the principal (independent) clause. In so far as the form is triggered by the meaning expressed in the main clause, we can say that the subjunctive form is non-meaningful; *comprends* and *comprenne* both mean the same thing. The morphological distinction between indicative and subjunctive is purely grammatical. The processing problem here is captured in the Meaning-Before-Nonmeaning Principle. Additionally, subjunctive verb morphology does not occur in a favoured processing position. VanPatten captured this problem as the Sentence Location Principle (P1f): 'learners tend to process items in sentence initial position before those in final position and those in medial position' (VanPatten, 2004b: 13–14). The other targeted linguistic item was causative construction with the verb *faire*. The surface level syntax and morphology do not transparently reflect the underlying relations between agents and actions. As we discussed in Chapter 1, this construction is an example of how learners use content words to make meaning: the Primacy of Content Words Principle (P1a), 'learners process content words in the input before anything else' (VanPatten, 2004b: 8). For these constructions, learners tend not to process the verb *fait* nor the marker *à*. Additionally, these constructions are subject to the First Noun Principle (P2): 'learners tend to process the first noun or pronoun they encounter in a sentence as the subject or agent' (VanPatten, 2004b: 15). For these constructions, learners take the first noun and make it the object of the first verb they process (after skipping over *fait*). The result is that they completely misinterpret the underlying relations between agents and actions.

Why are processing principles and the processing problems associated with them so important to second language acquisition? If learners are not processing a form, they cannot acquire it. If learners are not connecting a form with its meaning, then they are not acquiring it. We use the term 'form' to refer broadly to surface features of a language such as nominal morphology, verbal morphology of tense and mood, syntactic patterns, and object markers (for further discussion of what is a 'form', see also VanPatten *et al.*, 2004: 1–2). The relationship between our use of the term 'processing' and the roles of attention, conscious attention and awareness of form in language acquisition are still highly debated. Some take the position that conscious attention is necessary (e.g. Schmidt, 1990) whereas others take the position that various components of attention do not require awareness to operate cognitively. As Tomlin and Villa (1994: 93) state, ' ... information can be cognitively detected even though the individual is not aware of it having occurred'. In her overview of nine theories of second language acquisition, Ortega (2007) contrasts two theories, Associative-Cognitive CREED and Skill Acquisition Theory for their fundamental differences on the role of consciousness in learning. Associative-Cognitive CREED presents language learning as an implicit inductive undertaking and so emphasises incidental learning and unconscious representations of language (Ellis, 2007). Skill Acquisition Theory emphasises conscious processing, deliberate learning, and explicit representations of language (DeKeyser, 2007). Processing Instruction allows for an interface between explicit and implicit learning. Processing Instruction often contains explicit information about form and processing strategies. But there is also research that demonstrates that learners make gains in the absence of such explicit information. They make gains through doing structured input activities (Benati, 2004a; VanPatten & Oikennon, 1996; Wong, 2004b). Clearly, there needs to be further work at both the theoretical and empirical levels to clarify the issues surrounding conscious attention.

The Findings

Our point of departure in carrying out this work was a set of hypotheses Lee generated from his critical review of the PI research (Lee, 2004). They are as follows.

Hypothesis 7: PI will be effective for instilling target-language specific processing strategies, no matter the L1 of the learners.

Hypothesis 9: learners who receive training on one type of processing strategy for one specific form will appropriately transfer the use of that strategy to other forms without further instruction in PI.

Hypothesis 10: learners who receive PI will develop better intuitions about the L2 than learners who receive other types of instruction.

Hypothesis 11: the cumulative effects of PI will be greater than its isolated effects'. (Lee, 2004: 322)

We present a summary of our findings on the primary and transfer-of-training effects of PI and TI in Table 6.2. Our findings lend support to these hypotheses.

In support of Hypothesis 7 we offer our findings on the primary effects of PI on the acquisition of English simple past tense by native speakers of Korean. Benati (2005) had previously researched this particular form with native speakers of Greek and Chinese. For both groups of learners the PI groups improved significantly more than the MOI and TI groups on the interpretation test, and all three groups improved equally on the production test. Our present findings are identical in that the PI group outper-

Final Comments

Table 6.2 Summary of the primary and transfer-of-training effects of PI versus TI versus C (control)

Linguistic item: targeted	Results: Primary effects	Linguistic item: Transfer-of training	Results: Transfer effects	Subjects
Italian noun–adjective agreement	*Processing:* primary effect: yes PI > TI > C *Production:* Primary effect: yes (PI = TI) > C	Italian future tense	*Processing:* transfer effect: yes PI > (TI = C) *Production:* transfer effect: yes (PI = TI) > C	L1: English Age: university-level adults
English past tense -*ed*	*Processing:* primary effect: yes PI > TI *Production:* primary effect: yes PI = TI	English 3rd person singular, present tense -*s*	*Processing:* transfer effect: yes PI > TI *Production:* transfer effect: yes PI > TI	L1: Korean Age: middle school adolescents
French past tense, imperfective aspect	*Processing:* primary effect: yes PI > TI > C *Production:* primary effect: yes (PI = TI) > C	French subjunctive mood	*Processing:* transfer effect: yes PI > (TI = C) *Production:* transfer effect: yes PI > (TI = C)	L1: English Age: university-level adults
French past tense, imperfective aspect	*Processing:* primary effect: yes PI > TI > C *Production:* primary effect: yes (PI = TI) > C	French causative constructions with *faire*	*Processing:* transfer effect: yes PI > (TI = C) *Production:* transfer effect: yes PI > (TI = C)	L1: English Age: university-level adults

formed the TI group on the interpretation task but the two groups performed equally well on the production task. These combined results demonstrate that learners representing three different native languages can be taught to employ effectively a target-language specific processing strategy, i.e. pay attention to the ends of verbs in order to use a form not a lexeme to make meaning.

In support of Hypothesis 9 we offer our secondary transfer-of-training effects for PI. We isolated for examination two English verbal inflections that are affected by the Lexical Preference Principle (P1b). The temporal information encoded in these morphemes can also be expressed lexically through adverbs and adverbial phrases. The person-number information encoded in *-s* is also expressed in naming the subject of the verb, which English does obligatorily. In the PI instructional treatment we taught learners to attend to the verb final morpheme *-ed* and to use this form to make meaning. Meaning here refers to the concept of pastness. As the results of our analyses of primary effects show, learners successfully adopted this processing strategy for the target form. As the results of our analyses of the secondary transfer-of-training effects show, the learners successfully applied this processing strategy to another formal feature of English without further instruction on this form. Given the support we provided for the hypothesis, we would like to now term it The Secondary Transfer-of-Training Hypothesis. We would expect that future research will lend even greater support to the hypothesis.

In support of Hypothesis 10 we offer our findings on the secondary transfer-of-training effects we found for the acquisition of Italian by native speakers of English. We selected for examination both a nominal morpheme and a verbal one. These two types of morphemes are affected by different processing principles. The nominal morphology, agreement, is non-meaningful and redundant. The verbal morphology is quite meaningful as long as a lexical item does not also encode the same semantic information about tense/time. We found that learners who were taught to process the nominal morphology and to use it to make a form–meaning connection were then also able to better process the verbal morphology. How would learners transfer processing instruction on a redundant, non-meaningful nominal morpheme to a meaningful verbal morpheme except by having developed a better intuition about the target language? Processing Instruction forced the learners to use the nominal morphology, which is something they would not have done left to their own devices. PI alters those 'devices' and does so in a way that is useable to learners beyond the target item directly affected. The learners have begun to work with input differently as a result of PI.

Also in support of Hypothesis 10 we offer our findings on the acquisition of French verbal morphology by native speakers of English. We selected for examination two verbal morphemes that are affected by the Lexical Preference Principle, but are affected in different ways. For the tense marker, a lexical item could encode time but such a lexical item is not an obligatory part of the sentence. For the mood marker, the semantics of the entire main clause determine the use or not of the mood marker. The presence of the main clause and its meaning are obligatory. These two verbal morphemes are very different from each other in that one is meaningful and the other is not. One occurs in the main clause and the other in a dependent clause. Despite these differences the learners who received PI training on the tense marker were then better able to process the mood marker. PI has helped alter the way they approach the target language. These learners are developing different intuitions about the way French works.

In support of Hypothesis 11 we offer our cumulative transfer-of-training effects for PI. We isolated for examination French verbal morphology and a complex syntactic construction with two underlying agents. These two aspects of French do not present to learners the same or even similar processing problems. The verb morphology is affected by the Lexical Preference Principle whereas the syntactic construction is affected by the First Noun Principle and the Primacy of Content Words Principle. The isolated effect in this investigation was the primary effect that processing instruction aimed at teaching learners to process the verb morphology effectively taught them to do so. The cumulative effect is that this instruction carried over to a novel form. The PI learners have begun to work with French syntax in a different way from those who did not receive PI.

The Size of Things

We have previously presented the results of the statistical comparisons and discussed the statistically significant differences from pre-test to post-test scores. In Table 6.3 we present the increase in performance, as a percentage, of the PI groups across the three investigations we carried out. We provide the increase for the primary linguistic target as well as for the secondary and cumulative target items. We do this in order to give some perspective to our results. Collentine (2004) examined standard deviations of the means and found that the results of Processing Instruction were robust. When learners receive PI the direct effects on their processing and production of the form are fairly equal: 51% and 44%, respectively, for Italian noun adjective agreement, 46% and 42% for English simple past tense and 58% and 69% for French past tense. Both interpretation and production scores are increasing. The greatest area in which PI affects transfer-of-training is found in the interpretation task scores. These are consistently higher than the production scores, from a low of double to a high of triple. For secondary and cumulative effects, the impact of PI on language learners is greatest in the area of processing.

Table 6.3 Summary of the increases in performance of PI groups

Primary target	Primary effects	Secondary target	Transfer-of-training effects
Italian noun–adjective agreement	processing 51% production 44%	Italian future tense	processing 25% production 8%
English past tense -ed	processing 46% production 42%	English 3rd person singular, present tense -s	processing 22% production 11%
French past tense, imperfective aspect	processing 58% production 69%	French subjunctive mood	processing 20% production 10%
		French causative constructions with *faire*	processing 34% production 11%

Table 6.4 The increases in performance from when our secondary targets were primary targets

Target item	Previous research	Primary effects	Transfer-of-training effects
Italian future tense	Benati (2004)	processing 56% production 51%	processing 25% production 8%
French subjunctive mood morphology	Lee & Benati (2007b)	processing 67% production 58	processing 20% production 10%
French causative construction with *faire*	VanPatten & Wong (2004)	processing 69–71% production 61–79%	processing 34% production 11%

Another perspective to take on the transfer-of-training findings is to compare these results with those of previous research in which our transfer-of-training targets were the primary targets. This perspective is presented in Table 6.4, in which we compare the results of three previous studies with those presented in this book. Benati (2004a) investigated the direct effects of PI on Italian future tense. Lee and Benati (2007b) investigated the direct effects of PI on French subjunctive mood morphology. VanPatten and Wong (2004) examined the direct effects of PI on French causative constructions with *faire*. As is obvious from the figures presented in Table 6.4, the impact of PI is greater for direct effects than it is for transfer-of-training effects.

With direct training on Italian future tense morphology, learners improve on their processing scores by 56% whereas as a secondary effect they improve on these scores by 25%. This means that learners are almost half way to where they would be with direct instruction. With direct training on French causative constructions, learners improve on their processing scores by 69–71%, whereas as a secondary effect they improve on these scores by 34%. This means that learners are almost half way to where they would be had they received direct instruction on the form. The story is not so dramatic for French subjunctive mood morphology. With direct instruction learners' processing scores improved 67%, whereas as a secondary effect the improvement was 20% – the learners are less than one third of the way to where they would be with direct instruction. And, as stated above, the story with production is very different. No matter what the size of percentage increase, these statistically significant results point to the fact that PI instruction has both primary and transfer-of-training effects. The instruction has helped bring about changes in the learners' internal systems.

The Context of Other Processing Instruction Research

In its debut empirical investigation, Processing Instruction research took as its point of departure the aim of proving that PI was effective instruction vis-à-vis other types of instruction (VanPatten & Cadierno, 1993). This work spawned the first branch or research strand under which we can classify subsequent research. As shown by our review in Chapter 2 and the results of the research presented in this book, PI is an effective form of instruction. The next strand of research was established in 1996 when VanPatten and Oikennon investigated which component of PI was the causative factor in the positive findings. They explored the role of structured input activities (SIA) separate from the role of the explicit information (EI) given to learners (which included information about processing strategies). Although established in 1996, subsequent research on the roles of structured input and explicit information did not appear until VanPatten's 2004 edition. This research, almost uniformly but not quite, indicates that structured input activities alone have the same effect on learners as does the combination of explicit information plus structured input activities. Recently, two new research strands have opened up into which we can classify Processing Instruction research: enhancing structured input and modes of delivering PI. Lee and Benati (2007a) investigated the relationship between structured input and enhanced input (Wong, 2005). In a series of investigations, they compared the effects of structured input with those of textually or acoustically enhanced structured input. For the four target items they investigated, they found that enhanced and unenhanced structured input activities had equal effects on learners' performance. Lee and Benati (2007b) and their collaborators investigated the effects of delivering PI in a classroom, in a whole-group context and in a virtual context (i.e. learners working individually at computer terminals). In a series of investigations, they found that both classroom and computer delivery of PI were equally effective. With the research we have presented in the previous chapters, we have once again opened a research strand into which we can classify PI research: transfer-of-training effects. Across the investigations we presented here we have found consistently that PI instruction on one target leads to transfer-of-training effects on other targets. The new areas of investigation will require time to become more fully established so that a robust set of findings is available to those interested in Input Processing Theory as well as in Processing Instruction.

Methodological Considerations

With two exceptions, Processing Instruction research has examined adult learners. VanPatten and Oikennon (1996) was the first research to examine younger learners. For their study, they used teenagers enrolled in an American high school (years 9–12). We, too, have examined a group other than adult classroom learners. In our research on the acquisition of English, presented in Chapter 4, we used a group of adolescents enrolled in a Korean middle school. The results of these two investigations converge with all other investigations in establishing that PI is an effective intervention. While two studies is not a robust enough number from which to draw a generalisation or conclusion, we do feel we can propose the Age Hypothesis:

> *The Age Hypothesis:* PI will be just as effective as in intervention with younger learners as it is with older learners.

Future research that focuses on the age of learners will determine whether or not learners of primary school age will benefit from Processing Instruction, and whether or not they benefit from it to the same degree as older learners.

In 2004, Lee stated, 'I am confident regarding the generalisability of Processing Instruction to Romance Languages but reasonable questions could be posed regarding the generalisability of Processing Instruction beyond Romance languages' (Lee, 2004: 315). From 2004 to the present much new research on the effects of PI has emerged. Benati (2005) developed Processing Instruction for learners of English as a second language, and we have, in the present series of investigations, continued that research. Lee and Benati (2007a, 2007b) developed Processing Instruction for learners of Japanese. These findings are consistent with all other PI findings: that PI proved to be an effective intervention for English and Japanese. The reason is simple. PI focuses on a target-language specific processing problem and teaches learners to use the target-language appropriate processing strategy. The research on non-Romance languages is just beginning but the results are very encouraging. We can combine Lee's (2004) Hypotheses 1, 2 and 3 into one, the Target Language Hypothesis:

> *The Target Language Hypothesis:* PI can help learners of any target language develop an appropriate, target-language specific processing strategy to address a target-language specific processing problem.

In 2004, Lee stated:

> The PI research has examined three target languages, Spanish, French, and Italian, but only one native language, English. The homogeneity of the overall database lends weight to arguments of generalisability but is at the same time a limitation. Is Processing Instruction equally effective across a variety of native languages? (Lee, 2004: 318)

As noted above, we can now generalise the findings of PI research beyond Romance languages. Additionally, that same research allows us to generalise beyond native speakers of English. Benati (2005) examined native speakers of Chinese and Greek. We have examined native speakers of Korean. Lee and Benati (2007a, 2007b) examined native speakers of Italian. The reason PI is an effective intervention for native speakers of all these languages is that the instruction is based on a target-language specific processing problem. We have provided support for Lee's Hypothesis 7 (Lee, 2004: 318) and formulate it here as the Native Language Hypothesis:

> *The Native Language Hypothesis:* PI will be effective for instilling target-language specific processing strategies, no matter the native language of the learners.

Contributions to Input Processing Theory

VanPatten and Williams (2007a) have edited a volume in which nine contemporary theories of second language acquisition are presented by those most closely associated with the theories. In their introduction, VanPatten and Williams present a condensed list of 10 observable phenomena that need to be explained by theories of second language acquisition. One of the observed phenomena concerns incidental language acquisition. It states:

> *Observation # 2: A good deal of SLA happens incidentally.* This observation captures that various aspects of language enter learners' minds/brains when they are focused on communicative interaction (including reading). In other words, with incidental acquisition the learner's *primary* focus of attention is on the message contained in the input, and linguistic features are 'picked up' in the process. Incidental acquisition can occur with any

aspect of language (e.g. vocabulary, syntax, morphology [inflections], phonology). (VanPatten & Williams, 2007b: 10)

When Carroll (2007: 169) addressed this phenomenon she explained that '... most, if not all acquisition, as defined by the creation of a grammar in the learner's head, is incidental in that it happens as a byproduct of learners interacting with language in some kind of setting'. We would emphasise the concept of byproduct, as does VanPatten (2007:130): 'In a certain sense, acquisition is the byproduct of learners' actively attempting to comprehend input'. To that end, the research we have conducted on transfer-of-training effects speaks, to some degree, to the issue of incidental language acquisition.

We explain our transfer-of-training findings as an example of incidental acquisition. We found statistically significant differences from pre-test to post-test on four secondary target linguistic items. With this we can certainly conclude that change has taken place in the learners' minds/ brains (VanPatten & Williams, 2007b) or that a grammar in the learner's head is being created or at least added to (Carroll, 2007). The stimulus for the change in performance was receiving Processing Instruction on a primary target. Then, when learners took the post-tests for the secondary targets, they worked with the some of the input differently. We would argue that the interpretation test directed learners' primary attention toward the message contained in the input; they were actively trying to comprehend the input. They had to be 'picking up' on the linguistic features in that input in order for their performance to have changed significantly from pre-test to post-test. That the changes in interpretation scores were between 20% and 34% attests to how slow the process of second language acquisition is. We agree with Carroll (2007: 170) that 'explicit instruction and practice will not lead to changes in the learners' mental representation unless the instruction itself causes changes in processing of primary linguistic data'. Processing Instruction brings about changes in processing of primary linguistic data as evidenced in our transfer-of-training effects.

Another of the observed phenomena that VanPatten and Williams refer to is the role of learners' first language in second language acquisition:

Observation # 8: There are limits on the effect of a learner's first language on SLA. Evidence of the effects of the first language on SLA has been around since the beginning of contemporary SLA research in the early 1970s. It is clear, however, that the first language does not have massive effects on either processes or outcomes as once thought ... Instead, it seems that the influence of the first language is somehow selective and also varies across individual learners. (VanPatten & Williams, 2007b: 11)

Many of the authors in their volume address the issue of the L1. Bardovi-Harlig, who takes a concept-oriented approach, states that:

> A basic tenet of the concept-oriented approach to second language acquisition is that adult learners of second or foreign languages have access to the full range of semantic concepts from their previous linguistic and cognitive experiences. Von Stutterheim and Klein argue that 'a second language learner – in contrast to a child learning his first language – does not have to acquire the underlying concepts. What he has to acquire is a specific way and a specific means of expressing them' (1987: 194). (Bardovi-Harlig, 2007: 58)

Our learners came to us knowing that language can express futurite, past, causation and agency. They had to acquire the specific ways and means to express these in Italian, English or French.

Ellis, who works with associative and cognitive processing, states that ' ... the initial state for SLA is no longer a plastic system [as it is for first language acquisition]; it is one that is already tuned and committed to the L1' (Ellis, 2007: 83). As the pre-test scores demonstrate, our learners were not using target-language-appropriate processing strategies prior to instruction, perhaps because they are approaching the L2 with mental procedures tuned and committed to their native languages. Through Processing Instruction, these mental procedures are re-tuned and have to become committed to the L2.

VanPatten (2007) acknowledges three possibilities for the role of the L1 in parsing. First, he presents the possibility that the First Noun Principle is a universal processing strategy independent of learners' L1. Second, he formulates the L1 Transfer Principle, learners begin acquisition with L1 parsing procedures (VanPatten, 2007: 122). Third, VanPatten combines the positions stating that a possible scenario is that learners start with universal procedures for parsing but then the L1 parser is somehow triggered and either assists or inhibits correct interpretation. It does seem reasonable to consider that learners might approach the L2, at least initially, with inappropriate L1-based processing mechanisms. The question will remain open for further investigation.

Avenues for Further Investigation

The reason Lee (2004) proposed 11 hypotheses about the effects of Processing Instruction was to stimulate further research and to offer specific avenues for investigation. As indicated above, our research is in response to these hypotheses. In discussing our results we have proposed additional hypotheses that we hope will encourage future research. And so, in this final section, we would like to bring Lee's hypotheses and our own to the forefront for further future consideration. Several of Lee's hypotheses are not directly relevant to the research we presented. They are, however, worth mentioning as viable avenues for further investigation. We have given each hypothesis its own name and have revised it slightly in recognition of the amount of research that has been conducted since 2004.

Our present research did not include delayed post-testing, but the Processing Instruction literature illuminates this issue. We do know that the effects of PI are undiminished one week (e.g. Cadierno, 1995; Lee et al., 2007), two weeks (e.g. Farely, 2004a), three weeks (e.g. Benati, 2001; Cheng, 2002), one month (e.g. Benati, 2004a; VanPatten & Cadierno, 1993) and 14 weeks after instruction (Marsden, 2006). VanPatten and Fernández (2004) measured the longer-term effects. After eight months they found that the effects of PI had endured but had diminished. The research challenge is to control the input to which learners are exposed so that it does not include the target item. This challenge is a substantial one. A beginning point would be to test learners somewhere in between the one month and eight month marks that we currently have. Even so, we put forward the following hypothesis (adapted from Hypothesis 4).

> *The Longer Term Effects Hypothesis:* PI will have long-term durative effects on all types of processing strategies (word-order, perceptual and semantic).

In all the research on PI, only two studies have addressed individual differences among the learners. Lee et al. (2007) found differences among the learners in how much they improved from pre-test to post-test. The learners with the lower pre-test scores gained more than the learners with the higher pre-test scores so that both groups ended up near the same spot. VanPatten and Wong (2004) suspected there might be individual differences based on the different universities in which their subjects were enrolled. This difference was not found. VanPatten and Wong did find, however, that some learners employed a test-taking strategy that boosted their performance. They separated these learners out from their data pool. The nature of individual differences is a vast field of investigation.

> *The Individual Difference Hypothesis:* some learners benefit more from PI than do others.

In our research we employed sentence-level interpretation tasks and modified cloze passages for the production tasks. Sanz (1995, 1997, 2004) and Cheng (2002, 2004) demonstrated that PI was effective not only at the sentence level but also at the discourse level. For her production tasks, Sanz (2004) included a sentence completion task and a video-retelling task. PI proved effective in improving learners' scores on both tasks. Cheng (2002) used sentence production and a guided composition to measure the effects of PI. PI proved effective in improving learners' scores on both tasks. A very fruitful avenue for further research will be to continue to examine if PI will effectively improve the way learners use language to create connected discourse.

> *The Discourse Hypothesis:* PI will yield significant improvement on discourse-level tasks.

We would encourage the development of a new strand of research that focused on the ongoing effects of PI. We have already proposed the idea that processing strategies strengthen with repeated treatments. At what point does the processing strategy become the learner's default strategy, employing it 100% of the time rather than 20% (as in our transfer-of-training targets) or 70% of the time as the result of direct instruction?

> *The Strengthening Hypothesis:* second language learners who receive multiple PI treatments that address the same processing principle will increasingly strengthen their use of the more optimal processing strategy until it becomes their default strategy for processing second language input.

The second hypothesis we put forward has to do with affecting learners underlying approach to processing primary linguistic data. When we structure input to address the Lexical Preference Principle, we remove any adverbials or other cues to temporal framework. In the real world, however, or even in classroom interaction, interlocutors use adverbials. Second language learners must learn to use form even in the presence of a lexical marker. Doing so would be optimal for continued second language development.

> *The Optimal Hypothesis:* when learners transfer their PI training, they will be more likely to process new grammatical forms as opposed to relying on lexical items to get meaning, when both encode the same semantic information.

The present studies have contributed to the expanding base from which we generalise the findings of PI research. We have added native speakers of Korean to the list of languages other than English on which we have observed PI effects. Further research is required before conclusions can be drawn about the role of the native language in second language processing.

> *The Native Language Hypothesis:* PI will be effective for instilling target-language specific processing strategies, no matter the native language of the learners.

The processing problems that learners face with a target language are due to the specific structure of that language. PI takes as its point of departure what learners do with the input, that is, how they miscomprehend it. From those mis-comprehensions, we derive Processing Instruction to address the specific processing problem.

The Target Language Hypothesis: PI can help learners of any target language develop an appropriate, target-language specific processing strategy to address a target-language specific processing problem.

With only two studies on learners who were not adults, we can only hypothesise about the effects of PI with younger learners. The findings of the two studies do, however, offer us encouragement.

The Age Hypothesis: PI will be equally effective as in intervention with younger learners is it is with older learners.

Our results are based on three languages and three primary target items. Our instructional treatments essentially taught the learners how to direct their attention to the ends of words. They successfully used this strategy on other forms, the secondary targets. This new strand of PI research is very new, but quite worthy of further investigation.

The Secondary Transfer-of-Training Hypothesis: learners who receive training on one type of processing strategy for one specific form will appropriately transfer the use of that strategy to other forms without further instruction in PI.

We also established that PI had what we termed a cumulative effect. From learning to process verb morphology, learners began to attenuate their use of the First Noun Principle. Our evidence for cumulative effects resides in just one piece of research. We strongly encourage more work in this area. Lee (2004) hypothesised that the cumulative effects of PI would be greater than its isolated effects, and they are. Given our results, we are hypothesising something a bit different.

The Cumulative Transfer-of-Training Hypothesis: learners who receive training on one type of processing strategy will begin to work differently with primary linguistic data.

We believe the reason that underlies the change in how learners work with primary linguistic data is that PI helps them to develop other intuitions about how the language works. PI brings about changes in the internal processing mechanisms, and these then operate on the next input to which the learners are exposed.

The Intuition Hypothesis: learners who receive PI will develop better intuitions about how the target language works than will learners who receive other types of instruction.

Final Words

We have long asserted that PI is an effective type of instructional intervention for morphology (e.g. Benati, 2001), syntax (e.g. VanPatten & Wong, 2004) and semantic distinctions (e.g. Cheng, 2002). We know that learners' performance improves when measured with interpretation tasks, sentence- level production tasks and discourse-level production tasks (e.g. Sanz, 1997). We know that PI is an effective intervention for typologically-different target languages such as English, Japanese and Romance languages. We know that learners with different L1s (Italian, English, Korean, Chinese, Greek) benefit from PI. We now have another reason to assert that PI is an effective type of instructional intervention and this reason is perhaps the most persuasive of all. PI shows secondary and cumulative transfer-of-training effects. Learners benefit from Processing Instruction directly, that is, they improve on the targeted linguistic item, but they also benefit indirectly, in that they improve on other linguistic items as well.

Appendix A

Sample Materials for Processing Instruction: English Past Tense

Activity A1 (Referential)
Now and last summer

- Listen to the following statements and decide whether each statement refers to an activity that takes place now or took place last summer in London.

	Now	Last summer	[Sentences heard by learners]
(1)	☐	☐	People worked overtime at work.
(2)	☐	☐	People visit London for the first time.
(3)	☐	☐	People celebrated different festivals.
(4)	☐	☐	People handed out bread to the pigeons at Trafalgar Square.
(5)	☐	☐	People protest in London about the war.
(6)	☐	☐	People walked to work.
(7)	☐	☐	People danced at nightclubs.
(8)	☐	☐	People watch at lot of TV.
(9)	☐	☐	People started a new hobby.
(10)	☐	☐	People receive gifts from their friends and family.

Activity A2 (Referential)
David Beckham – now and before

- **Step 1**
  Listen to the following statements made by a journalist about the life of footballer David Beckham and decide whether each statement is referring to his past life as a Manchester United player or his life now as a Real Madrid player in Spain.

	Manchester United (past)	Real Madrid (now)	[Sentences heard by learners] David Beckham …
(1)	☐	☐	… receives a lot of money from advertising.
(2)	☐	☐	… donated money to charities.
(3)	☐	☐	… reserved more time for his family.

(*Activity A2 – continued*)

(4)	☐	☐	... talked with many world leaders.
(5)	☐	☐	... plays football with his son.
(6)	☐	☐	... created a football academy for young people.
(7)	☐	☐	... trained 5 days a week.
(8)	☐	☐	... promotes many good causes.
(9)	☐	☐	... phones his wife for a chat.
(10)	☐	☐	... visits friends as often as he can.

Step 2
Now read the sentences you have just listened to and decide if David Beckham was more famous when he was a Manchester United player or a Real Madrid player.

Activity A3 (Referential)

Your teacher's life!

- **Step 1**
  Read the following statements about things your teacher does, and decide whether he/she does them now or last weekend.

	He/she ...	*Now*	*Last weekend*
(1)	... played tennis.	☐	☐
(2)	... cooks Italian food.	☐	☐
(3)	... talked to his mother.	☐	☐
(4)	... argued with a friend.	☐	☐
(5)	... listened to his ipod.	☐	☐
(6)	... watches TV.	☐	☐
(7)	... works on the computer.	☐	☐
(8)	... finished his/her homework.	☐	☐
(9)	... explores the local town.	☐	☐
(10)	... stayed up past 1am.	☐	☐

Step 2
Now decide in pairs whether your teacher's weekend was an interesting or a boring weekend.

Activity A4 (Referential)

What's appropriate?

- **Step 1**
  Listen to each sentence. Select the appropriate time-related adverbials that can be added to the sentence you hear.

	Yesterday	Right now	[Sentences heard by learners]
(1)	☐	☐	I laughed at another student.
(2)	☐	☐	I arrive late to the lesson.
(3)	☐	☐	I play computer games.
(4)	☐	☐	I dressed in a T-shirt and jeans.
(5)	☐	☐	I checked homework.
(6)	☐	☐	I relaxed in bed.
(7)	☐	☐	I shout at another student.
(8)	☐	☐	I listened to pop music.
(9)	☐	☐	I work at a part-time job.
(10)	☐	☐	I return homework on time.

- **Step 2**
  Now read through each of the sentences that you have just heard. If you think the sentence is more acceptable for your friend, mark F next to the sentence. If you think the sentence is more acceptable for your teacher, mark T next to the sentence. If you think it is acceptable for both, mark B next to the sentence.

- **Step 3**
  Which sentence is the most unacceptable for your teacher to do? Why?

Activity A5 (Referential)

Stress!

- **Step 1**
  You will hear a series of sentences about things that make your teacher more stressed or help relieve his/her stress. Listen to each sentence and decide whether your teacher did the activity in the past or the present.

	Past	Present	[Sentences heard by learners]
(1)	☐	☐	I joined a yoga club near my house.
(2)	☐	☐	I talk with my friends about how stressed I am.
(3)	☐	☐	I needed more time to study.
(4)	☐	☐	I smoke a lot.
(5)	☐	☐	I cleaned my room.
(6)	☐	☐	I relaxed in bed.
(7)	☐	☐	I cycle to school.

Sample PI Materials (English Past Tense) 179

(**Activity A5** – *continued*)

(8) ☐ ☐ I finished a 3000-word essay.
(9) ☐ ☐ I learn to speak Chinese.
(10) ☐ ☐ I need more money for my rent.

- **Step 2**
  Now in pairs go through the sentences you have just heard and decide if they make your teacher more or less stressed.

- **Step 3**
  Looking at the sentences again, decide who is more stressed, you or your teacher?

Activity A6 (Referential)

In their teens ...

- **Step**
  Listen to the following sentences about John who is now 23 years old and at University. Decide whether John is talking about what his life was like as a teenager or his life now.

	Now at university	When he was a teenager	[Sentences heard by learners]
(1)	☐	☐	I argue with teachers.
(2)	☐	☐	I failed lots of tests.
(3)	☐	☐	I cheat on some exams.
(4)	☐	☐	I achieved top grades.
(5)	☐	☐	I stay up all night at parties.
(6)	☐	☐	I lived in another country.
(7)	☐	☐	I consumed a lot of alcohol.
(8)	☐	☐	I revise a lot for the exams.

- **Step 2**
  Imagine what your parent's life was like as a teenager many years ago. What about another relative? Your teacher? Can you imagine who enjoyed too many parties? Who argued with his or her teacher a lot? Read over the following statements and decide whether each individual (parent, relative, teacher) likely did these things or not.

	He/she ...	Parent	Relative	Teacher
(1)	... argued with a teacher.	☐	☐	☐
(2)	... failed one or more tests.	☐	☐	☐
(3)	... cheated on an exam.	☐	☐	☐
(4)	... protested about something.	☐	☐	☐
(5)	... achieved top grades.	☐	☐	☐
(6)	... consumed alcohol whilst under age.	☐	☐	☐

(**Activity A6** – *continued*)

(7) ... stayed up all night at parties. ☐ ☐ ☐
(8) ... revised the day before an exam. ☐ ☐ ☐

- **Step 3**
Find out if the teacher did the activities above. Are you surprised?

Activity A7 (Affective)

New Year Celebration

- **Step 1**
Read the following activities and indicate whether you did the same or different things at the last New Year celebrations:

		Yes	No
(1)	... I visited my relatives.	☐	☐
(2)	... I received gifts.	☐	☐
(3)	... I mailed New Year cards to friends.	☐	☐
(4)	... I celebrated in the street with friends.	☐	☐
(5)	... I enjoyed myself.	☐	☐
(6)	... I decorated my home.	☐	☐
(7)	... I danced at a club.	☐	☐
(8)	... I decided on a New Year resolution.	☐	☐

- **Step 2**
Compare your results with your partner to find out how many similar things you did.

Activity A8 (Affective)

My first day in London

- **Step 1**
Listen to the following story that a student told about his first day in London and decide which statements accurately describe what happened.

[*Instructor's script*]
I really wanted to see Madame Tussaud's, so early in the morning I took a quick shower and washed myself, and travelled by train to Baker Street station. I had my picture taken with David Beckham, well the wax model that is. I also visited Trafalgar Square and saw Nelson's Column. There were so many pigeons there I think they owned the place! In the afternoon I waited for ages for a train to take me to Covent Garden. I really hated London trains; they are awful. Covent Garden was fantastic, I watched the different street performers, and I really enjoyed listening to the musicians. I finished my

Sample PI Materials (English Past Tense) 181

(*Activity A8* – continued)

exploration and sunbathed for a bit in Hyde Park – London's most famous and largest open space. I arrived home quite late and called my parents back in China and talked about my day. All in all, I had a wonderful time today.

True or false The student ...

_____ (1) ... wanted to see Buckingham Palace.
_____ (2) ... showed pictures of Hyde Park to his parents.
_____ (3) ... stayed in bed most of the morning.
_____ (4) ... liked Covent Garden.
_____ (5) ... phoned his parents.
_____ (6) ... liked English trains.
_____ (7) ... visited Madame Tussaud's.
_____ (8) ... travelled on the bus.
_____ (9) ... really liked the clowns in Oxford Circus.
_____ (10) ... arrived home early.

- **Step 2**
  Now read the text you have just listened to and check your answers.
  Would you like to change any of your answers?
  Then ask your teacher to give you answers.

- **Step 3**
  Read the text again.
  Do you know any of the famous places mentioned above?
  Would you like to go to any of them?

Activity A9 (Affective)

A typical student's day?

- **Step 1**
  The following events are from a typical day in a student's life in London.
  Put the following events in chronological order

  She ...
  A ... returned home in her mother's car.
  B ... showed her homework to her teacher.
  C ... travelled to school in her mother's car.
  D ... researched in the library for her homework after school.
  E ... cooked a nice pasta meal for dinner.
  F ... exercised in the evening at a gym.
  G ... changed into her school uniform.
  H ... prepared her clothes and books for the next day.

(**Activity A9** – *continued*)

    I   ... skipped breakfast.
    J   ... washed her face in the morning.
    Answer:
    1____ 2____ 3____ 4____ 5____ 6____ 7____ 8____ 9____ 10____

- **Step 2**
  Is this routine similar to your routine?
  How many things are similar to your routine?

Activity A10 (Affective)

A horrible day

- **Step 1**
  Break into pairs and listen as your instructor reads a short narration about what Richard did last Saturday.

[*Instructor's script:*]
Last Saturday, Richard jumped out of bed at 8am. He felt tired because he had stayed up most of Friday night. He poured himself three strong cups of coffee to wake up fully. He watched TV and slowly felt more awake. He wanted to go back to sleep again, but he remembered that he had work on Saturdays. He worked part-time at Starbucks café and the manager was very strict. He walked quickly to the bus stop, but unfortunately there was a lot of traffic and so he waited for over an hour. He eventually arrived late and his manager was extremely angry. He shouted at him and said he was a useless employee. Things got worse when Richard spilled a customers coffee all over floor and his boss got really angry and informed him that he was sacked. Finally, Richard returned home feeling miserable and exhausted. What a horrible Saturday. At least he could sleep in on Sunday!

- **Step 2**
  In your pairs, give as many details as you can remember by completing the following sentences. The group with the most details wins. You have three minutes.

  (1) Richard jumped out _____.
  (2) Richard needed _____to wake up fully.
  (3) He wanted to go back to sleep but remembered _____.
  (4) He worked part time at _____.
  (5) He waited at the bus stop for _____.
  (6) His manager shouted at him and said _____.
  (7) Richard spilled _____ and his boss got really angry.
  (8) and informed Richard he _____.
  (9) Richard returned home feeling _____.

Appendix B

Sample Materials for Traditional Instruction: English Past Tense

Activity B1

- I will give you a verb in the present simple tense.
  I want you to then give me a correct sentence in the past simple.

  [*Teacher goes round class. Each participant must give a sentence for every verb.*]

- For example if I say 'play' to you, you could say 'John played football'.

  Verbs given to students:

  (1) cook, (2) talk, (3) phone, (4) work, (5) watch,
  (6) exercise, (7) shop, (8) finish, (9) listen, (10) walk.

Activity B2

- Listen to the following sentences, which are in the present tense. To change the sentence into the past tense, write down the verb in the past tense.
- Example: when you hear 'I listen to the radio', you write down '**listened**'.

    [*Sentences heard*]
    (1) He donates money to charity.   _____
    (2) I donate money to charities.   _____
    (3) The couple reserve a nice hotel room. _____
    (4) John and Mary talk a lot about football. _____
    (5) David Beckham plays football.   _____
    (6) I train at the gym.   _____
    (7) I visit my family in China.   _____
    (8) I receive gifts on New Year's day.   _____
    (9) He creates his own football team.   _____
    (10) David Beckham promotes many good causes. _____

Activity B3

- Put the following verbs provided in the simple past simple tense.

    [*Sentences heard*]
    (1) Last week, I (listen) to some music   _____
    (2) Yesterday, I (work) overtime at work.   _____
    (3) Last Christmas, I (celebrate) with my family. _____
    (4) Last night, I (dance) at a nightclub.   _____
    (5) Last week, I (smoke) too many cigarettes.   _____
    (6) Two years ago, I (protest) in London about the war. _____
    (7) Last summer, I (visit) London for the first time.   _____
    (8) On Christmas day, I (receive) lots of presents.   _____
    (9) 5 years ago, I (travel) to China.   _____
    (10) In 1999, I (start) smoking for the first time. _____

Activity B4

- Match a line in A with a line in B. Put the verb in B into the past simple (10 items)

A	B
I _____ (want) to join a yoga club	because I _____ (work) very long hours.
I _____ (start) work at 5:30 in the morning	but when I was a child I _____ (play) with my school friends.
I was always tired in my first job	but 10 years ago my mother _____ (clean) my room.
Now I play football with my university friends	he _____ (visit) China last year.
Now I clean my room	luckily, I _____ (join) one near my home.
Johns likes to travel to other countries	and I _____ (finish) at 9.00 in the evening.
I was only eight	we _____ (talk) for 2 hours.
I met up with John yesterday	when I _____ (learn) how to ride a bicycle.

Activity B5

- Put the following verbs in the sentences below. Put them in the past simple tense.

    relax   cook   phone   attend   dress   check   listen   watch   talk   need

    (1) Yesterday morning _____ with my lecturer about my essay mark.
    (2) This morning, John _____ in bed for a few hours.
    (3) Last night I _____ my homework before handing it in.
    (4) Last week, I _____ more time.

Sample TI Materials (English Past Tense)

(*Activity B5 – continued*)

(5) Two years ago, I _____ in different kinds of clothes.
(6) When I was 17, I _____ to pop music.
(7) Last weekend I _____ a really exciting film.
(8) Last Christmas I _____ a nice meal for my family.
(9) Two weeks ago, I _____ a meeting with my lecturers.
(10) Three days ago, I Tom for help with my homework.

Activity B6

- Fill in the gaps. Use the past simple form of the verbs below.

watch visit like call sunbathe travel like want hate arrive

I really **(1)** _____ to see Madame Tussaud's, so early in the morning I hopped on the train and **(2)** _____ on London underground to Baker Street. I had my picture taken with David Beckham, well the wax one that is. I also **(3)** _____ Trafalgar Square and saw Nelson's column. There were so many pigeons there, I think they **(4)** _____ the place! In the afternoon, I waited for ages for the train to take me to Covent Garden. I really **(5)** _____ travelling on the trains. Covent Garden was fantastic, I **(6)** _____ the different street performers, and I really **(7)** _____ listening to the musicians. At the end of the day it was still sunny so I lay down on the grass and **(8)** _____ for a bit in Hyde Park – London's most famous and largest green open space. I **(9)** _____ home quite late and **(10)** _____ my parents back in China and talked about my day. All in all, I had a wonderful time today.

Activity B7

- Complete the sentences below by changing the infinitive of the verbs in brackets to the past tense. For example: 'Yesterday, I met my friends and ... (to play)'. You could write down **'played football with them'**.

(1) Last Christmas I ... (to receive)
_____

(2) Last month it was my birthday and I ... (to celebrate)
_____

(3) London was great, I really ... (like)
_____

(4) This morning Tom was happy because he ... (to start)
_____

(5) The day before yesterday, at university ... (to learn)
_____

(*Activity B7 – continued*)

(6) In 1999, I ... (to party)

(7) Last summer Mary was unhappy because ... (to fail)

(8) This afternoon John ... (to telephone)

(9) Today in London I ... (to photograph)

(10) England was great I really ... (to enjoy)

Activity B8

- Write sentences by using the verbs in the brackets.
- For example, for (to fix) you could write: '**I fixed my car**'.

(1) (to join) _____
(2) (to need) _____
(3) (to cycle) _____
(4) (to clean) _____
(5) (to relax) _____
(6) (to finish) _____
(7) (to talk) _____
(8) (to dance) _____
(9) (to listen) _____
(10) (to dress) _____

Activity B9

- Complete the dialogue with the appropriate form of the following verbs.

    arrive   wait   start   pour   remember   shout   walk   stay   watch   drop

    A: Hi Richard, how was your day?
    B: Horrible!
    A: Why? What happened?
    B: Well it **(1)**_____ badly. In the morning, I felt tired because I **(2)**_____ up most of the night. I **(3)**_____ myself three strong cups of coffee to wake up.

Sample TI Materials (English Past Tense)

(**Activity B9** – *continued*)

- **A:** That's not so bad.
- **B:** No wait! It got worse. I **(4)**_____ TV for a few hours and then **(5)**_____ that I had to go to work.
- **A:** Oh no! so you were a bit late?
- **B:** Very late. I **(6)**_____ quickly to the bus stop but there was a lot of traffic so I **(7)**_____ for over an hour
- **A:** Did you get in trouble?
- **B:** Yes, my manager was really angry and **(8)**_____ at me and said I was a useless employee.
- **A:** Let me guess, things got worse right?
- **B:** Yes, I **(9)**_____ two people's drinks and the boss yelled at me and said I was the most clumsy person he had ever employed.
- **A:** Did he fire you?
- **B:** Luckily no. I **(10)**_____ home absolutely exhausted and miserable. I need sleep!
- **A:** What a horrible day!

Activity B10

- Write a sentence using one verb and one noun.
- For example:

Verb   **Noun**
spill   coffee

You could write down: **'This morning I spilled some coffee.'**

	Verbs:	Nouns:	
(1)	mail	car	_____
(2)	celebrate	mistletoe	_____
(3)	kiss	club	_____
(4)	achieve	anniversary	_____
(5)	consume	teacher	_____
(6)	cheat	letter	_____
(7)	quarrel	top grades	_____
(8)	repair	home	_____
(9)	return	alcohol	_____
(10)	danced	exam	_____

Appendix C

Sample Materials for Processing Instruction: French Imparfait

Activity C1 (Affective)
Cécile's holidays

- **Step 1**
  Read the following statements that Cécile made about her last holidays and decide whether there are similar *(similaire)* or different *(différent)* to your activities during your last holidays.

	Elle ...	*similaire*	*différent*
(1)	... allait à la plage tous les jours.	☐	☐
(2)	... faisait du ski nautique.	☐	☐
(3)	... se baignait dans la mer.	☐	☐
(4)	... mangeait au restaurant.	☐	☐
(5)	... dormait beaucoup.	☐	☐
(6)	... écoutait de la musique.	☐	☐
(7)	... sortait le soir avec ses amis.	☐	☐
(8)	... se couchait tard.	☐	☐

- **Step 2**
  Now decide in pairs whether it was an interesting or a boring holiday.

Activity C2 Referential activity
Zinédine Zidane: Avant et après

- **Step 1**
  Listen to the following statements made by a journalist about the life of Zinédine Zidane and decide whether each statement is referring to his past life as a professional football player or to his life now as a retired football player.

	professional football player	retired football player	[Sentences heard] Zinédine Zidane ...
(1)	☐	☐	... jouait au football dans le monde entier.
(2)	☐	☐	... gagnait beaucoup de coupes.
(3)	☐	☐	... passe du temps avec sa famille.

(Activity C2 – continued)

(4)	☐	☐	... participait à beaucoup de diners officiels.
(5)	☐	☐	... s'entrainait avec Ronaldo.
(6)	☐	☐	... s'occupe de ses enfants.
(7)	☐	☐	... est directeur de l'association ELA.
(8)	☐	☐	... téléphone à Thierry Henri pour discuter.
(9)	☐	☐	... marquait beaucoup de buts.
(10)	☐	☐	... était le meilleur joueur de football au monde.

- **Step 2**
  Now decide if Zinédine Zidane was busier when he was a professional football player or now that he is retired.

Activity C3 (Referential)

Things people were doing last summer or now

- Listen to the following statements and decide whether each statement refers to an activity that was taking place last summer or takes place now.

	Last summer	Now	[Sentences heard]
(1)	☐	☐	*On avait chaud.*
(2)	☐	☐	*On regarde beaucoup la télévision.*
(3)	☐	☐	*On allait à la plage.*
(4)	☐	☐	*On dansait.*
(5)	☐	☐	*On travaille beaucoup.*
(6)	☐	☐	*On voyage en train.*
(7)	☐	☐	*On visitait Paris.*
(8)	☐	☐	*On lisait le* DaVinci Code.
(9)	☐	☐	*On est fatigué.*
(10)	☐	☐	*On étudie beaucoup.*

Activity C4 (Affective)

Stress!

- **Step 1**
  You will hear a series of sentences about what Cécile was doing last week. Decide if what you hear is something that relieved her stress or contributed to her being stressed.

	Relieved stress	Contributed to stress	[Sentences heard]
(1)	☐	☐	*Je faisais du yoga.*
(2)	☐	☐	*Je parlais de mon stress à mes amies*

(*Activity C4* – *continued*)

(3)	☐	☐	J'avais besoin de plus de temps pour étudier.
(4)	☐	☐	Je venais à l'université en vélo.
(5)	☐	☐	J'avais besoin d'argent pour payer mon loyer.
(6)	☐	☐	Je fumais beaucoup.
(7)	☐	☐	Je me relaxais au sauna.
(8)	☐	☐	Je nettoyais mon appartement
(9)	☐	☐	Je travaillais beaucoup.
(10)	☐	☐	Je faisais du sport avec mon ami Charles

Step 2
Who was more stressed last week, you or Cécile?

Activity C5 (Affective):

What's appropriate?

- **Step 1**
  Read each sentence then decide whether or not it is typical of your lecturer's behaviour.

Mon professeur ...	*C'est typique*	*Ce n'est pas typique*
(1) ... dormait toute la journée.	☐	☐
(2) ... travaillait chez MacDonald.	☐	☐
(3) ... faisait la fête tous les soirs.	☐	☐
(4) ... notait les examens.	☐	☐
(5) ... venait à l'université en voiture.	☐	☐
(6) ... préparait sa classe..	☐	☐
(7) ... se couchait à 5 heures du matin..	☐	☐
(8) ... portait un jean et des baskets..	☐	☐
(9) ... écoutait de la musique «garage».	☐	☐
(10) ... lisait le journal tous les jours.	☐	☐

- **Step 2**
  Which statement do you think is the least typical for your lecturer to have done? And why?

Activity C6 (Affective)

Noël

- **Step 1**
  Read the following activities and indicate whether you were doing similar (*similaire*) or different (*différent*) things last Christmas.

	similaire	*différent*
(1) *J'étais avec ma famille.*	☐	☐
(2) *Je décorais le sapin de Noël.*	☐	☐
(3) *J'envoyais des cartes de Noël.*	☐	☐
(4) *J'allais à la messe de minuit.*	☐	☐
(5) *J'avais beaucoup de cadeaux.*	☐	☐
(6) *Je buvais du champagne.*	☐	☐
(7) *Je regardais un film classique à la télévison.*	☐	☐
(8) *Je faisais mon portfolio.*	☐	☐
(9) *Je jouais avec ma X-Box.*	☐	☐
(10) *Je mangeais de la dinde.*	☐	☐

- **Step 2**
  Compare your answers with your partner to find out how many similar things you were doing last Christmas.

Activity C7 (Referential)

First day at university, what a day!

- **Step 1**
  Listen to the following story a student told about his first day at university and decide which statements accurately describe what was going on.

  [Instructor's script]
  Mes premiers cours commençaient à 9.00 et je voulais vraiment arriver à l'université à l'heure. A 7h00 je me levais pour prendre une douche et je mettais ma plus belle chemise et ma plus belle veste. Je prenais un petit-déjeuner rapide et je partais de la maison aussi vite que possible. Il était déjà 8h00 donc je décidais de prendre le métro pour aller plus vite. Il y avait beaucoup de monde dans le métro, on ne respirait pas. Il y avait beaucoup de retard et les métros ne venaient pas. Je décidais donc de prendre le bus. Mais j'attendais, j'attendais et les bus ne venaient pas: il était maintenant 8h30. Je décidais finalement de prendre un taxi. Une fois dans le taxi je racontais mon histoire au chauffeur qui riait. A 9h00 j'arrivais enfin à l'université, je sortais du taxi pour payer mais je ne trouvais plus mon portefeuille, il était dans mon autre veste: pas d'argent ni de carte bancaire pour payer. A 9h02 je remontais dans le taxi et je repartais chez moi pour aller chercher mon portefeuille. Pas de chance et en plus j'étais TRES en retard pour mon premier cours.

(*Activity C7* – *continued*)

	Vrai	Faux
L'étudiant ...		
(1) ... *voulait arriver à l'heure à l'université.*	☐	☐
(2) ... *se levait à 6h30.*	☐	☐
(3) ... *mettait une vieille chemise.*	☐	☐
(4) ... *ne prenait pas de petit-déjeuner.*	☐	☐
(5) ... *voulait prendre le métro.*	☐	☐
(6) ... *prenait le bus.*	☐	☐
(7) ... *prenait un taxi.*	☐	☐
(8) ... *racontait son histoire au chauffeur de taxi.*	☐	☐
(9) ... *avait de l'argent pour payer le taxi.*	☐	☐
(10) ... *était beaucoup en retard.*	☐	☐

- **Step 2**
  Now read the script.
  Which do you think the student was the most frustrated about?
  Compare with your partner.

Activity C8 Affective activity
(Adapted from Farley, 2004)

In their teens ...

- **Step 1**
  Imagine what your parent's life was like as a teenager many years ago.
  What about another relative, or your instructor?
  Can you imagine who partied too much?
  Who argued with his/her teacher a lot?
  Read over each statement and decide whether each individual (parent, relative or instructor) did these things or not.

		Parent	Relative	Instructor
	Il/Elle ...			
(1)	... *se disputait avec son professeur.*	☐	☐	☐
(2)	... *ne passait pas son baccalauréat.*	☐	☐	☐
(3)	... *trichait aux examens.*	☐	☐	☐
(4)	... *avait de très bonnes notes.*	☐	☐	☐
(5)	... *buvait de l'alcool à 15 ans.*	☐	☐	☐
(6)	... *faisait la fête toute la nuit.*	☐	☐	☐
(7)	... *visitait beaucoup de pays.*	☐	☐	☐
(8)	... *organisait des soirées étudiantes.*	☐	☐	☐

- **Step 2**
  Find out if your instructor did any of the above. Are you surprised?

Activity C9 (Affective)

A typical student's day

- **Step 1**
  The following verbs are from a typical day in a student's life at university. Put the following events in chronological order.

  Elle ...
  (1) ... *rentrait chez elle en train.*
  (2) ... *faisait des courses au supermarché.*
  (3) ... *allait à l'université en vélo.*
  (4) ... *lisait ses cours avant de se coucher.*
  (5) ... *allait en classe.*
  (6) ... *cherchait des articles à la bibliothèque.*
  (7) ... *ne prenait pas de petit-déjeuner.*
  (8) ... *se levait à 7h30.*
  (9) ... *préparait un bon dîner.*
  (10) ... *regardait la television.*

- **Step 2**
  Is this routine similar to your routine?
  How many things are similar to your day?

Activity C10

A horrible day!
(Adapted from Lee & VanPatten, 2003)

- **Step 1**
  Break into pairs and listen as your instructor reads a short narration about what Charles did last Saturday.

  [Instructor's script]
  Quand Charles se levait à 8.00 ce matin là il se sentait fatigué parce qu'il s'était couché très tard la nuit dernière. Il buvait 3 tasses de café pour se réveiller. Il regardait la Télé et se sentait mieux petit à petit. Il voulait encore dormir mais il devait aller travailler. Il travaillait à mi-temps au Café Rouge et le directeur était très strict. Il marchait jusqu'à l'arrêt de bus mais malheureusement il y avait beaucoup de circulation et le bus n'arrivait pas. Il arrivait enfin au travail avec une heure de retard et son directeur n'était pas content. C'était sa dernière chance: le directeur ne voulait plus qu'il arrive en retard. Mais 10 minutes plus tard c'était encore pire: Charles cassait 2 verres et une tasse! Le directeur n'était vraiment pas content. En fin de journée, Charles rentrait enfin chez lui très fatigué et de mauvaise humeur. Quel samedi. Au moins le lendemain il pouvait dormir: c'était dimanche.

- **Step 2**
  In your pairs, give as many details as you can remember by completing the following sentences. The group with the most details wins. You have three minutes.

(**Activity C10**– *continued*)

(1) *Charles se levait* _____.
(2) *Il buvait*_____ *pour se réveiller.*
(3) *Il voulait encore* _____.
(4) *Il travaillait à mi temps au*_____.
(5) *Il arrivait au travail avec* _____*de retard.*
(6) *Son directeur n'était pas* _____.
(7) *Charles cassait* _____.
(8) *Charles rentrait chez lui* _____.

Appendix D
Sample Materials for Traditional Instruction: French Imparfait

Activity D1
- Follow the example to create sentences.
- Example:
  Maintenant je marche très peu, mais avant
  je marchais beaucoup.

(1) *Maintenant je fais peu de sport, mais avant*

(2) *Maintenant il se baigne peu, mais avant*

(3) *Maintenant tu manges peu, mais avant*

(4) *Maintenant elle dort peu, mais avant*

(5) *Maintenant j'écoute peu la radio, mais avant*

(6) *Maintenant il sort peu, mais avant*

(7) *Maintenant on se couche tôt, mais avant*

(8) *Maintenant je vais très peu au cinéma, mais avant*

Activity D2

Zinédine Zidane: *Avant et après*

- **Step 1**
  Fill in the blanks with what you think the ex-football player, Zinédine Zidane, does nowadays that he is retired. Use the following verbs. Some verbs may be used more than once.

  passer, s'occuper de, être, téléphoner

  Zinédine Zidane ...

  (1) _____ du temps avec sa famille.
  (2) _____ à beaucoup de diners officiels.
  (3) _____ de ses enfants.
  (4) _____ directeur de l'association ELA.
  (5) _____ à Thierry Henri pour discuter.

- **Step 2**
  Now fill in the blanks below, but this time think of Zinédine Zidane when he was a professional football player. Use the following verbs.

  jouer, gagner, participer, s'entrainer, marquer

  Zinédine Zidane ...

  (6) _____ au football dans le monde entier
  (7) _____ beaucoup de coupes.
  (8) _____ avec Ronaldo.
  (9) _____ beaucoup de buts.
  (10) _____ le meilleur joueur de football au monde.

Activity D3

What people used to do

- Follow the model and describe how people used to live before.

MAINTENANT	AVANT
(1) *Les femmes travaillent à l'intérieur.*	<u>Les femmes travaillaient à l'extérieur.</u>
(2) *On a une voiture.*	_____
(3) *Nous allons beaucoup en vacances.*	_____
(4) *Les enfants regardent beaucoup la télévision.*	_____
(5) *Les jeunes dansent beaucoup.*	_____
(6) *On voyage beaucoup.*	_____
(7) *On visite beaucoup de pays;*	_____

(**Activity D3** – continued)

(8) *Les jeunes étudient beaucoup.* _____
(9) *Les enfants lisent beaucoup.* _____
(10) *On est stressé.* _____

Activity D4

- Here are some things Caroline is doing today.
  Follow the model and what she used to do.

MAINTENANT	AVANT
(1) *Elle pèse 55 kilos.*	*Elle pesait 105 kilos.* _____
(2) *Elle fait une taille 38.*	_____
(3) *Elle ne fume pas.*	_____
(4) *Elle travaille beaucoup.*	_____
(5) *Elle a besoin de 1500 calories par jour.*	_____
(6) *Elle fait du sport.*	_____
(7) *Elle vient au travail en vélo.*	_____
(8) *Elle se relaxe au yoga.*	_____
(9) *Elle a besoin de manger peu.*	_____
(10) *Elle parle de se marier.*	_____

Activity D5

What's appropriate?

- **Step 1**
  Use the indicated verbs in brackets to describe the typical day of one of your lecturers.

  Mon professeur ...
  (1) ... *(préparer)* _____*sa classe.*
  (2) ... *(venir)* _____ *à l'université en voiture.*
  (3) ... *(noter)* _____ *les examens.*
  (4) ... *(porter)* _____*des vêtements chics.*
  (5) ... *(lire)* _____ *le journal tous les jours.*

(*Activity D5* – *continued*)

- **Step 2**
  Now use the indicated verbs in brackets to describe a typical student's day during the last holidays.

  Pendant les vacances d'été, Paul ...
  (1)   ... (dormir) _____ toute la journée.
  (2)   ... (travailler) _____ chez MacDonald.
  (3)   ... faire) _____ la fête tous les soirs.
  (4)   ... (se coucher) _____ à 5 heures du matin.
  (5)   ... (écouter) _____ de la musique «garage».

Activity D6

Noël

- Use the verbs given below and write 8 sentences about what you did last Christmas.

  être, décorer, envoyer, aller, avoir, boire, regarder, jouer

  (1)   Je _____
  (2)   Je _____
  (3)   Je _____
  (4)   Je _____
  (5)   Je _____
  (6)   Je _____
  (7)   Je _____
  (8)   Je _____

Activity D7

First day at university, what a day!

- Read the text below about a student's first day at university and fill in the gaps using the *imparfait*.

  Mes premiers cours commençaient à 9.00 et je (vouloir) _____ vraiment arriver à l'université à l'heure. A 7h00 je (se lever) _____ pour prendre une douche et je (mettre) _____ ma plus belle chemise et ma plus belle veste. Je (prendre) _____ un petit-déjeuner rapide et je partais de la maison aussi vite que possible. Il était déjà 8h00 donc je (décider) _____ de prendre le métro pour aller plus vite. Il y

Sample TI Materials (French Imparfait)

(***Activity D7** – continued*)

avait beaucoup de monde dans le métro, on ne respirait pas. Il y avait beaucoup de retard et les métros ne venaient pas. Je décidais donc de prendre le bus. Mais j'attendais, j'attendais et les bus ne venaient pas : il était maintenant 8h30. Je (prendre) _____ finalement un taxi. Une fois dans le taxi je (raconter) _____ mon histoire au chauffeur qui riait. A 9h00 j'arrivais enfin à l'université, je (sortir) _____ du taxi pour payer mais je ne (trouver) _____ plus mon portefeuille, il était dans mon autre veste : pas d'argent ni de carte bancaire pour payer. A 9h02 je remontais dans le taxi et je repartais chez moi pour aller chercher mon portefeuille. Pas de chance et en plus je (être) _____ TRES en retard pour mon premier cours.

Activity D8

In their teens ...

- Imagine what your parent's life was like as a teenager many years ago.
  Use the verbs below to write sentences about things they did in their teens.

  (1) Mon père (se disputer) _____ souvent avec son professeur.

  (2) Ma mère (passer) _____ ses vacances avec des amies.

  (3) Mon père (tricher) _____ aux examens.

  (4) Ma mère (avoir) _____ de très bonnes notes.

  (5) Mon père (boire) _____ de l'alcool à 15 ans.

  (6) Ma mère (faire) _____ la fête toute la nuit.

  (7) Mon père (visiter) _____ beaucoup de pays.

  (8) Ma mère (organiser) _____ des soirées étudiantes.

Activity D9

A typical student's day

- Transform each sentence according to the example.
- Example:
  Elle (étudier) _____ à l'université.
  Elle **étudiait** à l'université.

  (1) Elle (selever) _____ à 7h30.

  (2) Elle (prendre) _____ son petit-déjeuner.

  (3) Elle (aller) _____ à l'université en vélo.

  (4) Elle (aller) _____ en classe.

  (5) Elle (chercher) _____ des articles à la bibliothèque.

  (6) Elle (faire) _____ des courses au supermarché.

(**Activity D9** – *continued*)

    (7) Elle (rentrer) _____ chez elle en train.
    (8) Elle (préparer) _____ un bon dîner.
    (9) Elle (regarder) _____ la télévision.
    (10) Elle (lire) _____ ses cours avant de se coucher.lisait ses cours avant de se coucher.

Activity D10

A horrible day!
(Adapted from Lee & VanPatten, 2003)

- Read the following text.
  Use the indicated verbs in brackets to fill in the gaps using the *imparfait*.

Quand Charles (se lever) _____ à 8.00 ce matin là il se sentait fatigué parce qu'il s'était couché très tard la nuit dernière. Il (boire) _____ 3 tasses de café pour se réveiller. Il regardait la Télé et se sentait mieux petit à petit. Il (vouloir) _____ encore dormir mais il devait aller travailler. Il (travailler) _____ à mi-temps au Café Rouge et le directeur était très strict. Il marchait jusqu'à l'arrêt de bus mais malheureusement il y avait beaucoup de circulation et le bus n'arrivait pas. Il (arriver) _____ enfin au travail avec une heure de retard et son directeur ne (être) _____ pas content. C'était sa dernière chance: le directeur ne voulait plus qu'il arrive en retard. Mais 10 minutes plus tard c'était encore pire: Charles (casser) _____ 2 verres et une tasse! Le directeur n'était vraiment pas content. En fin de journée, Charles (rentrer) _____ enfin chez lui très fatigué et de mauvaise humeur. Quel samedi. Au moins le lendemain il pouvait dormir: c'était dimanche.

Appendix E

Sample Materials for Processing Instruction: Italian Adjective Gender Agreement

Activity E1

- Listen to each sentence in which a person is described and determine which person is described. Then you must indicate whether you agree or disagree. You must pay attention to the adjective ending in order to understand who and what we are referring to. In addition to that, you need to understand the meaning of the sentence containing the adjective.

	Sofia Loren	Luciano Pavarotti	*son d'accordo*	*non sono d'accordo*	[Sentences heard]
(1)	☐	☐	☐	☐	*È bella.*
(2)	☐	☐	☐	☐	*È brutto.*
(3)	☐	☐	☐	☐	*È antipatico.*
(4)	☐	☐	☐	☐	*È simpatica.*
(5)	☐	☐	☐	☐	*È alta*
(6)	☐	☐	☐	☐	*È basso.*
(7)	☐	☐	☐	☐	*È grasso.*
(8)	☐	☐	☐	☐	*È magra..*
(9)	☐	☐	☐	☐	*È dinamico.*
(10)	☐	☐	☐	☐	*È dinamica.*

Activity E2

- Listen to each sentence in which a person is described and determine which person is described.

	Claudia Schiffer	Brad Pitt	[Sentences heard]
(1)	☐	☐	*È bella.*
(2)	☐	☐	*È bello.*
(3)	☐	☐	*È Americano*

(**Activity E2** – *continued*)

(4)	☐	☐	È Tedesca.
(5)	☐	☐	È bruno.
(6)	☐	☐	È bionda.
(7)	☐	☐	È viva.
(8)	☐	☐	È antipatico.
(9)	☐	☐	È alto.
(9)	☐	☐	È magra
(10)	☐	☐	È alto.

Activity E3

- **Step 1**
  Read the following statements and indicate whether you agree or disagree.

		Sono d'accordo	Non sono d'accordo
(1)	Clinton è bello.	☐	☐
(2)	Alessandro è bravo.	☐	☐
(3)	Greenwich è suggestiva.	☐	☐
(4)	Tony Blair è simpatico.	☐	☐
(5)	George Bush è antipatico.	☐	☐
(6)	Londra è noiosa.	☐	☐
(7)	Londra è caotica.	☐	☐
(8)	L'Università è organizzata.	☐	☐
(9)	Pizza Espress è caro.	☐	☐
(10)	L'Inghilterra è bella.	☐	☐

- **Step 2**
  Compare your views with a classmate.

Activity E3

- **Step 1**
  Read the following statements and indicate whether you agree or disagree.

		Sono d'accordo	Non sono d'accordo
(1)	Clinton è bello.	☐	☐
(2)	Alessandro è bravo.	☐	☐
(3)	Greenwich è suggestiva.	☐	☐
(4)	Tony Blair è simpatico.	☐	☐
(5)	George Bush è antipatico.	☐	☐
(6)	Londra è noiosa.	☐	☐

Sample PI Materials (Italian Adjective Gender Agreement)

(**Activity E3** – continued)

(7) Londra è caotica. ☐ ☐
(8) L'Università è organizzata. ☐ ☐
(9) Pizza Espress è caro. ☐ ☐
(10) L'Inghilterra è bella. ☐ ☐

- **Step 2**
  Compare your views with a classmate.

Activity E4

- **Step 1**
  Listen as your instructor makes a statement. Decide whether the statements refer to your professor (male or female?).

	La professoressa	Il professore	[Sentences heard]
(1)	☐	☐	È noiosa.
(2)	☐	☐	È noioso.
(3)	☐	☐	È bravo.
(4)	☐	☐	È brava.
(5)	☐	☐	È simpatico.
(6)	☐	☐	È simpatica.
(7)	☐	☐	È stupido.
(8)	☐	☐	È stupida.
(9)	☐	☐	È bello.
(10)	☐	☐	È bella.

- **Step 2**
  Discuss with your partner whether you agree or disagree with each statement.

Activity E5

- **Step 1**
  Read the following statements about Uma Thurman and indicate whether it is true or false.

		Vero	Falso
	Uma Thurman ...		
(1)	... è brutta.	☐	☐
(2)	... è alta.	☐	☐
(3)	... è una brava attrice.	☐	☐
(4)	... è grassa.	☐	☐
(5)	... è Italiana.	☐	☐
(6)	... è dotata.	☐	☐

(**Activity E5** – *continued*)

(7) ... è aperta. ☐ ☐
(8) ... è innamorata di Tarantino. ☐ ☐
(9) ... è timida. ☐ ☐
(10) ... è una persona calda. ☐ ☐

- **Step 2**
  Compare your answers with a classmate.

  Sei d'accordo? _____ *Non sono d'accordo?* _____

Activity E6

- **Step 1**
  Listen to each sentence in which an adjective is used to describe life in a city or a small town. First determine which one of the two is described.

- **Step 2**
  Indicate whether you agree or disagree.

	Vivere in citta	Vivere in un paese	[Sentences heard]	Si	No
(1)	☐	☐	È calmo.	☐	☐
(2)	☐	☐	È frenetica.	☐	☐
(3)	☐	☐	È tranquillo.	☐	☐
(4)	☐	☐	È caotica.	☐	☐
(5)	☐	☐	È cosmopolita.	☐	☐
(6)	☐	☐	È noioso.	☐	☐
(7)	☐	☐	È moderna.	☐	☐
(8)	☐	☐	È antico.	☐	☐
(9)	☐	☐	È bello.	☐	☐
(10)	☐	☐	È bella.	☐	☐

References

Allen, L.Q. (2000) Form–meaning connections and the French causative. *Studies in Second Language Acquisition* 22, 69–84.

Barcroft, J. and VanPatten, B. (1997) Acoustic salience of grammatical forms: The effect of location stress, and boundedness on Spanish L2 input processing. In W.R. Glass and A.T. Pérez-Leroux (eds) *Contemporary Perspectives on the Acquisition of Spanish: Production, Processing and Comprehension* (pp. 109–121). Somerville, MA: Cascadilla Press.

Bardovi-Harlig, K. (2007) One functional approach to second language acquisition: The concept-oriented approach. In B. VanPatten and J. Williams (eds) *Theories of Second Language Acquisition: An Introduction* (pp. 97–113). Mahwah, NJ: Erlbaum.

Benati, A. (2001) A comparative study of the effects of processing instruction and output-based instruction on the acquisition of the Italian future tense. *Language Teaching Research* 5, 95–127.

Benati, A. (2004a) The effects of structured input and explicit information on the acquisition of Italian future tense. In B. VanPatten (ed.) *Processing Instruction: Theory, Research, and Commentary* (pp. 207–255). Mahwah, NJ: Erlbaum.

Benati, A. (2004b) The effects of processing instruction and its components on the acquisition of gender agreement in Italian. *Language Awareness* 13, 67–80.

Benati, A. (2005) The effects of PI, TI and MOI in the acquisition of English simple past tense. *Language Teaching Research* 9, 67–113.

Bernhardt, E.B. (1992) *Reading Development in a Second Language.* Norwood, NJ: Ablex.

Bever, T.G. (1970) The cognitive basis for linguistic structures. In R. Hayes (ed.) *Cognition and Language Development* (pp. 279–362). New York: Wiley & Sons.

Bransdorfer, R. (1991) Communicative value and linguistic knowledge in second language oral input processing. PhD thesis, University of Illinois at Urbana-Champaign.

Brown, J.D. (1988) *Understanding Research in Second Language Learning: A Teacher's Guide to Statistics and Research Design.* London: Cambridge University Press

Cadierno, T. (1995) Formal instruction from a processing perspective: An investigation into the Spanish past tense. *The Modern Language Journal* 79, 179–93.

Carroll, S. (2004) Commentary: Some general and specific comments on input processing and processing instruction. In B. VanPatten (ed.) *Processing Instruction: Theory, Research, and Commentary* (pp. 293–309). Mahwah, NJ: Erlbaum.

Carroll, S. (2007) Autonomous induction theory. In B. VanPatten and J. Williams (eds) *Theories of Second Language Acquisition: An Introduction* (pp. 155–173). Mahwah, NJ: Erlbaum.

Cheng, A. (2002) The effects of processing instruction on the acquisition of *ser* and *estar*. *Hispania* 85, 308–323.

Cheng, A. (2004) Processing instruction and Spanish *ser* and *estar*: Forms with semantic-aspectual value. In B. VanPatten (ed.) *Processing Instruction: Theory, Research and Commentary* (pp. 119–141). Mahwah, NJ: Erlbaum.

Collentine, J.G. (1998) Processing Instruction and the subjunctive. *Hispania* 81, 576–587.

Collentine, J.G. (2004) Commentary: Where PI research has been and where it should be going. In B. VanPatten (ed.) *Processing Instruction: Theory, Research, and Commentary* (pp. 119–141). Mahwah, NJ: Erlbaum.

DeKeyser, R. (1997) Beyond explicit rule learning: Automatizing second Language morphosyntax. *Studies in Second Language Acquisition* 19, 195–221.

DeKeyser, R. (2007) Skill acquisition theory. In B. VanPatten and J. Williams (eds) *Theories of Second Language Acquisition: An Introduction* (pp. 97–113). Mahwah, NJ: Erlbaum.

Echevarría, M.S. (1978) *Desarrollo de la comprensión infantil de la sintaxis española*. Concepción: Universidad de Concepción.

Ellis, N. (2007) The associative-cognitive CREED. In B. VanPatten and J. Williams (eds) *Theories of Second Language Acquisition: An Introduction* (pp. 77–95). Mahwah, NJ: Erlbaum.

Ervin-Tripp, S. (1974) Is second language learning like the first? *TESOL Quarterly* 8, 111–127.

Farley, A.P. (2001a) The effects of processing instruction and meaning-based output instruction. *Spanish Applied Linguistics* 5, 57–94.

Farley, A.P. (2001b) Authentic processing instruction and the Spanish subjunctive. *Hispania* 84, 289–299.

Farley, A. (2004a) The relative effects of processing instruction and meaning-based output instruction. In B. VanPatten (ed.) *Processing Instruction: Theory, Research and Commentary* (pp. 143–168). Mahwah, NJ: Erlbaum.

Farley, A. (2004b) Processing instruction and the Spanish subjunctive: Is explicit information needed? In B. VanPatten (ed.) *Processing Instruction: Theory, Research, and Commentary* (pp. 227–239). Mahwah, NJ: Erlbaum.

Farley A. (2005) *Structured Input: Grammar Instruction for the Acquisition-Oriented Classroom*. New York: McGraw-Hill.

González, N. (1997) A parametric study of L2 acquisition: Interpretation of Spanish word order. In A.T. Pérez-Leroux and W.R. Glass (eds) *Contemporary Perspectives on The Acquisition of Spanish (Vol. 1): Developing Grammars* (pp. 133–148). Somerville, MA: Cascadilla Press.

Houston, T. (1997) Sentence processing in Spanish a background knowledge. In W.R. Glass and A.T. Pérez-Leroux (eds) *Contemporary Perspectives on the Acquisition of Spanish: Production, Processing and Comprehension* (pp. 123–134). Somerville, MA: Cascadilla Press.

Klein, W. (1986) *Second Language Acquisition*. Cambridge University Press.

Krashen, S. (1982) *Principles and Practice in Second Language Acquisition*. London: Pergamon.

Lee, J.F. (1987) Comprehending the Spanish subjunctive: An information processing perspective. *Modern Language Journal* 71 (1), 50–57.

Lee, J.F. (1990) Constructive processes evidenced by early stage non-native readers of Spanish in comprehending an expository text. *Hispanic Linguistics* 4, 129–148.

Lee, J.F. (1998) The relationship of verb morphology to second language reading comprehension and input processing. *Modern Language Journal* 82 (l), 33–48.

Lee, J.F. (1999) On levels of processing and levels of comprehension. In J. Gutiérrez-Rexach and F. Martínez-Gil (eds) *Advances in Hispanic Linguistics* (pp. 42–59). Somerville, MA: Cascadilla Press.

Lee, J.F. (2002) The incidental acquisition of Spanish future tense morphology through reading in a second language. *Studies in Second Language Acquisition* 24, 55–80.

Lee, J. (2003) Cognitive and linguistic perspectives on the acquisition of object pronouns in Spanish. In B. Lafford and R. Salaberry (eds) *Spanish Second Language Acquisition: State of the Science* (pp. 98–129). Washington, DC: Georgetown University Press.

Lee, J. (2004) On the generalizability, limits, and potential future directions of processing instruction research. In B. VanPatten (ed.) *Processing Instruction: Theory, Research, and Commentary* (pp. 311–323). Mahwah, NJ: Erlbaum.

Lee, J. and Benati, A. (2007a) *Second Language Processing: An Analysis of Theory, Problems and Solutions*. Continuum: London.

Lee, J. and Benati, A. (2007b) *Delivering Processing Instruction in Classrooms and Virtual Contexts: Research and Practice*. Equinox, London.

Lee, J.F., Benati, A., Aguilar-Sánchez, J. and McNulty, E.M. (2007) Comparing three modes of delivering processing instruction on preterite/imperfect distinction and negative informal commands in Spanish. In J. Lee and A. Benati *Delivering Processing Instruction in Classrooms and Virtual Contexts: Research and Practice* (pp. 73–98). Equinox: London.

Lee J., Cadierno, T., Glass, W. and VanPatten, B. (1997) The effects of lexical and grammatical cues on processing past temporal reference in second language input. *Applied Language Learning* 8, 1–27.

Lee, J.F. and Rodriguez, R. (1997) The effects of lexemic and morphosyntactic modifications on L2 reading comprehension and input processing. In W.R. Glass and A.T. Perez-Leroux *Contemporary Perspectives on the Acquisition of Spanish* (pp. 135–157). Somerville, MA: Cascadilla Press.

Lee, J.F. and Rossomondo, A. (2004) Cross experimental evidence for the incidental acquisition of Spanish future tense morphology. Paper presented at the Annual Symposium on Hispanic Linguistics. Minneapolis, October.

Lee, J. and VanPatten, B. (1995) *Making Communicative Language Teaching Happen*. New York: McGraw-Hill.

Lee, J. and VanPatten, B. (2003) *Making Communicative Language Teaching Happen* (2nd edn). New York: McGraw-Hill.

LoCoco, V. (1987) Learner comprehension of oral and written importance of word order. In B. VanPatten, T. Dvorak and J.F. Lee (eds) *Foreign Language Learning: A Research Perspective* (pp. 119–129). Rowley, MA: Newbury House.

Long, M. (1991) Focus on form: A design feature in language teaching methodology. In K. De Bot (ed.) *Foreign Language Research in Cross-Cultural Perspectives*. Philadelphia, PA: John Benjamins.

Mangubhai, F. (1991) The processing behaviours of adult second language learners and their relationship to second language proficiency. *Applied Linguistics* 12, 268–297.

Marsden, E. (2005) Exploring input processing in the classroom: An experimental comparison of processing instruction and enriched input. *Language Learning* 56, 507–566.

Mitchell, R. and Myles, F. (2004) *Second Language Learning Theories* (2nd edn). London: Hodder Arnold.

Morgan-Short, K. and Bowden, H.W. (2006) Processing instruction and meaningful output-based instruction: Effects on second language development. *Studies in Second Language Acquisition* 28, 31–65.

Musumeci, D. (1989) The ability of second language learners to assign tense at the sentence level: A cross-linguistic study. PhD thesis, University of Illinois at Urbana-Champaign.

Nam, E. (1975) Child and adult perceptual strategies in second language acquisition. Paper presented at the annual TESOL Convention, Los Angeles.

Ortega, L. (2007) Second language learning explained? SLA across nine contemporary theories. In B. VanPatten and J. Williams (eds) *Theories in Second Language Acquisition* (pp. 225–250). Mahwah, NJ: Erlbaum.

Paulston, C. (1972) Structural patterns drills: A classification. In H. Allen and R. Campbell (eds) *Teaching English as a Second Language* (pp. 129–138). New York: McGraw-Hill.

Peters, A.M. (1985) Language segmentation: Operating principles for the perception and analysis of language. In D. Slobin (ed.) *The Crosslinguistic Study of Language Acquisition: Theoretical Issues*. Mahwah, NJ: Lawrence Erlbaum Associates.

Pienemann, M. (2007) Processability theory. In B. VanPatten and J. Williams (eds) *Theories in Second Language Acquisition: An Introduction* (pp. 137–154). Mahwah, NJ: Erlbaum.

Rosa, E., and O'Neill, M. (1998) Effects of stress and location on acoustic salience at the initial stages of Spanish L2 input processing. *Spanish Applied Linguistics* 2, 24–52.

Rossomondo, A.E. (2007) The role of lexical temporal indicators and text interaction format on the incidental acquisition of Spanish future tense morphology. *Studies in Second Language Acquisition* 29, 39–66.

Salaberry, M.R. (1997) The role of input and output practice in second language acquisition. *The Canadian Modern Language Review* 53, 422–451.

Sanz, C. (1997) Experimental tasks in SLA research: Amount of production, modality, memory, and production processes. In W.R. Glass and A.T. Perez-Leroux (eds) *Contemporary Perspectives on the Acquisition of Spanish: Production, Processing, and Comprehension* (pp. 41–56). Sommerville, MA: Cascadilla Press.

Sanz, C. (2004) Computer delivered implicit versus explicit feedback in processing instruction. In B. VanPatten (ed.) *Processing Instruction: Theory, Research, and Commentary* (pp. 241–255). Mahwah, NJ: Erlbaum.

Schmidt, R. (1990) The role of consciousness in second language learning. *Applied Linguistics* 11, 129–158.

Sharwood-Smith, M. (1986) Comprehension versus acquisition: Two ways of processing input. *Applied Linguistics* 7, 239–274.

Sharwood-Smith, M. (1991) Speaking to many minds: On the relevance of different types of language information for the L2 learner. *Second Language Research* 7, 118–132.

Sharwood-Smith, M. (1993) Input enhancement in instructed SLA: Theoretical bases. *Studies in Second Language Acquisition* 15, 165–179.

Slobin, D.I. (1966) Grammatical transformations and sentence comprehension in childhood and adulthood. *Journal of Verbal Learning & Verbal Behaviour* 5, 219–227.

Slobin D. I. (1973) Cognitive prerequisites for the development of grammar. In C.A. Ferguson and D.I. Slobin (eds) *Studies of Child Language Development*. New York: Holt, Rinehart & Winston.

Tomlin, R. and Villa, V. (1994) Attention in cognitive science and second language acquisition. *Studies in Second Language Acquisition* 16, 183–204.

VanPatten, B. (1985) Communicative value and information processing in second language acquisition. In E. Judd, P. Nelson and D. Messerschmitt (eds) *On TESOL '84: A Brave New World* (pp. 88–99). Washington, DC: TESOL.

VanPatten, B. (1990) Attending to content and form in the input: An experiment in consciousness. *Studies in Second Language Acquisition* 12, 287–301.

VanPatten, B. (1993) Grammar instruction for the acquisition rich classroom. *Foreign Language Annals* 26, 433–450.

VanPatten, B. (1996) *Input Processing and Grammar Instruction: Theory and Research*. Norwood, NJ: Ablex.

VanPatten, B. (2000) Processing instruction as form–meaning connections: Issues in theory and research. In J.F. Lee and A. Valdman (eds) *Form and Meaning: Multiple Perspectives* (pp. 43–68). Boston: Heinle & Heinle.
VanPatten, B. (2002) Processing Instruction: An update. *Language Learning* 52, 755–803.
VanPatten, B. (2003) *From Input to Output: A Teacher's Guide to Second Language Acquisition*. New York: McGraw-Hill.
VanPatten, B. (ed.) (2004a) *Processing Instruction: Theory, Research and Commentary*. Mahwah, NJ: Erlbaum.
VanPatten, B. (2004b) Input processing in second language acquisition. In B. VanPatten (ed.) *Processing Instruction: Theory, Research, and Commentary* (pp. 5–31). Mahwah, NJ: Erlbaum.
Van Patten, B. (2007) Input processing in adult second language acquisition. In B. VanPatten and J. Williams (eds) *Theories in Second Language Acquisition* (pp. 115–135). Mahwah, NJ: Erlbaum.
VanPatten, B. and Cadierno, T. (1993) Explicit instruction and input processing. *Studies in Second Language Acquisition* 15, 225–243.
VanPatten, B. and Fernández, C. (2004) The long-term effects of processing instruction. In B. VanPatten (ed.) *Processing Instruction: Theory, Research, and Commentary* (pp. 273–289). Mahwah, NJ: Erlbaum.
Van Patten, B. and Houston, T. (1998) Contextual effects in processing L2 input sentences. *Spanish Applied Linguistics* 2, 53–70.
VanPatten, B., Lee, J.F. and Ballman, T. (2006) *Viztazos: Un curso breve*. New York: McGraw-Hill.
VanPatten, B. and Oikennon, S. (1996) Explanation vs. structured input in processing instruction. *Studies in Second Language Acquisition* 18, 495–510.
VanPatten, B. and Sanz, C. (1995) From input to output: Processing instruction and communicative tasks. In F.R. Eckman, D. Highland, P.W. Lee, J. Mileham and R.R. Weber (eds) *Second Language Acquisition Theory and Pedagogy* (pp. 169–185). Mahwah, NJ: Erlbaum.
VanPatten, B. and Williams, J. (2007a) *Theories in Second Language Acquisition: An Introduction*. Mahwah, NJ: Erlbaum.
VanPatten, B. and Williams, J. (2007b) Introduction: The nature of theories. In B. VanPatten and J. Williams (eds) *Theories in Second Language Acquisition: An Introduction* (pp. 1–16). Mahwah, NJ: Erlbaum.
VanPatten, B., Williams, J. and Rott, S. (2004) Form–meaning connections in second language acquisition. In B. VanPatten, J. Williams, S. Rott and M. Overstreet (eds) *Form–Meaning Connections in Second Language Acquisition* (pp. 1–26). Mahwah, NJ: Erlbaum.
VanPatten, B. and Wong, W. (2004) Processing instruction and the French causative: Another replication. In B. VanPatten (ed.) *Processing Instruction: Theory, Research, and Commentary* (pp. 97–118). Mahwah, NJ: Erlbaum.
Wong, W. (2004a) The nature of processing instruction. In B. VanPatten (ed.) *Processing Instruction: Theory, Research, and Commentary* (pp. 33–63). Mahwah, NJ: Erlbaum.
Wong. W. (2004b) Processing instruction in French: The roles of explicit information and structured input. In B. VanPatten (ed.) *Processing Instruction: Theory, Research, and Commentary* (pp. 187–205). Mahwah, NJ: Erlbaum.
Wong, W. (2005) *Input Enhancement: From Theory and Research to the Classroom*. New York: McGraw-Hill.
Wong, W. and VanPatten, B. (2003) The evidence is IN: Drills are OUT. *Foreign Language Annals* 36, 403–423.

Author Index

Aguilar-Sanchez, J., 47
Allen, L.Q., 18, 99, 127

Barcroft, J. 16
Bardovi-Harlig, K., 56, 171
Benati, A., 2, 13, 38, 39, 43, 44, 47, 48, 51, 58, 62, 64, 67, 74, 83, 86, 88, 90, 91, 93, 94, 104, 117, 123, 126, 127, 162, 166, 167, 168, 169, 172, 175
Bernhardt, E.B., 6, 7
Bever, T.G, 18
Bowden, H.W., 41, 93
Bransdorfer, R., 14
Brown, J.D., 75

Cadierno, T., 35, 36, 37, 42, 43, 93, 104, 110, 131, 135, 138, 172
Carroll, S. 10, 23, 170
Cheng, A., 38, 172, 175
Collentine, J.G., 99, 123, 165

DeKeyser, R., 84, 162

Ellis, N., 56, 60, 84, 91, 96, 129, 162, 171
Ervin-Tripp, S., 18

Farley, A.P., 1, 39, 43, 98, 99, 100, 101, 123, 126, 192
Fernández, C., 35, 52, 87, 119, 157, 172

Gonzalez, N., 18

Houston, T., 20, 21

Klein, W., 23
Krashen, S., 24

Lee, J., 2, 4, 5, 6, 8, 9, 10, 11, 13, 14, 18, 23, 24, 33, 34, 39, 41, 44, 46, 47, 48, 51, 53, 58, 62, 64, 65, 66, 67, 85, 86, 89, 90, 95, 98, 100, 103, 119, 122, 123, 124, 126, 127, 132, 156, 162, 166, 167, 168, 169, 171, 172, 174
LoCoco, V., 18, 19
Long, M., 24

Mangubhai, F., 23
Marsden, E., 172
McNulty, E.M., 47
Mitchell, 1, 2
Morgan-Short, K., 41, 93
Myles, 1, 2
Musumeci, D., 12, 57

Nam, E., 18

Oikennon, S., 93, 162, 168
O'Neill, M., 16
Ortega, L. 162

Paulston, C., 24, 25
Peters, A.M., 23
Pienemann, M., 91, 92

Rodriguez, R., 5
Rosa, E., 16
Rossomondo, A.E., 5, 6, 11
Rott, S., 161

Salaberry, R., 99
Sanz, C., 32, 67, 93, 99, 172, 175
Schmidt, R., 161
Sharwood-Smith, M., 35, 50
Slobin, D.I., 3, 18

Tomlin, R., 161

Villa, V., 161
VanPatten, B., 1, 2, 3, 4, 5, 6, 7, 8, 10, 12, 13, 14, 15, 16, 18, 19, 20, 21, 22, 23, 24, 25, 26, 27, 29, 32, 33, 34, 35, 36, 37, 39, 41, 42, 43, 46, 48, 50, 52, 54, 55, 56, 57, 62, 65, 66, 83, 84, 85, 86, 87, 89, 90, 92, 93, 97, 98, 99, 100, 103, 104, 105, 110, 116, 119, 120, 121, 122, 124, 125, 127, 131, 132, 157, 158, 160, 161, 162, 166, 167, 168, 169, 170, 171, 172, 175

Williams, J., 1, 169, 170
Wong, W., 1, 7, 8, 18, 19, 27, 38, 44, 50, 52, 65, 98, 99, 100, 103, 105, 124, 125, 127, 162, 166, 167, 172, 175

Subject Index

Age hypothesis, 168, 174
Availability of resources principle/strategy, 3, 14, 17, 90

Contextual constraint principle/strategy, 4, 22
Cumulative effects/hypothesis, 22, 53, 86, 121, 129, 142, 143, 151, 152, 153, 154, 155, 156, 157, 158, 162, 165, 174

Developing system, 22, 25, 25, 36, 37, 46, 52, 86, 93, 124, 155

Event probabilities principle/strategy, 4, 21

First noun principle/strategy, 3, 4, 16, 18, 20, 21, 35, 37, 41, 121, 124, 161, 165, 174
Form-meaning connections/mappings, 1, 2, 4, 14, 15, 16, 22, 27, 43, 44, 46, 50, 56, 64, 84, 90, 93, 94, 95, 99, 101, 134, 163

Input, 1, 2, 3, 6, 8, 14, 22, 24, 25, 26, 37, 31, 32, 33, 35, 36, 39, 41, 42, 47, 50, 52, 62, 65, 84, 93, 94, 95, 103, 122, 134, 143, 155, 167, 169
Input processing, 1, 2, 4, 10, 11, 14, 21, 22, 25, 26, 46, 92, 122, 158, 168,
Intake, 25, 26, 27, 124, 155,
Intuition hypothesis, 156, 157, 174

Lexical preference principle/strategy, 3, 10, 11, 13, 17, 27, 36, 37, 41, 44, 51, 54, 57, 58, 89, 90, 91, 92, 103, 106, 110, 116, 119, 121, 122, 123, 157, 160, 163, 165, 173
Lexical semantics principle/strategy, 4, 21

Meaning-based output instruction (MOI), 35, 36, 39, 41, 42, 47, 52, 93, 94, 95, 96, 104, 126, 127, 162
Meaning-before-non meaning principle/strategy, 3, 17, 29, 56, 84, 124, 160, 161

Optimal hypothesis, 119, 173
Output, 25, 26, 36, 42, 46, 62, 67,

Processing Instruction (PI) 13, 22, 27, 28, 35, 36, 37, 39, 41, 42, 43, 44, 46, 47, 50, 51, 52, 53, 54, 55, 56, 58, 59, 60, 61, 62, 64, 67, 68, 73, 74, 76, 77, 78, 79, 81, 82, 83, 84, 85, 86, 87, 88, 89, 91, 93, 94, 95, 96, 97, 98, 99, 100, 101, 102, 103, 104, 106, 110, 111, 112, 113, 114, 116, 117, 118, 119, 120, 121, 122, 123, 124, 126, 127, 128, 129, 131, 132, 134, 135, 143, 145, 146, 147, 148, 150, 151, 152, 154, 155, 156, 157, 158, 160, 162, 163, 165, 166, 167, 168, 169, 171, 172, 173, 174, 175
Preference for nonredundancy principle/strategy, 3, 13, 17, 29, 31, 37, 43, 50, 54, 56, 84, 89, 91, 92, 123, 160
Primacy of meaning principle/strategy, 13, 16, 17, 27, 29
Primacy of content words principle/strategy, 3, 17, 18, 56, 161, 165
Primary effects, 35, 39, 41, 52, 58, 59, 75, 82, 83, 84, 89, 93, 95, 98, 111, 116, 117, 118, 128, 145, 147, 154, 157, 162, 170

Second Language Acquisition (SLA) 1, 2, 3, 18, 25, 26, 59, 161, 169, 170, 171
Sentence location principle/strategy, 3, 15, 16, 17, 29, 31, 32, 39, 43, 47, 50, 51, 91, 92, 93, 103, 116, 122, 123, 124, 157, 161
Strengthening hypothesis, 119, 156, 173
Structured input activities/practice (SIA), 27, 28, 29, 32, 33, 35, 39, 42, 43, 44, 46, 50, 51, 52, 58, 61, 64, 65, 66, 67, 94, 98, 99, 100, 103, 132, 167

The discourse hypothesis, 173
The individual difference hypothesis, 172
The longer term effect hypothesis, 172
The native language hypothesis, 169, 173
The target language hypothesis, 168, 169, 173
Traditional instruction (TI), 35, 37, 39, 41, 42, 44, 46, 52, 55, 59, 60, 61, 62, 64, 67, 68, 73, 77, 78, 79, 81, 82, 83, 84, 85, 89, 93, 95, 96, 97, 104, 106, 110, 111, 112, 113, 114, 116, 117, 118, 128, 129, 131, 134, 143, 146, 148, 149, 150, 151, 152, 154, 155, 157, 162
Transfer-of-training effects/secondary/hypothesis, 22, 53, 55, 58, 59, 60, 70, 73, 78, 80, 82, 84, 85, 86, 88, 89, 91, 95, 96, 98, 106, 110, 113, 114, 116, 117, 118, 119, 121, 128, 129, 136, 138, 143, 148, 149, 153, 154, 155, 156, 157, 158, 162, 163, 165, 166, 167, 168, 170, 173, 174, 175

For Product Safety Concerns and Information please contact our EU Authorised Representative:

Easy Access System Europe

Mustamäe tee 50

10621 Tallinn

Estonia

gpsr.requests@easproject.com